SIDELIGHTS AND LIGHTER SIDES OF THE WAR BETWEEN THE STATES

A Feast of History Cooked Up in Small Bites!

by
Ralph Green

BURD STREET PRESS
SHIPPENSBURG, PENNSYLVANIA

The acid-free paper used in this book meets the guidelines for permanence and durability of the Committee on Production Guidelines for Book Longevity of the Council on Library Resources.

For a complete list of available publications
please write
Burd Street Press
Division of White Mane Publishing Company, Inc.
P.O. Box 708
Shippensburg, PA 17257-0708 USA

Library of Congress Cataloging-in-Publication Data

Green, Ralph, 1927-
   Sidelights and lighter sides of the War between the States : a feast of history cooked up in small bites! / by Ralph Green.
      p. cm.
   ISBN-13: 978-1-57249-394-0 (pbk. : alk. paper)
   ISBN-10: 1-57249-394-1 (pbk. : alk. paper)
   1. United States--History--Civil War, 1861-1865--Anecdotes. 2. United States--History--Civil War, 1861-1865--Social aspects--Anecdotes. 3. United States--History--Civil War, 1861-1865--Quotations, maxims, etc. 4. United States--History--Civil War, 1861-1865--Humor. I. Title.

   E655.G77 2007
   973.7--dc22

                                                                        2007010874

PRINTED IN THE UNITED STATES OF AMERICA

Contents

PREFACE

As a comedy the War Between the States would be a complete failure. It has been called many things, but I suspect that either "funny" or "amusing" was rarely found among the adjectives or phrases used. Yet there were many events and incidents that could be so described. Also, there were many occurrences, speeches, and written items that illustrated the hardships faced by the gallant people of the South, their efforts to cope, their spirit, and the nature of the conflict. Other available information showed how the true history of the ineptly phrased "inevitable conflict" has been warped and obscured.

Through the years I have gathered and recounted many such items in talks and in the *Rebel Rouser*, monthly publication of the General W. L. Cabell Camp of the Sons of Confederate Veterans. While there is much interest in the era of the war, many of the stories were too long for my use. Generally the items I have mentioned or published have been those that I could condense to essentials and still have something to inform or amuse my audience or readers. I presume that the results were appreciated as I have recognized my styling in republication of articles by some of my readers.

It has often been suggested that I publish these short narratives in a book, so now I have! My primary sources have been old books, magazines, newspapers, and letters. You won't find a bibliography because I gathered the information over many years for the pleasure of my readers, with no plans for a book or academic purposes. The content hereof is not presented in a strictly organized format, but randomly in the way many important events of the war took place. Whether you ingest these tales as occasional hors d'oeuvres or as a smorgasbord, I hope this food-for-thought feeds your interest in a critical period of Southern history.

In Defense of Confederate Symbols

Mark Twain once noted that the Mississippi River was 242 miles shorter than it had been 176 years earlier, giving an average reduction of one and one-third miles per year. According to that, he continued, anyone could see that in 742 years the

Lower Mississippi would be only a mile and three-quarters long, and Cairo and New Orleans would have joined their streets together and be plodding comfortably along under a single mayor and a mutual board of aldermen. Warning against extrapolations made without concern for context or common sense, Twain commented, "There is something fascinating about science. One gets such wholesale returns of conjecture out of such a trifling investment of fact."

The fact that some blacks object to the Confederate battle flag has been extrapolated to produce a finding that the flag is racist and should be removed from all public display, gatherings, and buildings. Must Old Glory and our national anthem be discarded lest we offend our citizens of English descent? Will Texans be required to raze the San Jacinto Monument and lower the Lone Star flag to avoid offending anyone of Mexican ancestry? Another extrapolation declaring the battle flag to be racist and divisive is based on the display of the flag by the KKK. That organization also displays the U.S. flag and the Christian cross. The Confederate flag flew over slavery for four years, but the U.S. flag did so before, during, and after the Confederacy. The cross of Christianity was prominent throughout the last 1800 years of slavery. Do we cast out the U.S. flag and the cross? Should history be ignored? Or preserved? The Confederate flags are neutral about race; to discard them because someone *says* they are racist would be the same as agreeing they *are* racist.

While on a business trip across the Pacific, I became aware of a problem we Southerners share with Hawaiians and the Maoris of New Zealand. The histories of all these peoples have become "fuzzy" and need to be preserved. The young people know all about the history of their conquerors, but not that of their own people. In the South, many young people are more familiar with Daniel Webster and Abraham Lincoln than with John Calhoun and Jefferson Davis. Anyone who reads a newspaper or watches TV can see the assaults on Southern history and heritage, with the proposals to remove Confederate memorials, delete Confederate holidays, and obliterate the memory of the Confederacy and its leaders. So-called "docudramas" pervert history in the name of entertainment or in the interest of "making a point" in support of a viewpoint or belief not supported by the facts. We are faced with one demand after another to ignore or rewrite history. No one could be more hypocritical than the groups and leaders who accuse Southerners of racism for wanting to recognize and honor their heritage. It is naive, if not downright dishonest, to contend that all the Martin Luther King holidays, boulevards, and centers are just honoring a civil rights leader and do not carry any current racial burden. It will be a sign of improvement and reason when blacks and others are just as uncomfortable as whites with these constant efforts to deny whites the pride deemed a natural right for blacks.

In England I was questioned about my Sons of Confederate Veterans lapel pin. After receiving an explanation of the pin's significance, my questioner exclaimed, "You Southerners are the Welsh of the United States." It took a moment for the accuracy of the statement to sink in. Just as the Welsh of Great Britain, we Southerners are proud of our country. At meetings of the Sons of Confederate Veterans, we salute the Confederate flag, but we pledge allegiance to the flag of the United States. While we recognize the outcome of past conflict, we don't forget why our forefathers fought. We resist the belittling efforts of those with only surface acquaintanceship with that cause, and resent insults to the gallant people of the Confederacy, black and white. The loss of the War Between the States by the South does not lessen the honor and respect due the Confederacy. We are told we should forget the Confederacy and its heroes, since the war ended over 125 years ago. Well, Christ died 2,000 years ago and the Ten Commandments are much older. I believe honor and principles have no expiration date. I shall continue to fly the battle flag. I shall continue to observe Confederate Memorial Day. I shall continue to honor the Confederacy. These are obligations to my ancestry, responsibilities to my descendants, and pleasures to myself.

APPETIZERS

It's the Truth

From the appendix, Congressional Globe, 1st Session, 30th Congress, January 12, 1848, page 94:

"People have the right to rise up and shake off the existing government." — Abraham Lincoln

Sorry About That

When the first Confederate shot hit Fort Sumter, the war could have started a month earlier than it actually did. Shortly after dawn on March 8, 1861, a Southern battery was conducting a drill, practicing the motions of firing its guns. Suddenly a mortar roared as an actual shot was fired at the fort. As the fort's garrison manned its guns to reply, the commander of the battery rushed over in a small boat under a flag of truce to apologize for the accidental firing.

Foretold

On December 12, 1862, Generals John B. Hood and Stonewall Jackson were riding to Lee's headquarters for consultation. The conversation turned to the future. Jackson asked Hood if he expected to live to see the end of the war. Hood answered that he didn't know, but he was inclined to think he'd be badly shattered before the struggle ended. When asked the same question, Jackson said without hesitation that he did not expect to live to the end of the contest, adding that he could not say he desired to do so. The casually spoken words foresaw the fate of each man: Hood was crippled before the close of the war; Jackson died following his wounding during a battle.

A Question of Legality

The requirement of the Yankee government for "re-admission" of Southern states is a rebuttal of any claim that secession was illegal, that the South was in rebellion against the legal government. Unless such states had left the Union, "re-admission"

1

could not occur. The requirement was a tacit admission that the Yankees waged a war of conquest against a foreign country.

States Rights Not a New Idea

George Washington, president of the United States, visited Boston during John Hancock's term as governor of Massachusetts. Hancock refused to call upon the president. He contended that any man who came into a state must yield rank to the governor of that state.

Well Said

From the preamble to Resolution No. 2, March 11, 1862, first session of the first Confederate Congress:

"Whereas the United States are waging war against the Confederate States, with the avowed purpose of compelling the latter to reunite with them under the same Constitution and Government; and whereas the waging of war with such an object is in direct opposition to the sound republican maxim that 'all good government rest upon the consent of the governed,' and can only tend to consolidation in the General Government and the consequent destruction of the rights of the States; and whereas the result being attained, the two sections can only exist together in the relation of the oppressor and the oppressed, because of the great preponderance of power in the Northern section, coupled with dissimilarity of interest."

Lincoln's View

The Great Emancipator did nothing in his so-called "Emancipation Proclamation" to free slaves in any area where he had any actual authority. The reason for such inaction may be inferred from Lincoln's words spoken in Charleston, Illinois, on September 18, 1858, and quoted in the September 1858 issue of *The Indiana Journal* of Indianapolis.

"I will say, then, that I am not, nor ever have been, in favor of bringing about in any way the social and political equality of the white and black races; that I am not, nor ever have been, in favor of making voters or jurors of Negroes, nor of qualifying them to hold office, nor to intermarry with white people; and I will say, in addition to this, that there is a physical difference between the white and black races which I believe will forever forbid the two races living together on terms of social and political equality. And inasmuch as they cannot so live, while they do remain together there must be the position of superior and inferior, and I as much as any other white man am in favor of having the superior position assigned to the white race...I will add to this that I have never seen, to my knowledge, a man, woman, or child who was in favor of producing a perfect equality, social and political between Negroes and white men."

If a Southerner made such a statement it would forever be used to illustrate the depths of regional racial prejudice.

Jackson at VMI

From 1851 until the outbreak of Civil War, Thomas J. Jackson taught at Virginia Military Institute in Lexington, Virginia. He served as professor of natural and experimental philosophy and instructor of artillery tactics. Natural philosophy in modern terms was roughly equivalent to physics. It included astronomy, mechanics, acoustics, optics, and other sciences, and was a difficult part of the mid-nineteenth century curriculum.

Many cadets found it almost impossible to master the subject under the best of circumstances. Unfortunately, Major Jackson, as he was known at VMI, was a mediocre teacher. Although highly intelligent, he could not convey the concepts to students. This inability, along with his humorless demeanor, soon branded Jackson as an unpopular faculty member, one who was the target of many student pranks. His ungainly appearance, strictness, and lack of humor provided fuel for much juvenile wit and merriment. Cadets delighted in drawing caricatures on the blackboard in Jackson's classroom, often a sketch depicting an officer with enormous feet. His exceptionally large shoe size inspired "Square Box," one of his several nicknames; others were "Old Jack," "Tom Fool," "Old Hickory."

Other incidents included throwing spitballs in class, making noises when his back was turned, dropping a brick as he passed underneath a barracks window, and pulling linchpins from cannon wheels during artillery drill.

Francis H. Smith, VMI superintendent during Jackson's era, wrote in his *History of the Virginia Military Institute*: "As Professor of Natural and Experimental Philosophy, Major Jackson was not a success. He had not the qualifications needed for so important a chair. He was no teacher, and he lacked the tact required in getting along with his classes...His genius was in the Science and Art of War. He found a field for the display of this genius when the war opened in 1861."

Black Days Ahead

On November 13, 1860, the *New Orleans Daily Crescent* commented on the situation facing Southerners:

"The history of the...Black Republican party of the North is a history of repeated injuries and usurpations, all having in direct object the establishment of absolute tyranny over the slave-holding states. And all without the smallest... justification...Every appeal and expostulation has only brought upon us renewed insults and augmented injuries. They have robbed us of our property...they have set at naught the decrees of the Supreme Court, they have invaded our States and killed our citizens, they have declared their unalterable determination to exclude us altogether from the Territories, they have nullified the laws of Congress, and finally they have capped the mighty pyramid of unfraternal enormities by electing Abraham Lincoln...on a platform and by a system which indicates nothing but the subjugation of the South and the complete ruin of her social, political and industrial institutions."

Bad Timing?

Abraham Lincoln was elected president of the United States on November 6, 1860. He was not inaugurated until March 4, 1861. Nearly a third of a year had elapsed before his inauguration. During that time most of the Southern states had seceded, led by their firebrand militants. If Lincoln had been inaugurated in mid-January as the president is today, there would have been less time to secede, select leaders, organize a government, and initiate rudiments of an army. It is possible that many of those firebrands would have been politically isolated from the moderates. Compromises might have been crafted and armed conflict avoided. We may have gone to war because we were slow to install a new president.

Origins

Critics of the South who decry Southern slave-owning before the war conveniently ignore the origins of our country's freedom. Our country sprang from seeds sown centuries ago. In feudal England, and much earlier in Athens and Rome, societies that did not consider owning slaves were incompatible with living in a democracy or a republic.

How True!

Jeremiah 1:14 foretold the future: "Out of the north an evil shall break forth upon all the inhabitants of the land."

Nobly Said

On Monday, April 29, 1861, President Jefferson Davis addressed the Confederate Congress. Among notable points of his speech:

"We feel that our cause is just and holy. We protest solemnly in the face of mankind that we desire peace at any sacrifice save that of honor and independence; we seek no conquest, no aggrandizement, no concession of any kind from the States with which we were lately confederated; all we ask is to be let alone; that those who never held power over us shall not attempt our subjugation by arms. This we will, this we must, resist to the direst extremity."

Rawle on the Constitution

In 1822 a textbook was introduced into the course of studies at West Point. This book, *Commentaries on the Constitution of the United States*, was popularly known as *Rawle on the Constitution*. Rawle was a Northern lawyer of great ability. His work was the very essence of States' Rights and the right of secession was distinctly set forth by him. The legislatures of New York, Vermont, Connecticut, and Massachusetts had previously asserted this right, so the book violated no Northern sentiment at the time it was introduced. The book remained at West Point as a standard textbook until 1861. When Jefferson Davis, Robert E. Lee, and Albert Sidney Johnston left the Union with their states, they were not only obeying their natural instinct and dictates of duty; they were obeying the instruction they had received at West Point.

The Solid North?

From an editorial in the *New York Tribune* in 1861:

"If it (the Declaration of Independence) justified the secession from the British Empire of three millions of colonists in 1776, we do not see why it would not justify the secession of five millions of Southerners from the Federal Union in 1861. If we are mistaken on this point, why does not someone attempt to show wherein and why?"

Truly Prophetic

General Winfield Scott knew that defense of their homes would harden the Southerners' spirit of dissidence. He warned Lincoln, "If you invade the South, I guarantee you that at the end of a year you will be further from a settlement than you are now."

What's in a Name?

Many politicos gathered in Montgomery were pleased at the birth but unhappy with the name they had settled on for the newborn nation, THE CONFEDERATE STATES OF AMERICA. That name was finally adopted only because they could agree on no other. Inspired by the concept of each state's sovereignty was one unaccepted suggestion, THE LEAGUE OF NATIONS.

A View of the Yankee People

A Confederate officer captured at Gettysburg writing to some friends about Yankees:

"They believed their manners and customs more enlightened, their intelligence and culture immeasurably superior. Brimfull of hypocritical cant and puritan ideas, they preach, pray and whine. The most parsimonious of wretches, they extol charity; the most inveterate blasphemers, they are the readiest exporters; the worst of dastards, they are the most shameless boasters; the most selfish of man, they are the most blatant philanthropists; the blackest-hearted hypocrites, they are religious fanatics. They are agitators and schemers, braggarts and deceivers, swindlers and extortioners, and yet pretend to Godliness, truth, purity and humanity. The shibboleth of their faith is, "The union must and shall be preserved", and they hold on to this with all the obstinacy peculiar to their nature. They say that we are a benighted people, and are trying to pull down that which God himself built up. Many of these bigots express great astonishment at finding the majority of our men could read and write; they have actually been educated to regard the Southern people as grossly illiterate, and little better than savages.

"The whole nation lives, breathes, and prospers in delusions; and their chiefs control the spring of the social and political machine with masterly hands. I could but conclude that the Northern people were bent upon the destruction of the South. All appeared to deprecate the war, but were unwilling to listen to a separation of the old union. They justified the acts of usurpation on the part of their government, and seem submissive to the tyranny of its acts on the plea of military necessity; they say that the union is better than the Constitution, and bow their necks to the yoke in the hope of success against us.

"A great many, I believe, act from honest and conscientious principles; many from fear and favor; but the large majority entertained a deep-seated hatred, envy and jealousy towards the Southern people and their institutions. They know (yet they pretend not to believe it) that Southern men and women are their superiors in everything relating to bravery, honesty, virtue and refinement, and they have become more convinced of this since the present war; consequently, their worst passions have become aroused, and they give way to frenzy and fanaticism. We must not deceive ourselves; they are bent upon our destruction, and differ mainly in the means of accomplishing this end. However, much as sections and parties that hate each other, yet, as a whole, they hate us more. They are so entirely incongruous to our people that they and their descendants will ever be our natural enemies."

Southern Views

"Resolved, that the several States composing the United States of America, are not united on the principle of unlimited submission to their General Government."—Thomas Jefferson, 1798

"Our present condition, achieved in a manner unprecedented in the history of nations, illustrates the American idea that governments rest upon the consent of the governed, and that it is the right of the people to alter or abolish governments whenever they become destructive of the ends for which they were established."—Jefferson Davis, inaugural address as president of the Confederate States, 1861

"Although the South would have preferred any honourable compromise to the fratricidal war which has taken place, she now accepts in good faith its constitutional results, and receives without reserve the amendment which has already been made to the constitution for the extinction of slavery. This is an event that has long been sought, though in a different way, and by none has it been more earnestly desired than by citizens of Virginia."—General R. E. Lee, 1866

English Views

"The Northern onslaught upon slavery was no more than a piece of specious humbug designed to conceal its desire for economic control of the Southern states."—Charles Dickens, 1862

"I deemed that you were fighting the battles of our liberty, our progress, and our civilization; and I mourn for the stake which was lost at Richmond more deeply than I rejoice over that which was saved at Waterloo."—British historian of liberty Lord Acton to General R. E. Lee, 1866

Lincoln's Views

"Any people anywhere, being inclined and having the power, have the right to rise up and shake off the existing government, and form a new one that suits them better. This is a most valuable, a most sacred right—a right which we hope and believe is to liberate the world. Nor is this right confined to cases in which the whole people of an existing government may choose to exercise it. Any portion of such people, that can, may revolutionize, and make their own so much of the territory as they inhabit."—Abraham Lincoln, 1848

"What then will become of my tariff?"—Abraham Lincoln to Virginia compromise delegation, March 1861

"If I could save the Union without freeing any slave I would do it, and if I could save it by freeing all the slaves I would do it; and if I could save it by freeing some and leaving others alone I would do that. What I do about slavery, and the colored race, I do because I believe it helps to save the Union, and what I forbear, I forbear because I do not believe it would help to save the Union."—Abraham Lincoln to Horace Greeley, 22 August 1862

Pro-Southern Activists Needed

"It does not require a majority to prevail, but rather an irate, tireless minority keen to set brush fires in people's minds."—Samuel Adams (1722–1803)

Clear Views from Overseas

English novelist Charles Dickens noted in 1861, "Union means so many millions a year lost to the South; secession means the loss of the same millions to the North. The love of money is the root of this, as of many other evils. The quarrel between the North and the South is, as it stands, solely a fiscal quarrel."

Karl Marx went to the heart of the matter when he said, "The war between the North and the South is a tariff war. The war is further not for any principle, does not touch the question of slavery, and in fact turns on the Northern lust for sovereignty."

Fought for the Southern Cause

When the War Between the States broke out, the majority of able-bodied men in East Texas went to war. Although most slaves stayed home to help look after the soldiers' families, some army-bound owners took their slaves along to serve as orderlies or cooks. However, East Texas slaves Penn Manuel and Turner Armstrong volunteered as combat soldiers and were accepted for service in Ross's Cavalry Brigade, a unit made up chiefly of Texans. They saw action in Alabama, Mississippi, and Tennessee. After the war the two former slaves, their loyalty unshaken, returned to East Texas to work for their former owners. The only difference was that they were now salaried workers. They belonged to the United Confederate Veterans and were granted veterans' pensions. They died about 1920 within a few months of each other and were buried along with other Confederate soldiers in the Mount Vernon Cemetery east of town. Their white friends turned out in great numbers for the funeral services and their graves were banked high with floral offerings from both races. It was an impressive gesture of respect for the two ex-slaves who had been ready to give their lives for the Southern cause.

Jefferson Davis, 1861

From his inaugural address as president of the Confederate States:

"Our present condition, achieved in a manner unprecedented in the history of nations, illustrates the American idea that governments rest upon the consent of the governed, and that it is the right of the people to alter or abolish governments whenever they become destructive of the ends for which they were established."

Honor Thy Forefathers

"He alone deserves to be remembered by his children who treasures up and preserves the memory of his fathers."—Edmund Burke (1729–1797)

Southern History Stolen

Why do Americans think of Lexington and Concord when they think of our nation winning its independence? Why not Sullivan's Island in South Carolina? Why has the British rout of the militia in Massachusetts become some sort of American triumph while in fact the first decisive American victory over the British has been forgotten? Because the loss of the War Between the States resulted in New Englanders writing our nation's history, i.e., writing off the Southern contributions. Even though the war began in Massachusetts, the British abandoned Boston and sailed to South Carolina to quell the rebellion. War there was far more savage and personal than anything fought in the North. British troops slaughtered their opponents all over South Carolina. Their atrocities aroused the emergence of partisan bands who doggedly and ably fought for liberty. Lord Cornwallis wrote that "there was scarce an inhabitant ... that was not in arms against us." There were 137 battles, actions, and engagements in South Carolina. In no other state was there so much fighting and bloodshed. Much more than New England, South Carolina deserves the credit for the colonies winning their independence.

To Be Precise

"The United States did not undergo Civil War in 1861—a collection of states did."—Professor James I. Robertson

No Wonder We Had to Fight

When asked, "Why not let the South go in peace?" Abraham Lincoln replied, "I can't let them go. Who would pay for the government?"

A Lousy Shot, Thank Goodness!

Captain Robert E. Lee endured a very close call during the Mexican War when a nervous sentry fired at him. The bullet came close enough that it actually singed Lee's uniform.

A Moral Leader

Ben "Beast" Butler gave early indications of his moral fiber. After enrolling as a divinity student in 1834 at Colby College, Maine, with a major as a divinity student, Butler petitioned the school administration to be excused from attending the college's compulsory church services.

Sumter a Pretext

Abraham Lincoln needed an incident to inflame and unite the population in the North. He knew that provisioning Sumter could provoke a war. In a letter to Gustavus Fox on 1 May 1861, he made it clear that he was pleased by the result of the firing on Fort Sumter. "You and I both anticipated that the cause of the country would be advanced by making the attempt to provision Ft. Sumter, even if it should fail; and it is no small consolation now to feel that our anticipation is justified by the result."

The Real Reason the North Opposed Secession

The Northern states used import taxes to protect their manufacturers from overseas competition. With a non-export-oriented economy the North paid minimal taxes into the Federal treasury. Heavily dependent upon exporting cotton (on which they paid excise taxes) and importing manufactured goods (on which they paid import taxes), the Southern states paid *87 percent* of the Federal treasury's tax revenues in 1860.

Lincoln and Civil Liberties

His admirers generally overlook Abraham Lincoln's suppression of civil liberties. Lincoln suspended the writ of habeas corpus, closed 300 opposition newspapers, arrested and jailed some 20,000 political opponents, and even threatened to arrest all of the Supreme Court when the justices expressed displeasure at his actions.

Slavery in the Southern View

The state of Virginia was the very first political body in the entire world to enact legislation to end the slave trade. On October 5, 1778, the General Assembly passed "An act for preventing the further importation of slaves," in which "any slave brought into the state contrary to the law would be then and forevermore free." In keeping with such opposition to the slave trade, the Constitution of the Confederate States of 1861 permanently abolished the practice in Article 1, Section 9, Clause 1. Confederate President Jefferson Davis made clear his plans for the infant country when he stated, "The slave must be made fit for his freedom by education and discipline and thus be made unfit for slavery."

WBTS

Alexander Stephens, vice president of the Confederate States of America, is believed to have originated the term "War Between the States."

Don't Pet the Pet

Lieutenant Colonel Robert E. Lee kept an unusual pet during his tour of duty with the 2nd U.S. Cavalry in Texas in the late 1850s. Fed frogs and mice, the "pet" was a rattlesnake.

Location of Constitution

The main library on the campus of the University of Georgia in Athens houses the original Constitution of the Confederate States of America.

Wartime English Comment

The Wigan Examiner, an English newspaper

"For the contest on the part of the North is now undisguisedly for empire. The question of slavery is thrown to the winds. There was hardly any concession in its favor that the South could ask which the North would refuse, provided only that the seceding States would re-enter the Union...Away with the pretence on the North to dignify its cause with the name of freedom to the slave!"

Fort Sumter Not U.S. Property

When Beauregard's troops fired on Fort Sumter on the morning of 12 April 1861, he was firing on land belonging to South Carolina, not the United States. To provide protection for Charleston, the land for the fort was ceded to the U.S. by the State of South Carolina in 1805, with certain conditions. Unless the conditions were met, the land reverted to the state. The conditions were that the fortifications were to be completed by a certain date and the fort would be continuously garrisoned thereafter. The fortifications were never completed and the fort was never garrisoned, therefore the Federal troops' move there in December of 1860 was illegal.

The conditional conveyance to the USA of land in the harbor of Charleston may be found in the reference library of the South Carolina Department of Archives and History. It is on pages 501 and 502 of *The Statutes At Large of South Carolina,* edited by Thomas Cooper, the fifth edition, printed in 1839 in Columbia. The act is entitled *"An Act to Cede to the United States Various Forts and Fortifications, and sites for the Erection of Forts"* and was passed December 19, 1805. Section three is the section requiring the U.S. to build the forts and maintain garrisons.

Still True

"Any society which suppress the Heritage of its conquered minorities, prevents their history, and denies them their symbols, has sewn the seed of its own destruction."—Sir William Wallace, 1281 AD

The Principle of Secessionism

The right of states to secede was an accepted principle throughout the United States until the War of Northern Aggression. The dominant view was that the Union was a marriage between sovereign states, binding until separation. There were seven unsuccessful secession movements between 1798 and 1856, with five of those in Northern states who wished to leave what they saw as an oppressive "unity."

A Keen Observer in 1860

"If we submit, the South is done. The concentration of absolute power in the hands of the North will develop the wildest democracy ever seen on earth."— Lawrence Keitt, South Carolina Congressman

Not a Matter of Principles

Northern states were in the midst of a depression before the war broke out. The United States Treasury was bankrupt. Northern Congressional representatives wanted high protective tariffs. The vast bulk of the Federal income came from those tariffs and was paid by the South, which depended heavily on imports. Therefore the South always fought the North's pet desires for such unjust protective tariffs. However, with the departure of the Southern states, this obstacle was removed and one of the first acts of the Republican-dominated 37th Congress was the immediate passage of the Morrill Tariff. At 47 percent this tariff was the highest in the history of the country. It went into effect in early March of 1861. At the same time, the Confederate Congress instituted a low 10 percent tariff, true to the South's historic aversion to protective tariffs. The natural result of the difference between these tariffs would be to divert trade from New York and Boston to the Southern ports.

If the secession of the South was allowed to stand, the tariff in the North would have to be lowered to match that of the South, or the Northern states would suffer financial ruin. Lincoln had already vowed in his Inaugural Address to enforce the Morrill Tariff at Charleston and other Southern ports. As representatives of the Virginia Convention, Mr. John Baldwin and Mr. A. H. H. Stuart went to Washington and met with Abraham Lincoln. They urged him to delay action that opened the war. In reply, Lincoln asked, "What is to become of my revenue in New York if there is a 10 percent tariff at Charleston?"

When war did occur, overseas observers easily discerned the principal reason. As Karl Marx and Friedrich Engels stated in 1861, "The war between the North and the South is a tariff war. The war is further, not for any principle, does not touch the question of slavery, and in fact turns on the Northern lust for sovereignty."

A War of Firsts

The WBTS marked the beginning of modern warfare. It was the first war with trenches and wire entanglements, the use of observation balloons and the telegraph, and the use of railroads for troop movements. First use armament included rifled cannon, armored ships, the submarine, and repeating rifles. This war was the first use in America of the military draft.

Ominous

For centuries brilliant fiery comets were deemed by many to be omens signaling impending disaster. In April 1861, such a comet lighted the skies of northern Virginia and Washington, D.C. An old Virginia slave named Oola had piercing eyes and was feared by other servants for her "evil eye" and apparent ability to "conjure spells." The blazing comet inspired Oola to make a dire prediction. She warned that it meant a great war was coming. Calling the comet a "great fire sword" with the handle toward the North and the point toward the South, she said it meant the North would take the sword and cut the heart out of the South. She added that if Lincoln took the sword he would perish by it. Word of her prediction spread and one of Lincoln's sons told him of it. He seemed greatly concerned and watched the comet intently, deep in thought.

International Recognition

Although the Confederacy had diplomatic representatives abroad, the only country that officially recognized the Confederate States of America was the Duchy of Saxe-Coburg-Gotha, which did so on July 30, 1861. (The ruler there had married a Southern belle.)

Prayer of a Texas Ranger

Texas Ranger Captain Jerome B. McGowan, 1846:

"Oh Lord! we are about to do battle with vastly superior numbers of the enemy, and Heavenly Father, we would mightily like for you to be on our side and help us, but if you can't do it, for Christ sake don't go over to the enemy, but just lie low and you'll see one of the damnedest fights you ever saw in all your life. Amen."

MAIN DISHES

How Appetizing!

The Civil War was the first American conflict that saw soldiers issued canned rations. "Embalmed beef" was the Union soldier's term for canned beef. "Panada" was a hot gruel made of corn meal and army crackers mashed in boiling water, ginger or "bully" soup. "Salt horse" was the name given army-issued beef, so heavily salted it had to be soaked for days before it could be eaten.

A Tad Hungry

Private George Watson enlisted in the W. P. Lane Rangers in April 1861. In September 1863, Watson had been on short rations for quite a spell. He vowed to his friends that if he ever got back to his father's house in Texas, he would "take a hundred biscuits and two large hams, call it three days rations, then go down on Goat Island and eat it all at one meal!"

Hard to Decide What to Eat

A Southern soldier wrote to his mother that he had a delightfully varied menu available to him:

Breakfast: Coffee, hardtack, pork
Dinner: Pork, coffee, hardtack
Supper: Hardtack, pork, coffee

A Thinking Man

General Albert Sidney Johnston was known as a deliberate man. When a friend started to dart across the street just in front of an approaching carriage, Johnston calmly told him, "I believe there is more room behind that carriage than in front of it."

Sounds Reasonable

Prior to entering the Confederate army, James H. Lane was a professor at the North Carolina Military Institute. Although less than thirty years of age, the future Confederate general was totally bald. Teased by cadets about his lack of hair, he responded that he dwelt on a higher plane than his more hirsute friends, there being not a hair between him and heaven.

An Inspiration

General Joseph Johnston always enjoyed the confidence of his men. They were reported to say as Johnston rode by, "There goes old Joe; he don't look like he's whipped, and I ain't till he is."

Taylor and Texans

General Richard Taylor was one of the most literate of the Confederate generals. He was also one of the most talented "cussers" in the Southern armies. During the rearguard action around Pleasant Hill, Taylor met some of Tom Green's Texans who told him, "We'll ride with you, General, if you won't cuss us." Taylor often cursed his Texans because of their lack of discipline and the familiarity between officers and enlisted men. Taylor said, "Distinctions of rank were unknown among my Texans. Officers and men addressed each other as Tom, Dick, or Harry, and had no more conception of military gradations than of the celestial hierarchy of the poets."

Had To Be a Reason

Riding briskly along, a cavalryman overtook an old straggling infantryman trudging wearily on the road and called out, "Hurry up there, old webfoot; the Yankees are coming!" The infantryman asked, "Did you see 'em, Mister?" "Yes, they are coming on right behind us!" The infantryman, no fan of the cavalry, responded, "Say, mister, was your hoss lame, or wus your spurs broke?"

Our English Friends

In October of 1864, Liverpool, England, was the site for a huge fund-raiser in behalf of Confederates in Union prisons. Held in the magnificent St. George's Hall on Lime Street, the event was designated "The Southern Bazaar." Stalls named after the various Southern states were staffed by local social leaders and members of the nobility. The affair was a brilliant success, with men and women competing to spend money. Approximately 30,000 pounds were raised in three days of the bazaar. No problem in connection with this project arose until the money was delivered; when Northern ladies who received the money tried to help the imprisoned Southerners, Union authorities caused never-ending delays and hindrances.

Why They Fought

Reverend Randolph H. M'Kim, DD, LLD:

"I was a soldier in Virginia in the campaigns of Lee and Jackson, and I declare I never met a soldier who had drawn his sword to perpetuate slavery...What he had chiefly at heart was the preservation of the supreme and sacred right of self-government...it was a very small minority of the men who fought in the Southern armies who were financially interested in the institution of slavery."

First Shot at Bethel

According to the *State Journal*, Raleigh, North Carolina, June 26, 1861, and Clark's *North Carolina Troops*, Vol. 1, page 96, the first shot fired at Bethel by a member of Captain Ashe's Company D was by Sam Mayho, a black servant of Lieutenant R. B. Saunders. The shot was fired at Major Theodore Winthrop, a member of Butler's staff, who was leading a charge of Massachusetts and Vermont troops.

Brotherly Love

At 4 p.m. on Christmas Day in 1861, Val C. Giles of the 4th Texas Infantry was on picket duty at Cockpit Point, Virginia, on the Potomac River. Suddenly he heard his name being called by his brother, Lewis, who was supposed to be in Tennessee with the 8th Texas Cavalry. Val looked in every direction but Lewis was nowhere around. At 4 p.m. on Christmas Day in 1861, Lewis L. Giles passed away in Gallatin, Tennessee, from wounds received eight days earlier.

Considerate

After a battle during which a farmhouse had been destroyed, pigs and chickens were wandering about the area. The Southern troops had not eaten in forty-eight hours, but strict orders had been issued against foraging the livestock of farmers around there. With a dry humor one of the troopers commented that someone should take care of the homeless creatures. Within moments his suggestion was heeded and the men took care of every one they could catch!

Don't Ask

A newly inducted Georgia company was on its first march, walking to Evergreen, Alabama. Their feet were sore and their untried muscles weary. Some civilians they met were asked the distance to Evergreen and said "about five miles." Marching onward, the company met another traveler who said "six miles" when asked the same question. Tramping along the dusty road they met another man. Before anyone could ask the distance to Evergreen, Tom Eve yelled, "For the Lord's sake, don't inquire again. The road gets longer every time you ask!"

Couldn't Take Chances

Abolitionist Wendell Phillips was visiting Charleston, South Carolina, and ordered breakfast served in his hotel room. When a slave brought the food, Phillips seized on the opportunity to impress on the man that he regarded him as a brother and wanted to free all slaves. The slave seemed more interested in serving the food than in his own social position. Discouraged, Phillips finally told him to leave, saying he could not bear to be served by a slave. "You must excuse me," the slave replied, "I am obliged to stay here 'cause I'm responsible for the silverware."

Flying the Colors

During the first day at Gettysburg the flag of the 26th North Carolina was shot down fourteen times as each bearer was killed or wounded.

We Had Them, Too

Although the galvanized Rebs (captured Confederates who donned the Union blue) are fairly well known, little publicity has been given to the galvanized Yankees. In 1864 two battalions of captured Federals were enlisted in the Confederate army. One company of these troops fought gallantly against Grierson's raiders, holding out for hours under hopeless conditions before becoming prisoners of war.

Giving Credit Where Due

After six tremendous Union assaults on his position on August 29, 1862, Stonewall Jackson's troops still held Stony Ridge. That night a friend told Jackson, "We have won this battle by the hardest kind of fighting." Jackson replied, "No, no, we have won it by the blessing of Almighty God!"

Inspired Eloquence

During the beginning of the conference with Sherman for the surrender of Joseph E. Johnston's troops, John C. Breckinridge sat devoid of animation. Due to an early morning start he had missed not only his sleep but also his customary bourbon. Following an invitation by Sherman to have a drink, Breckinridge poured a tremendous drink and downed it with satisfaction. He then began arguing with such eloquence, marshalling facts, laws, and precedents, that Sherman protested, "See here, gentlemen, who is doing the surrendering, anyhow? If this goes on, you'll have me sending a letter of apology to Jeff Davis!"

A Record Trip

Following the Confederate seizure of a large supply of Federal whiskey at Hagerstown, Maryland, John Bell Hood demanded and got some of the liquor for his Texans. The brigade was marching from Virginia across the narrow neck of Maryland on its way to Gettysburg, Pennsylvania. Although Hood specified a distribution of one-fourth pint of whiskey per man, non-drinkers passed on their allowance to their drinking buddies. The combination of a long march, scanty rations, and a few gills of whiskey was disastrous. One member of the brigade said that within half an hour there were more drunken men than he had seen in his entire life, describing them as "drunk all over, through and through, up and down, side, edge and fore and aft. It kept the sober boys busy to keep the drunk ones from killing each other. Some soon fell by the wayside helpless and were dumped into wagons and ambulances and hauled the balance of the day. Some others were not seen for 15 hours afterwards and when they caught up with their commands they were quite sober but their eyes looked like two burnt holes in a blanket." After reforming into some semblance of order, the brigade moved on to a site near Greencastle, Pennsylvania, where they cooked supper and camped for the night. The brigade set a record by being in four states in one day: they ate breakfast in Virginia, lunch in the state of Maryland, supper in the state of Pennsylvania, and slept that night in a state of intoxication.

A Certainty

"I wish all Yankees were in hell," said a tired, lean member of the Stonewall Brigade. "I don't," said another, "because Old Jack would have us standing picket at the gate before night and in there before morning."

A Secret Friend

In York, Pennsylvania, in late June of 1863, a little girl, about twelve years old, ran up and handed a large bouquet of flowers to General John B. Gordon. In the center of the bouquet was a note outlining numbers and dispositions of Union forces in Wrightsville, toward which Gordon was moving, and making suggestions for a plan of attack. Written in a woman's delicate handwriting the note was unsigned. It gave no assurance of sympathy for the South, but was so terse and detailed it inspired Gordon's confidence. Nearing Wrightsville, Gordon went to a high ridge as the note instructed and used field glasses to scan the town and protecting troops. Everything checked, including strategic physical items, such as a gorge extending around the flank of the enemy. Gordon followed suggestions of the note and forced the Union troops to retreat or surrender. He never discovered the identity of the writer of the note.

The Fifth General

You may have heard of the bodies of five generals lying on the porch at Carnton after the Battle of Franklin. Information for this story of the "fifth general" was provided by Tim Burgess of White House, Tennessee.

Grandson of a captain in the Continental Cavalry, Robert Butler Young was born in 1828 in South Carolina. He graduated from the Georgia Military Academy. A major in the Georgia Militia, in 1848 he commanded its 338th Battalion. Robert experienced financial problems and by 1859 had moved wife and daughter to Bosque County, Texas. He considered joining the Texas Rangers, but he decided he would rather fight the Yankees than the Indians. Commissioned captain in the 6th Texas Volunteers in 1861, he reported to the 10th Texas Infantry as major, becoming its lieutenant colonel in September 1862. Wounded and captured with his unit in late 1862, he was very ill while in prison at Camp Chase in Ohio. When he was exchanged in 1863, he was met by his younger brother, Pierce, who never forgave the Yankees for their treatment of Robert. A major general of cavalry under Robert E. Lee, Pierce was shocked at seeing an emaciated Robert, "a living skeleton with clothes dropped over him."

Colonel Young went to his family's plantation near Carterville, Georgia, to recuperate from his wound, his illness, and the shameful treatment he had received from the Yankees. Crushed, haggard, and spiritless, he was nursed back to health by his family and rejoined his unit. By September of 1864, the 10th Texas numbered only 96 out of its original 1,050 men. During his fighting against Sherman in the bloody Atlanta Campaign, Colonel Young was again wounded. He was cited by General Granbury for his gallantry in battle. At the Battle of Franklin on 30 November 1864, while serving as Granbury's chief of staff, Colonel Young was killed along with more than one hundred of his fellow Texans. After the battle, the body of Colonel Young was placed tenderly on the porch of the McGavock mansion "Carnton" along with the bodies of Generals Cleburne, Strahl, Granbury, and Adams. A Confederate flag covered each body. This scene led to the misconception that all five generals killed outright at Franklin were laid side by side on the porch. The generals and Young and some of their staff were buried first in Rose Hill Cemetery in Columbia, Tennessee, then reburied in the Ashwood church cemetery nearby. Although the generals were later moved to their home states, Lieutenant Colonel Robert Butler Young remains under his original grave marker.

Blacks in the Union Army

Blacks in the Union army were terribly mistreated. They were given white officers and paid one-half the rate of whites. They were assigned guard duty, jobs, and risks that whites didn't want or refused. Their death rate was almost unbelievable. Of the 186,000 who served in the Federal army, 68,000 died: 2,000 in battle, over 65,000 from sickness and disease, often from duties served in place of whites.

The Treatment of President Davis
(an editorial in the May 26, 1866, issue of the *New York World*)

"It is no longer a matter of newspaper rumor that the treatment which Jefferson Davis has received during his incarceration in Fortress Monroe has been such as to break down his constitution and to put him, after twelve months of protracted suffering, in imminent peril of death. The President of the United States recently ordered the post surgeon at Fortress Monroe to make a...thorough report upon the condition of Mr. Davis' health. That report can not be read by any honorable and right-minded American, no matter what his sectional feelings or his political opinions may be, without a sickening sensation of shame for his country and a burning flush of indignation against the persons who have prostituted their official position to inflict upon the American name an ineffaceable brand of disgrace by the wanton and wicked torture of an invalid lying a helpless prisoner in the strongest fortress of the Union."

An Honest Man

General Edward P. Alexander was approached near Hagerstown by an elderly member of the Dunkard faith. Confederate Scouts had taken the man's only horse. The Dunkard told the general that without a horse his crop would be lost. He asked the general to trade him one of the hoof-sore horses that the Confederates would be leaving behind anyway. Recognizing the man as a born gentleman and anxious that the war not grind the poor fellow into poverty, the general suggested that the man take two or three of the horses. The man said that the rule of his church was an eye for an eye, a tooth for a tooth, a horse for a horse, and he could not break the rule. The general told the Dunkard that the Lord had made all horses and knew a good horse was worth a dozen old scrubs. He finally prevailed upon the man to take two by calling one a gift. Late that night the Dunkard returned one horse. He tied the horse to a fence and rode off after saying, "You made it look all right to me today when you were talking, but after I went to bed tonight I got to thinking it all over, and I don't think I could explain it to the church and I'd rather not try."

Dying to Join the South

At the outbreak of the War, Confederate General G. W. Smith and M. Lovell were street commissioners in New York City. Finding their means of escape practically cut off, they developed a daring plan with the aid of a friendly doctor. Smith supposedly fell ill. The doctor pronounced Smith's condition so serious that no one but Lovell could see him. Smith's health became worse and he finally "died." While a handsome coffin filled with bricks was buried with honor, Smith made his way in disguise into the Southern lines. Lovell soon found a way to join him.

Took No Chances

On July 13, 1862, Terry's Texas Rangers, the 8th Texas Cavalry, with Nathan Bedford Forrest and two battalions of Confederate troopers, arrived at the headquarters of Union Brigadier General Thomas Turpin Crittenden in Murfreesboro, Tennessee. The outnumbered Forrest ordered Crittenden to surrender his large garrison, telling him, "If you refuse I will charge you with the Texas Rangers under the black flag." One thousand forty Federals surrendered, along with mountains of stores and four pieces of artillery.

Unquestionably

Q. Why did the vipers leave the Yankee alone when he fell in their nest?

A. Professional courtesy.

Q. A Yankee and a pope arrived in Heaven at the same time. The Yankee got the most lavish accommodations possible, but the pope received the bare minimum. Why?

A. There were plenty of popes in Heaven, but they had never had a Yankee!

Q. What's the first thing to do if you see a Yankee up to his neck in concrete?

A. Order more concrete!

Too Slow

Captain Rufus F. Dunn, of Company F, 3rd Texas Dismounted Cavalry, was a gallant soldier, pleasant companion, and always a jokester. Dunn had his leg broken by grapeshot and was being cared for at Iuka, Mississippi. When a volunteer nurse asked him how he received his injury, he solemnly told her, "Well, madam, I am captain of a company, and when we got into the battle the Yankees began shooting cannonballs at us, and to protect my men I got out in front of them and would catch the cannonballs as they came and throw them back at the Yankees; but when the battle grew real hot they came so fast I couldn't catch all of them, and one of them broke my leg."

Men of Honor

The wording of a parole did not interest most men. However, two Texans captured at Iuka would not accept paroles describing them as officers in the "so-called Confederate States Army." Colonel H. P. Mabry of Hebert's Brigade and Captain Lee of the 3rd Texas chose to go to an Illinois prison rather than sign a parole carrying the "so-called" reference.

Actually Southern

Among the best-known music in the United States is that of a Southern hymn. William Steffe wrote "Say Brothers Will We Meet You Over On The Other Shore?" for an 1852 revival camp meeting in Charleston, South Carolina. A U.S. infantry regiment at Fort Warren in Massachusetts found the melody good for marching and fitted new words to it, starting with "John Brown's body lies a-moldering in the grave." While visiting Washington, Julia Ward Howe heard an army unit playing and singing their version. The next day she wrote new words and the Southern hymn became the bitter attack on the South, "Battle Hymn of the Republic."

A Better Choice

J. Q. Quattlebun was appointed major of the 5th Texas. A non-Texan, he was deeply disliked by the Texans to whom he was equally hostile. After a very short time, he left the regiment, saying that if he had to associate with devils he would wait till he went to hell where he could select his own company.

Close Up Those Ranks

A Virginia captain shouted at his straggling, worn men, "Close up, boys, hang you, close up! If the Yanks were to fire on you when you're straggling along that way, they couldn't hit one of you!" And the boys closed up.

Spirited Cause

Union General William T. Sherman lamented:

"No amount of poverty or adversity seems to shake these Rebels' faith. Their wealth and luxury is gone, their money is worthless, starvation is within view, and their causes enough to make the bravest tremble yet I see no sign of let-up in their spirit. They are tired of war, but they are determined to fight it out."

Journalistic Integrity

In June 1863, Colonel John B. Frick was in charge of Union forces at Wrightsville, Pennsylvania. To keep General John B. Gordon's Southern troops from using a bridge there to cross the Susquehanna River and advance on Lancaster, Frick ordered the bridge destroyed. After an explosion failed to bring the bridge down, Frick ordered it burned, careless of danger to the town. The fire spread to lumber yards on the river's edge, then to the town. Southern troops entering the town formed bucket brigades around the burning district, passing buckets of water to combat the raging fire. The Southerners worked long into the night and eventually saved both the town and the bridge.

Mrs. L. L. Rewalt was a resident of the town and her husband was away in the Union army. However, before Gordon and his weary men left in the morning, she was one who expressed heartfelt thanks to them for gallantry in saving her home and the town, recognizing that from a military standpoint only the bridge needed saving. When reporting on the fire, the Northern press showed the same freedom from bias, which it still displays. It stated that Gordon and his men had set it!

Careful What You Wish For

On August 2, 1862, a hot fight erupted in Orange Court House, Virginia. Defenders and Yankee invaders fought hand-to-hand in the streets. Watching the combat, local residents cheered on the Confederates. During a respite in the fighting, a fiery young lass cried out, "Oh, I wish I was a man!" A cavalryman who had been in the thick of the fighting retorted: "If you was, you would wish you was a gal again mouty soon!"

Cooperation Needed

In May of 1864, U. S. Grant crossed the Rapidan and made his headquarters in a deserted farmhouse. Speaking to some reporters, Grant reviewed the situation. He stated that Lee must know by then of his advance although not necessarily of the extent of the movement. A reporter asked him how long it would take him to get to Richmond. Grant promptly responded, "I will agree to be there in about four days—that is, if General Lee becomes party to the agreement. But if he objects, the trip will undoubtedly be prolonged."

Two Brothers

Charlie and Sam Futch, Alabama brothers, enlisted at the same time, but wound up in different regiments. When parting, each promised to write often. Sam wrote first. Charlie responded: "Sam, I have carried your letter through two regiments trying to find someone who can read it but there ain't a man who can even make out the day of the month." Sam waited a while, then wrote back, "I have not heard from you in four weeks. If you are dead please write and let me know so I won't waste my time writing you anymore."

Played It Close

While under the command of General Rosser in early 1864, Harry Gilmore came back from a raid on Union rail facilities with a feeling he was on borrowed time. In his left breast pocket, under two coats, he carried a deck of cards that had been almost completely penetrated by a rifle bullet. Only the card nearest his skin had escaped defacement, an ace of spades. From his return, a standing query from Rosser was, "Major, are spades trumps?"

Stick to the Facts!

Early one morning in late February 1865, Jesse McNeill and his Rangers quietly entered Cumberland, Maryland, captured Union Generals George Crook and Benjamin F. Kelley, and then withdrew to Virginia with their prisoners. Two nights later Mary Clara Bruce, the future bride of General Kelley, was scheduled to sing at a local theater. As she began her first song, "He Kissed Me When He Left," an inebriated member of the audience loudly exclaimed, "No, I'll be damned if he did! McNeill didn't give him time!"

A Partisan Conversation

A voracious reader, one Union officer always tried to work a discussion of books into any conversation. He once read Victor Hugo's *Les Miserables* in an English translation since he spoke no French. Shortly afterward while passing a house near the Bloody Angle at Spotsylvania he saw a young lady sitting on the porch. He stopped, bowed to her, and endeavored to engage her in conversation. After a few words with her, he remarked, "By the way, have you seen 'Lee's miserables'?" anglicizing pronunciation of the book's title. Indignant, the lady replied, "Don't talk to me that way. They're a good deal better than Grant's miserables anyhow!"

Close!

From the *Confederate Baptist*, Wednesday, December 3, 1862:

"In the absence of field officers, and after the wounding of the senior captain, the command of the 15th Virginia Regiment at Sharpsburg devolved on Reverend E. J. Willis, formerly pastor of the Leigh St. Baptist Church and now Captain of Company A. At one time, seeing that the flag-bearer had been shot down, he seized the colors himself. Waving them, he was in advance when the staff was cut in two by a bullet. Eleven bullets passed through various portions of his clothing, one through his cap, and one carried off a portion of the scabbard of his sword."

Inspired Nomenclature

Colonel Hal Simpson always delighted in the interesting names of Texans who enlisted in Hood's Brigade. Company A boasted "Argyle Campbell," "Winkfield Shropshire," and "Glen Drumgoole," all good Scots. Company G (the Reagan Guards) had "Smith Bottoms," "Jasper Stalcup," and "Elbert E. Pugh." Company H listed "Romulus T. Rhome," "George Washington Culpepper," "John Steincipher," and "Ignatz Honingsburger." Company M included "Reason Hutto," "Bolewar J. Capps," "J. Pink O'Rear," "Buttons Evans," "Mutt Morgan," and "Shady Roach."

Keep It Quiet

During the night of May 21–22, 1864, near Front Royal, Virginia, 200 members of the 15th New York Cavalry held a party that ended in a riot. Officers from a reserve post half a mile away had to ride in and settle the dispute. After a brief quiet, Union Captain Michael Auer heard several shots from the same site and galloped into the camp shouting and cursing, demanding to know the meaning for "all this fuss." The answer stunned him: "It means Mosby's got you." While the attention of the Yankees had been on the riot, John S. Mosby and 99 of his Rangers had captured the picket post and then the camp, taking 75 horses and 16 prisoners. Auer became number 17.

Red Alert

Returning from a raid on Union troops at Belle Plain, Virginia, Lieutenant Alfred Glascock and other Mosby's Rangers were pursued by a regiment of Union cavalry. Approaching a railroad spur near Fredericksburg, they found Yankee infantry barring their escape route. Acting quickly, Glascock waved his men on at a gallop, shouting, "Mosby is after us! Get out of the way!" Mistaking the Rangers for Union cavalry, the Yankees scurried for cover as the Rangers raced to safety over the unguarded road.

Not a Failure

Following their defeat of Union forces at the Battle of Monocacy on June 9, 1864, the troops of Jubal Early had carried the war to the gates of Washington, D.C. For two days, on June 11–12, Early and his men probed and tested the fortifications that encased that city. Early always knew he could not really capture the city. After calling off the attack, he evaluated the results: "we haven't taken Washington, but we've scared Abe Lincoln like h———l."

Camp Ford

In 1862 a training camp for Confederate recruits was established about four miles northeast of Tyler, Texas. Named after John S. "Rip" Ford, Camp Ford became a military prison in 1863. It held the largest concentration of Union prisoners west of the Mississippi, up to 4,000 at one time. The camp had a mortality rate of less than 5 percent, one of the lowest rates of all prisons during the war. Prisoners were allowed to ease their boredom by engaging in commercial enterprises and sold their products to guards or to civilians of the area. Some baked cakes, cookies, and pies. One published *The Old Flag*, a newspaper. Others utilized crude machinery to produce goods including axe handles, baskets, caps and hats, brooms, candles, chairs, eating utensils, chessmen, pails, pipes, and soap. The prison operated until May 1865, when remaining prisoners were escorted to Shreveport by the 15th Texas Cavalry. The stockade was destroyed after the war by members of the 10th Illinois Cavalry, who had been imprisoned there.

No Problem

The battle had been difficult, fought over terrible terrain in a freezing rain. The Southerners had advanced through a swollen river and climbed a vertical embankment to attack the foe. Later an officer asked a hill-country farm lad in his company how difficult he had found the battlefield. The young man replied that at home he had crossed rougher country than that to get to the barn!

Hood's Texas Brigade

Private J. S. W. Cooke, Company B, 4th Texas, was the only non-volunteer member of Hood's Texas Brigade. He was conscripted June 6, 1862, at Culpeper Court House, Virginia.

Private Rube Blalock, Company D, 1st Texas, was the only member of the brigade to die from a bayonet thrust. He was slain at Spotsylvania Court House, on May 10, 1864.

Captured September 17, 1862, at Antietam, Lieutenant J. M. Alexander, Company K, 5th Texas, escaped and rejoined his company. Captured at Gettysburg on July 2, 1863, he escaped and rejoined his company. On October 8, 1864, he was captured at Darbytown Road. Once more he escaped and rejoined his company, this time staying with it until his parole at Appomattox.

Only 348 rifles were surrendered to the Federals at Appomattox by the 602 survivors of the brigade. Many of the troops smashed their guns against trees rather than give them up.

In the first half of 1863 the versatile foot soldiers of the brigade fought against gunboats and engaged in the first trench warfare in American history. One regiment, the 3rd Arkansas, was briefly mounted as a cavalry unit.

Thomas Jonathan Jackson
1824–1863

Soldierly
Thorough
Orderly
Natural
Eccentric
Wise
Adaptive
Laconic
Levelheaded
Judicious
Abstemious
Capable
Knightly
Solemn
Omnipotent
Noble

On Second Thought…

Union soldiers, camped on Cemetery Hill, near Moorefield, West Virginia, were surrounded by members of Hanse McNeill's Rangers. When a six-foot Georgian called on a Federal officer to surrender, the Ranger was shocked to hear, "I am an officer and will only surrender to an officer." The Southerner had his own ideas on the subject however. Raising his gun he barked, "We'll see! At this moment we are on equality, sir, officer or no officer." Without further remark the Federal submitted.

Uninvited Guests

Cleanliness was not a normal attribute of, nor readily available option to, many WBTS soldiers. It is said that from privates to generals most of them suffered infestation by "body varmints." One Virginian wrote home that before going to sleep one night he had removed his shirt and dropped it on the ground. The next morning he awoke and saw the shirt jerking about as though a rat had become trapped under it. However, it turned out merely to be fleas darting around wondering where he had gone!

Inspired Responses

In 1862 when he took command of the Union Army of Virginia, Union General John Pope boasted to the troops, "I have come to you from the West, where we have always seen the backs of our enemy." When he heard the statement, Richard Ewell joked, "Pope would not want to see the backs of my men. Their pantaloons are out at the rear!" Stonewall Jackson was more grim, "They say this new general claims my attention. Well, please God, he shall have it!" (And he did!)

As Seen by Our Enemies

A Yankee soldier's critique of Confederate troops: "In manners, in the conduct of soldiers and the discipline, these bundles of rags, these cough-wrecked, diseased, and starved men excel our well-fed, well-clothed, our best soldiers."

Quick Heat

It was a bitterly cold night but the 13th Virginia had been ordered to light no fires so as to avoid drawing enemy cannon fire. Billy Smith reached his limit of endurance and said he would have a fire if all the shells in the Yankee army were fired at him. Suiting action to words, he piled up logs and built a fire. Promptly a 20-pound shell passed over him. "Let 'em come, I'm going to get warm, damn the Yankees!" Hardly had he spoken when a shell struck the fire in the center. With a quick decision that he had warmed himself sufficiently, Smith covered the scattered embers and spent the balance of the night behind a nearby tree.

A Difference

In late April 1862, enraged by a terse reply by which Stonewall Jackson dismissed an elaborate scheme of Ewell's, General Richard Ewell exploded to a fellow officer, "Did it ever occur to you that General Jackson is crazy? He is as crazy as a March hare!" About six weeks later he told the officer, "I take it all back...Old Jackson's no fool. He keeps his own counsel, and does curious things, but he has method in his madness." Grinning, he added, "He's disappointed me entirely!"

Ladies of the South

The women of the wartime South have been described as the "staunchest Rebels." Some worked at home to make life more comfortable for the men at the front; Mrs. A. H. Gay of Decatur, Georgia, knitted a sock a day and packaged each pair separately, enclosing other items of clothing, gloves, and notes of encouragement. Others worked in war industries, in garment and textile plants, in hospitals, and on farms and plantations. Some, such as Rose O'Neal Greenhow and Belle Boyd, provided valuable service as spies and couriers. A few were not content to play any type of passive role, but cut their hair, disguised their identities, and followed the men into the fighting ranks. In addition to her service as a spy, Nancy Hart led an attack that captured a Union garrison at Summerfield, West Virginia, and helped Jackson in his famous Valley campaign; she escaped arrest in 1862 by killing a Yankee guard. While their men were away at war, the women of Bascom, Georgia, formed a female military company to protect the home front. The activities of the women of the South were essential to the life of the Confederacy.

Confederate Indians

Even before the War Between the States, hostile Indians raided Texans, stealing horses, cattle, women, and children, and left a trail of fire and ruin. In contrast the Tonkawa Indians sought friendship with Texans. During the war they were valued allies, scouting against hostile tribes and guarding against signs of Federal invasion. A few Tonkawa scouts were considered more useful than two or three companies of regular soldiers; they could stalk enemies better than bloodhounds. Old Texas Indian fighters in wartime asked for Tonkawa scouts. From the Red River to the Rio Grande, commanders valued them so much that they fed them at personal expense when necessary to obtain their help. The Tonkawas paid dearly for their Confederate loyalty. On October 25, 1862, their camp near Anadarko, Oklahoma, was attacked by hostile Indians who slew 137 men, women, and children. Granted a tribal home at Fort Griffin, Texas, they returned to Oklahoma in 1884.

Not an Even Swap

Colonel Robert Ingersoll of the 11th Illinois Cavalry was noted for his ability to talk long and loudly about any subject at any time. Captured at Lexington, Tennessee, by General Nathan Bedford Forrest, Ingersoll immediately began making fiery speeches for the Union to his captors. Exasperated, Forrest finally told Ingersoll that if he didn't shut up he would be exchanged for a U.S. Army mule!

Not a Well Man

Prior to his appointment as commissary general of the Confederate army, Colonel Lucius B. Northrop had been on sick leave from the U.S. Army for twenty-two years.

Stonewall Jackson

Thomas J. "Stonewall" Jackson regarded duty as a calling, not an elective. He remained close to his men and suffered with them. Soldiers arising with snow on their blankets would see their commander rise a few feet away. Jackson ignored grumbling by his men. While he did not remonstrate, neither did he relent; soldiers were meant to endure hardships. Combat and comfort did not coexist in his army. Jackson's concept of war was a simple one: "Armies are not called out to dig trenches, to throw up breastworks, to live in camps, but to find the enemy and strike him..." While many of his men thought him peculiar, they trusted and respected him. They cheered whenever he rode past them, even on forced marches. The Stonewall Brigade fought with distinction from First Manassas to Appomattox. Jackson's most famous nickname never appealed to his troops, who regularly referred to him as "Old Jack," "Old Blue Light," "Hickory," or even "Square Box" (because of his large shoe size).

Ordered to take command of Confederate forces in the Shenandoah Valley, Jackson was reluctant to leave the brigade. When he did so, he gave a farewell address at the request of his troops. Rising in his stirrups before the troops, he yelled: "In the Army of the Shenandoah you were the First Brigade! In the Army of the Potomac you were the First Brigade! In the Second Corps of the army you are the First Brigade! You are the First Brigade in the affection of your general, and I hope by your future deeds and bearing you will be handed down as the First Brigade in this our Second War of Independence. Farewell!"

Misbehaving

Ex-Governor Chapman of Alabama suffered spiteful depredations on his property near Huntsville by Yankee soldiers. Thinking such actions must be beyond orders, he went to see the colonel in charge of the troops. The colonel interrupted his account, stating, "Well, Governor, I don't think you have any property about here." "Well, sir, if it is not mine, be so kind as to inform me whose it is." "It is the property of the Government of the United States." "Ah, very well, Colonel, I have come to inform you then that your soldiers are treating the property of the United States Government damned badly. Good day!"

Eccentric

General John B. Gordon once described General Richard Ewell as "the most eccentric genius in the Confederate Army." However, it may be that his eccentricity was actually a facet of his tendency to concentrate only on his thoughts rather than his surroundings. Ewell's principal aide and stepson, Campbell Brown, told of an incident illustrating his single-mindedness. The two men stopped at a farmhouse for some buttermilk. While the lady there went to get some, Ewell picked up her scissors and began to cut his own hair. Only half-done when she returned, Ewell laid down the scissors, drank the milk, then rode off with the hair short on one side of his head and untouched on the other. Several days passed before Brown could get Ewell to finish the job.

Points of View

Two soldiers lay in their blankets staring up into the darkness. One asked, "What made you go into the army, Tom?" "Well," said Tom, "I had no wife and I loved war, Jack, so I went. What made you go?" "Well, I had a wife, and I loved peace, Tom, so I went."

The Texas Legislature

During the War Between the States, Texas legislators were in almost continuous session. Poor pay and inflated Confederate money caused many members to live in tents and covered wagons on the capitol grounds and cook over campfires. The legislators passed laws to raise, equip, and supply Texas soldiers fighting on all fronts. They also provided for the defense of the state's 2,000-mile frontier and coastline against Indians and Federal invaders. As the Federal naval blockade reduced imports, the legislature established plants to make guns, powder, cloth, and salt. Contracts, subsidies, and land grants were provided to encourage private industry to help meet heavy wartime demands for arms, supplies, clothing, and food. The lawmakers taxed property and business and required farmers to turn in tithes of produce to meet the crisis. Funds were voted to buy cotton to be exchanged for goods in Mexico to aid soldiers' dependents and to provide hospitals and medical care for troops in and out of the state.

Dedicated Workers

Afflicted with arthritis, Joseph M. Sparkman lay on a cot to run a shop making shoes for the Confederate army. This was near his home, on the Old Gilmer Road a couple of miles north of present-day Highway 80 at Longview, Texas. The boys and old men who made the shoes were taught and supervised by "Uncle Ben," a skilled slave shoemaker who had come with Sparkman from Georgia. Such men typify the home-front workers who made cloth and clothing, mined salt, and hunted the woods for medicinal herbs to meet the pressing needs of the South. Both Sparkman and "Uncle Ben" are buried in the family plot near where they served their country.

Texas Salt

Local salt production declined throughout the South between 1850 and 1861, as salt began to be imported from England. When the Federals set up their embargo in 1861, local production began again. A major source of salt in East Texas was the Neches Saline, southwest of Tyler and now covered by Lake Palestine. Here salt was produced by evaporating water drawn from shallow wells. Indispensable in the human diet, salt had many other uses. It was used in preserving meat and other foods. It was used to cure hides and set dyes in cloth. It was a necessity for the care of cavalry horses and army dray teams. Texas Rangers used salt as an antiseptic for wounds. Rattlesnake bites were lanced and the raw incisions filled with salt. Troops deloused their clothing and blankets by boiling them in strong salt solutions. The operation of the Neches Saline plant was so essential during the war that state troops were detailed to help run its twelve furnaces and produce 100 sacks of salt a day.

Feminine Secessionists

Secession was enthusiastically advocated and greeted by Southern women, who then pressured their men to enlist. Mrs. Joseph Johnston responded to a letter from Chief of Staff General Winfield Scott requesting her aid in persuading her husband to stay with the U.S. Army: "My husband can not stay in an army which is about to invade his native country." Later, Northern soldiers found Southern ladies outspoken to the point of being insulting. One girl noted in her diary that according to a Union officer, "We damned women had put the men up to fighting, and we were the ones to blame for the fuss."

Harvey Sanders

Harvey C. Sanders was a native of Kentucky. During the WBTS, he fought at Shiloh, Chickamauga, and other battles, and was wounded twice. He then became a guard at the Confederate White House. When Richmond fell in April of 1865,

Sanders was a member of the escort for the departing President Jefferson Davis. The party rode several weeks toward Florida, followed by thieves wishing to steal the Confederate treasury, the horses and the wagons. The Federal offer of a reward of $100,000 after Lincoln's assassination caused many adventurers to hunt for the Davis party. On May 10, 1865, near Irwinsville, Georgia, Federals captured the president and his party, including Postmaster General John H. Reagan and former Texas Governor F. R. Lubbock. All of the men were imprisoned. Sanders was released in a year. Later he came to Texas, living in Bowie County near New Boston from 1887 until his death in 1925. He was honored during his final years as the last man of the Davis bodyguard.

Always Ready

In the frosty pre-dawn of October 7, 1864, General Robert E. Lee sat on horseback, waiting impatiently for his forces to assemble to try to retake Fort Harrison, Virginia. When an aide approached him, Lee asked if all the commands were ready for the advance. "None but the Texas Brigade, General," replied the aide. Said General Lee, "The Texas Brigade is always ready!"

Shortage

Describing a battle, a private told his family how he had hugged the ground to avoid being shot. As he had said the fight took place in some woods, his mother asked why he didn't hide behind a tree. "Trees?" he exclaimed. "Why, there weren't even enough trees for all the officers!"

Gotta Know Where to Look

The Southern army was in great need of horses and mules as it moved into Pennsylvania prior to the Battle of Gettysburg. CSA quartermasters were ordered to scour the country for them and pay for them in Confederate money. Local farmers, averse to such transactions when not paid with Yankee money, were quite inventive in their efforts to hide the animals. Major John Campbell of General Harry Hays' brigade went to a fine house where he had been informed there was a splendid horse. Just as the homeowner denied having any horse, a neigh sounded from an adjoining room. When the major opened the door to the elegant parlor, he found standing there a noble steed, in close proximity to a costly rosewood piano. The horse quickly enlisted in the service of the South.

The Cotton Road

When the Federals took Vicksburg in 1863, they sealed off the Mississippi, dividing the Confederacy. The Texas-Mexico trade route, the "Cotton Road," became the South's major military supply line in the Trans-Mississippi. The road led from Alleyton, railhead of the Buffalo Bayou, Brazos and Colorado Railroad, to the Confederacy's back door on the Rio Grande. From north and east Texas, Arkansas, and Louisiana, cotton came to Alleyton. From Alleyton, it was carried to a point on the Colorado River, and ferried across to start a long, tortuous journey to the Rio Grande. Bales were hauled on big-bedded wagons and high-wheeled Mexican carts, pulled by mules, horses, or oxen. The road led to Goliad, San Patricio, the King Ranch, and on to Brownsville. The trail of the wagon trains was marked by shreds of white fluff on bush and cactus. From Brownsville the cotton moved across the river to Matamoros or Bagdad. Thousands of speculators waited in those Mexican border towns, clamoring for cotton, offering in exchange valuable European goods. In return for cotton, the wagon trains returned north with rifles, swords, shirts, pants, shoes, medicines, and munitions needed by the Confederates.

Recognized Danger

In April 1864, as a result of a conference at Fortress Monroe between Union Generals U. S. Grant and Benjamin F. Butler, prisoner exchanges were discontinued. General Butler explained in "Butler's Book": "Many a tribute has been paid to the soldier of the South by those for whom he fought, by those of the same blood and faith, by those who gloried in his splendid courage and pitied his terrible sufferings; but the highest compliment that ever was paid to the tattered and half-starved wearer of the gray was that of the Commander-in-Chief of the Union armies who, in a council of war, took the ground that the Confederate prisoner was too dangerous to be exchanged."

Jefferson, Texas

Jefferson was an important center of activity in Confederate East Texas. Established in 1862, a quartermaster depot supplied the army with camp equipment and clothing, such as boots and shoes from a factory in the town. Two iron works made cannonballs, skillets, kettles, and plows. A Cotton Bureau station bought cotton for export. Cattle and sheep were driven here for slaughter. This was a debarkation center for troops leaving Texas. The bustling town of the 1860s was quite a contrast with today's small, quiet town of antebellum homes, antique shops, and yesteryear atmosphere.

Texans and the Cavalry

Texans of military age were unaccustomed to walking and eschewed the Confederate infantry. They preferred the daring and mobility of the cavalry, which was used to scout the enemy, screen troop movements, and make lightning raids. Sixty percent of Texans recruited for Confederate service joined the cavalry, riding horses of their own or ones donated by citizens' groups. Many of the 325,000 horses Texas provided went to other states. As infantry troops were needed, Texas set up military camps to teach Texans to walk and fight. By mid-1862, the need for infantry was so great that many units were unhorsed despite strong protest by the troops. Among these were the 6th Texas Cavalry Battalion, and the 13th, 16th, 18th, 22nd, 24th, 25th, and 28th Texas Cavalry Regiments. On 15 August 1863, part of A. W. Terrell's Cavalry Regiment at Richmond, Texas, was ordered to dismount and march to defend Galveston. On September 11, an order to dismount more men caused a mutiny. Ninety-one men rode off with their prized horses, either returning to their homes or joining other cavalry units. When 25 of the men were tried later, only the officers were punished. Enlisted men returned to the regiment and fought in such later actions as the Red River Campaign, which prevented a Federal invasion of Texas.

A Recognized Need

During the occupation of Carlisle, Pennsylvania, by Confederate troops, citizens of the town asked General Richard Ewell, the Southern commander, if the Lutheran church could open on the next Sunday. Ewell responded, "Certainly, I'll attend myself if I'm here." The group was shocked at the prospect of Ewell being at their services. After a lengthy silence, the spokesman told Ewell that during the services prayers were offered for the president of the United States, and asked if they could do so this time. Barked Ewell, "Who do you mean, Lincoln? Certainly pray...I don't know anybody that stands more in need of prayer."

Changed His Mind

Stonewall Jackson's leadership in the Valley Campaign was evaluated by General Richard S. Ewell: "Well, sir, when he commenced it, I thought him crazy; before he ended it, I thought him inspired."

Devotion Was Inspired

In the spring of 1863, the 6th Louisiana held one bank of the Rappahannock River and the enemy held the other. There was no firing between the pickets and they often exchanged friendly salutations. One Confederate picket had grown up in Albany, New York, and had lived in the South only two years before the war. On one occasion he discovered the Yankee pickets opposite his post were from his hometown and included old friends and acquaintances. He accepted their invitation to cross the river and visit with them so he could inquire about his aged parents, of whom he knew nothing since the war began. The Yankee captain and his men reminded him of his tattered clothing, his scanty and indifferent food, and tried hard to induce him to desert, promising safe conduct to Albany and exemption from service in the Union army. The ragged and hungry soldier spurned the offer. He told his tempters that he had often braved danger and death with his fellow "rebs," had shared with them exposure, suffering and privation, was fully aware of the superior condition of the Federal troops, but that he would not desert his colors for all the gold the Federals had. He said that he had embarked in a righteous cause and that if God so willed it, he would die for it! This was the self-sacrificing devotion that fired the hearts and nerved the arms of the Confederate soldier.

Not Funny

On November 22, 1862, as his army was leaving Winchester, General Stonewall Jackson was stopped by an old woman asking for her boy, "Johnnie." Jackson asked her son's command. Obviously unaware of Jackson's identity, she replied, "Cap'n Jackson's company." Jackson respectfully identified himself as her son's commander and asked for more information to help locate him. Surprised that "Cap'n Jackson" didn't know all about her son, she tearfully repeated the little she knew, that he was in "Cap'n Jackson's company." Some young officers behind the general laughed about the old woman's expecting Jackson to know all of his men. Jackson turned and with fierce anger made them aware this was no laughing matter, immediately sending them to search until "Johnnie" was found.

A Walking Catalog

Under a truce in December of 1862, burial parties from both sides gathered on the desolate field at Fredericksburg. A young private from Alabama picked up a new Enfield rifle in the neutral ground. Sternly a mounted Federal officer ordered him to put it down, telling him he had no right to it. Wordlessly the young man examined the rifle and tested its sights, then calmly walked around the Federal, appraising every piece of the officer's clothing and accoutrements. Placing the rifle on his shoulder and walking back to his own lines, he coolly informed the Northerner, "Tomorrow I'll shoot you and get them boots."

As Long As One Is Wishing

When the artillery fire was at its height at Gettysburg, a brawny Southerner seemed happy at the prospect of doing battle. He broke into song: "Backward, roll backward, O time in thy flight; Make me a child again, just for this fight!" A less resolute companion commented, "Me too, and a gal child at that!"

A Sergeant Major Disappointment

In January 1864, Colonel Lloyd Beall, Commandant of the Confederate States Marine Corps, requested recruitment of a sergeant major for the corps a new position.

At his request, the following was included in a want ad in the *Mobile Advertiser & Register*: "A thoroughly drilled sober and intelligent man for the position of Sergeant Major of the Confederate States Marine Corps. Apply immediately at the Marine Barracks on Commerce St." Recruiter Captain Meiere was impressed by Edwin Wallace, a Scot and ex-Royal Marine, whose father was Sergeant Major of the Royal Marines. Edwin had been educated at the Duke of York Military School in London and seemed to be qualified. Already serving in the C.S. Navy, he was discharged from the navy, enlisted as a private, and promoted immediately to sergeant major on the same day, February 1, 1864. One week later he left Mobile for Drewry's Bluff on the James River in Virginia. Captain Meiere wrote that he regretted not being able to retain Wallace for a few months, complimenting Wallace's knowledge of drills, sword exercises, neatness, etc. After Wallace arrived in Virginia, something went drastically wrong. By March 27, Colonel Beall had inquired of Captain Meiere as to what promises had been made to Wallace. Meiere replied there had been none, other than comfortable arrangements at Drewry's Bluff for Wallace and his wife, as for other married men there. Whatever the disagreement, it evidently was not resolved. On July 25, 1864, Wallace was reduced to the ranks and assigned to Company B. Five days later he deserted, ending the record of one of the few Scots to serve the CSA on both sea and land.

A Good Enough Substitute

When a Federal officer captured a wounded Southerner at Spotsylvania, the Southerner said he was coming in to take the oath of allegiance. The officer told him he didn't have any of the proper forms for signing, adding that he did have some whisky. With no hesitation, the Southerner replied, "That will do just as well!"

Confederate Midshipmen

Midshipmen in the Confederate States Naval Academy led no life of ease. Their day began at 6 a.m. and ended at 10 p.m. They had two meals per day. Breakfast at 8 a.m. was hardtack and tea or coffee made from beans or sweet potatoes. Dinner at 2 p.m. was salt tack, vegetables, and cornbread. During the balance of the day, they studied naval tactics, practical seamanship, naval gunnery, artillery, infantry tactics, grammar, mathematics, French, Spanish, geography, and astronomy.

Had Earned Their Respect

One day Stonewall Jackson rode up to a Confederate picket on the Rappahannock River and was greeted as usual by a cheer. From across the river came a shout from Northern troops, "What's the matter over there, Johnny?" "General Stonewall Jackson!" yelled a Southern sentry. An astonishing yell came over the river from the "bluebellies": "Hurrah for Stonewall Jackson!"

Salt a Necessity

At the time of the WBTS, there were only two ways to preserve meat: salting or smoking. When the South levied a meat tithe, salt was necessary to cure bacon and beef for the military. Salt was also a must for horses and mules used by the cavalry and artillery and supply wagons. Hides to make leather required salt for their preservation. With such demand, salt works were operated along the Texas coast and in seven counties in Central, East, and West Texas. In South Texas the principal source of salt was "El Sal del Rey," a large salt lake in Hidalgo County. It provided salt to families, the Texas military board, the Confederate army, and wagons returning north on the vital Cotton Road trade route. Due to their military and domestic importance, the salt works were periodically raided and wrecked by the Federals. The Hidalgo County salt works were used for a base for the 1864 Confederate recapture of Brownsville.

In Defense of Their Homes

Texans rallied to the defense of the South against the Northern invaders. In addition to the various state guard and home guards organized to protect the frontier, Texas supplied the Confederate army with 28 regiments of cavalry, four battalions of cavalry, 22 regiments of infantry, 5 infantry battalions, and 16 artillery batteries.

Millican, Texas

Millican, in Brazos County, was born in 1859 with the coming of the Houston and Texas Central Railroad. It was the northernmost railroad terminus in Texas when the war began in 1861. Confederate troops came by rail to nearby Camp Speight, a training and rendezvous point. Some marched overland from there for duty in Arkansas and Louisiana; others entrained for Houston and Beaumont for service elsewhere. Millican was a vital shipping point for an area from the Red River on the north to the frontier settlements on the west. Products of that region went by rail to Houston, Beaumont, Galveston, and Alleyton for the Cotton Road. Returning from Brownsville, wagons brought military supplies and merchandise to Alleyton where they would be shipped by rail to Millican for further distribution. After enjoying prosperity due to its railhead position, the town declined when the railroad was extended northward beginning in 1866.

They Had Read the Papers

The mention of the CSS *Alabama* immediately brings to mind the name of Raphael Semmes, the ship's captain. Few seem aware that the marine officer for the ship was Becket K. Howell, brother-in-law of Confederate President Jefferson Davis. Incidentally, Howell was a non-swimmer. The ship's crew included many English seamen, about whom the Northern press printed many less than complimentary comments. Such comments were remembered by the seamen. When shells from the *Alabama* hit a Yankee ship, the English accent rang clearly,"That's from the scum of England!" "That's a British pill for you to swallow!"

Had a Good Reason

It was August of 1862. High on the side of Cedar Mountain, a group of Confederate chaplains and surgeons found a relatively safe vantage point from which to view the battle far below them. When Union soldiers saw the group of riders and began a noisy but harmless volley, the party fled. Leading the race for cover was a black servant of one of the surgeons. When the doctor caught up with him, he berated his servant for riding his horse so hard. The lad responded, "I didn't like the whizzing of them things any better than the rest did. And I don't think you ought to blame me, Doctor, 'cause my horse can beat yours running."

Hispanic Confederates

Hispanics of Texas were good Confederates. In the 32nd Texas Cavalry, only Company G had Anglos. All the rest had Spanish surnames.

9th Texas Cavalry

In October of 1861, the 9th Texas Cavalry, this distinguished regiment of Ross' Texas Brigade, was organized in Grayson County, under Colonel William B. Sims. Companies A and D were from Tarrant County, Company B was from Fannin County, Company C from Grayson County, Company E from Red River County, Companies F and I from Titus County, and Companies G and K from Hopkins County. As part of Van Dorn's army in December of 1863, the 9th almost captured U. S. Grant. In 1864 the 9th was a unit in the cavalry assault that captured and burned the Federal gunboat *Petrel*.

Creuzbaur Battery

Also known as "The Big Guns of Fayette," this battery was formed in 1861 in Fayette County by former Prussian artillery officer Edmund Creuzbaur. Composed of around 150 men, 4 cannon, 72 horses, and 30 mules, the unit served as both light and heavy artillery at various points in Texas and Louisiana. In May 1864, the unit attacked and captured two Federal gunboats at Calcasieu Pass, Louisiana. In that 75-minute fight, the battery hit one ship 65 times. Soon afterwards, Creuzbaur resigned and Captain Charles Welhausen assumed command.

If At First

A very large man, Jim Ferris of the 5th Texas, found himself in a dilapidated state of dress as Second Manassas ended. His pants were too short and his ankles were lacerated and bleeding. Deciding that the estate of a dead Yankee might provide him a pair of leggings, he roamed over the field of the dead, searching for a corpse of appropriate size and wondering if there really were ghosts. Finding a body of suitable size, he began to remove the leggings. Suddenly the "corpse" sat up and exclaimed, "Great God alive, man! Don't rob me before I'm dead, if you please!" The horrified Ferris sprang about twenty feet at one bound before recovering himself and apologizing. He gave the wounded man his canteen before leaving. Rather than risk waking another "corpse" he decided to do without leggings and just return to his camp. On the way he came across another large man lying full length on the ground and wearing leggings. Ferris put his hand on the man's shoulder, gave it a shake, and asked, "Say, mister, are you dead or alive?" Receiving no response, Ferris was soon the proud possessor of a magnificent pair of linen leggings.

Thank Goodness for the Dark

Captain Charles M. Blackford rode on scout duty with Stonewall Jackson one dark night. Jackson led the party over by-paths and unused roads all through the night, with no evident destination or purpose. Blackford muttered comments from time to time to Sandie Pendleton, who was riding beside him. At one point Blackford drowsed off in the saddle, then awoke and spoke in a petulant undertone to Pendleton, "Sandie, where is that old fool taking us?" From the dark figure on the next horse, the unmistakeable voice of Jackson responded, "What?" Thankful for the darkness, Blackford reined in his horse and continued the trip, wide awake once more.

Battle Dress

When the 2nd Texas arrived for the battle at Pittsburg Landing, it was almost without provisions or even uniforms. Prior to battle it was supplied with ill-fitting, undyed wool uniforms. A Federal prisoner later inquired, "Who were them hellcats that went into battle in their grave coats?"

The Flag of the Alamo City Guards

Made by ladies of San Antonio, the flag of the Alamo City Guards was a traditional "Bonnie Blue Flag" with a white star on a light blue field. It bore the name "ALAMO CITY GUARDS" and the motto "FIAT JUSTITIA RUAT COELUM" (Though the Heavens Fall, Let Justice Be Done).

Not the Best Meat

The beef distributed to one Southern army in late 1861 was so tough that a Louisiana colonel threatened to requisition files so his men could sharpen their teeth enough that they could eat the meat. When the same officer discovered shanks and necks ground into the meat, he told the quartermaster, "For God's sake, don't throw in the hoofs and horns!" Another soldier wrote that he and his friends had carried their meat ration for the very first time, explaining that up 'til then the maggots had toted it.

Fit to Be a Soldier

Disgusted with life as an infantryman, the young ex-cavalryman was deep in thought as he walked along hands in pockets. A newly commissioned lieutenant, irked by the lack of a salute from the young man, yelled after him, "Soldier, didn't you see this uniform?" Without pausing, the young man called over his shoulder, "Don't complain, look at the one they gave me!"

No Help for the Yankees

Santos Benavides, a member of a powerful family of Laredo, was offered a brigadier general's commission if he joined the Union army. He rejected this to accept a Confederate commission. With his brothers he helped raise the 32nd Texas Cavalry Regiment. When Federals approached Laredo in March of 1864, he ordered his brother Cristobal to burn all Confederate property, including his own home and 5,000 bales of cotton, if the Federals captured the city. He proclaimed, "Nothing of mine shall pass to the enemy. Let their victory be a barren one!" His stubborn defense of Laredo started the Yankees into retreat, resulting in the Confederate liberation of the Rio Grande.

Good Southerners

Company G of the 15th Tennessee Infantry was organized in 1861 with Thorndike Brooks as captain and Dr. John Wall as first lieutenant. This would not be so unusual but for the fact that it was recruited basically from Williamson and Jackson Counties in Illinois. The Illinois company participated in the heaviest fighting in the western campaigns and its casualties were heavy. The earliest muster, on October 31, 1861, showed 75 officers and men. The last roll, three years later, showed one officer, one sergeant, one private.

The Path of Duty

Alexander H. Stephens, Vice President, Confederate States of America:

"I would rather be defeated in a good cause than to triumph in a bad one. I would not give a fig for a man who would shrink from the discharge of duty for fear of defeat."

John R. Baylor

Born in Kentucky in 1822, John R. Baylor came to Texas in 1839. Over the next few years he fought Indians, was a member of the Texas legislature, and served as an Indian agent. He was a delegate to the Texas Secession Convention from Weatherford. As commander of a detachment of the 2nd Texas Mounted Rifles, he occupied Fort Bliss in June 1861, during the campaign to extend the Confederacy westward. On July 25, 1861, his troops repulsed the Federals at Mesilla, New Mexico. Two days later, at San Augustin Springs, New Mexico, Baylor and 200 men captured 700 Federals, with their transports, arms, munitions, 200 horses, 270 beeves, and four cannon. He proclaimed Mesilla the capital of Confederate Arizona and himself the governor. He supervised the mining of gold and silver for the Confederacy and sent the C.S. Treasury $9,500 captured at Fort Fillmore. His order to kill rather than capture troublesome Apaches incensed authorities and he was recalled to Texas, stripped of rank. As a private he served guns in the heated battle to recapture Galveston on New Year's Day, 1863. Salvaging parts from U.S. warships, he made cannon light enough to go into battle on the back of a mule. He served in the Confederate Congress from 1863 to early 1865, when he was made a brigadier general and given a new command. His frontier defense of Northwest Texas pinned down thousands of troops in Arizona and California. After the war, he lived in San Antonio and farmed and ranched in Uvalde County before his death in 1894.

A Soldier No Longer

In February 1861, Colonel Robert E. Lee of the U.S. Army arrived in San Antonio on his way to Washington, D.C., on orders from General Winfield Scott. When he learned there that General David Twiggs had surrendered the U.S. forces in Texas, Lee was astonished. Emotionally he exclaimed, "Has it come so soon to this?" The realization of what was happening was traumatic. Lee paced the floor of his room all that night. The next morning he met Captain Reuben Potter and commented, "When I get to Virginia, I think the world will have one soldier less. I shall resign and go to planting corn."

Justice

An English agent in Texas sold a large amount of goods and bought cotton with the proceeds. Before he could take the cotton to Matamoros, Mexico, a cotton bureau official took it from him, giving him in exchange a Confederate receipt. The official then took the cotton to Matamoros to dispose of it. There the English agent appeared and presented his bill of sale to the Mexican authorities. They would recognize only the ownership on the bill of sale, and the Confederate official had no jurisdiction in Mexico. The Englishman recovered his cotton without the problem and expense of transporting it.

Forgetful

As a young man, Confederate Lieutenant General Richard Ewell deeply loved a girl who wed another, a man named Brown. Ewell remained single but carried the lady in his heart for many years. Evidencing his continued affection, he even placed her son on his staff. Fate led to Ewell being wounded during the War and subsequently being nursed by Mrs. Brown, who had been a widow many years. During the weeks of her gentle care, Ewell wooed Mrs. Brown. He finally realized his dream of marriage to her and became a devoted husband. However, he never seemed aware their marriage had changed her name. He would proudly introduce her as "My wife, Mrs. Brown, sir."

6th Texas Infantry

The 6th Texas Infantry Regiment was formed in October 1861. Company A of Port Lavaca, and Company B, Victoria, were joined by troops from surrounding areas. The regiment trained at Camp Henry E. McCulloch, four miles from Victoria, a camp of instruction commanded by Colonel R. R. Garland. After training for eight months, on 22 May 1862 the 6th was ordered to General Van Dorn at Arkansas Post. There it was captured. Of the 643 men who made up this regiment, less than 100 lived through the war.

A Dedicated Man

According to a report of Union soldiers, a black Southern marksman at Yorktown did more injury to the Yankees there than any dozen of his fellow Southerners. He would climb a tree and hide behind the trunk to pick off the Federals. Eventually, the Union sharpshooters located him and called on him to surrender. Even though he was aware they knew just where he was, he refused. One Union sharpshooter drew aim on his known location and waited for him to appear. When eventually he moved, he was immediately killed.

Natural Choice

In late December of 1862 Nathan Bedford Forrest attacked a Union force at Parker's Crossroads. While Forrest was sending a message demanding immediate surrender, a second Union detachment attacked Forrest's rear. "What will we do, General?" asked a subordinate. The rapid response was, "We'll charge both ways!" (They did.)

Feeling the Enemy

After the battle at Williamsburg, General Joseph Johnston sent orders to General Hood stating that several thousand Union troops had landed on the York River and that Hood's Texans were to feel the enemy gently and draw back, drawing the enemy from the protection of their gunboats. Greatly outnumbered, the Texans charged the Yankees and forced them to retreat, killing or capturing several hundred. "Old Joe" questioned Hood later, wondering what would have happened if Hood had been ordered to charge if this was the Texas idea of feeling the enemy gently. Hood told him they would have captured the gunboats too!

General Polecat

Early in 1864 one brigade of Texans almost mutinied when placed under the command of the French Prince de Polignac. They said they wouldn't serve under a foreigner whose name they couldn't pronounce. The Texans derisively called their leader "General Polecat," often in his hearing, but he said nothing about it until the Texans were about to attack the Federals on the Washita. Standing in his stirrups he brandished his saber and called out, "You call me Polecat. I will show you whether I am a Polecat or a de Polignac! Follow me! Follow me!" By his coolness under fire de Polignac gained the confidence of his men. He and the Texans got along famously thereafter.

Wartime Medicines

As the Federal blockade cut off imports, the Confederate government was forced to establish medical laboratories. The army's medicines were ones of desperation, mainly mineral salts and such medicinal herbs as mistletoe, jimsonweed, snakeroot, poke root, mullein, Jerusalem oak, nightshade, and cherry bark. Of its nine laboratories, the only one west of the Mississippi River was the one about six miles east of Tyler, Texas. The site, "Headache Springs," was noted for its healing mineral waters. The laboratory made medicines and whiskey.

Texas Saltpeter

As mixed with small parts of charcoal and sulphur, saltpeter from a mine six miles southwest of Concan in Uvalde County powered Confederate cannons and smaller arms on both sides of the Mississippi. The mine had vast deposits of bat guano which by decay became saltpeter, main ingredient of gunpowder of the period. Inhabited by the bats that provided the guano, the cave extends about 23 miles. One "room" in the cave is 585 by 325 feet and has a 45-foot ceiling. A narrow gauge railway was used to haul the guano from the cave. The mules drawing the cars on the railway lived in corrals within the cave.

Wartime Marshall, Texas

Marshall, Texas, was a major center of activity for the Confederacy west of the Mississippi. Located here were military headquarters for the Trans-Mississippi Department, headquarters for the departmental medical bureau, headquarters for the departmental postal service, two military hospitals, a commissary bureau, and an ordnance bureau, laboratory, depot, and arsenal that produced and distributed powder, pistols, saddles, harness, and clothing. From November 1863 to June 1865, the wartime Confederate capital of Missouri was located in Marshall. In 1863, military and civil authority in the TM Department was consolidated under General E. Kirby Smith. During the war, departmental military officials and governors of the four states met here in three conferences. Among prominent Confederates from Marshall were wartime Texas governors Edward Clark and Pendleton Murrah, Senator Louis T. Wigfall, four brigadier generals (Matthew D. Ector, Elkanah Greer, Walter P. Lane, and Horace Randal), and Lucy Holcomb Pickens, the only woman whose portrait graced Confederate currency. A number of highranking military and civil officials left Marshall to go to Mexico at the end of the war, rather than surrender to the Yankees.

Parsons' Cavalry

Parsons' Cavalry was originally comprised of men from Ellis and nearby counties. It was organized at Rockett's Spring, northeast of Waxahachie. The unit was trained and commanded by Colonel William H. Parsons, a Mexican War veteran, editor, merchant, and lawyer. Parsons' Cavalry was joined with the 12th, 19th and 21st Texas Cavalry Regiments, Morgan's Battalion, and Pratt's Battery, forming a Confederate brigade that scouted and fought in Missouri, Arkansas, Louisiana, and the Indian Territory. During the 1864 Red River Campaign, the unit was famed for attacks on Federal ironclad ships.

Freedman's Village

During the war, General Robert E. Lee's home at Arlington was used as a Union military headquarters and then as a cemetery. The 1,100-acre estate also was the site of a sprawling encampment for black refugees. This village provided much-needed housing, hospitals, churches, commissaries, and other community services. At its peak nearly 3,000 people lived there. The village was dismantled in 1890. Today there is no memorial in the grounds to the village that once shared the estate with the dead.

Age No Problem

A sample of 11,000 Confederate troops showed the following age distribution:

5%	17 or younger
9%	18
64%	19–29
16%	30–39
4%	40–49
1%	50 and over

(To save you adding it up, the sum of the above is only 99 percent due to rounding.)

Relatively Bitter War

Cousin to Major H. B. McClellan, General Jeb Stuart's chief of staff, was Union General George B. McClellan.

The father-in-law of Robert Anderson, Union commander at Fort Sumter, was governor of Georgia.

Stonewall Jackson's sister, Laura, was a staunch Unionist. She nursed wounded Yankees and claimed she could take care of them as fast as brother Thomas could wound them.

Confederate General James Terrill was killed in 1864 at Bethesda Church. His brother, Union General William Terrill, was killed at Perryville in 1862.

The 7th Tennessee Regiment, CSA, captured the 7th Tennessee Regiment, USA.

Thirty-nine Missouri regiments fought at Vicksburg. Seventeen were Confederate; twenty-two were Union.

Seven grandsons of Senator Henry Clay fought in the war. Four fought for the South, while three were on the wrong side.

Think We Can Trust Him?

During the 1861–62 winter, Robert E. Lee lived quietly with no martial pomp in a little place called Coosawhatchie. He had hardly any staff and his clothing bore no mark of rank, giving little indication that he was a soldier. Given to solitary afternoon rambles, he wandered alone around the camp's stables and through the gun park. Few of the men knew who he was. One evening a sergeant who did know Lee was accompanied by a partially deaf teamster when they met the general. The sergeant saluted Lee, causing the teamster to call out loudly, in the manner of many deaf people, "I say, Sergeant, who is that durned old fool? He's always a-pokin' round my horse just as if he meant to steal one of 'em."

That's Not What He Told Me

Prior to the Battle of Prairie Grove, two Irishmen from St. Louis pledged to each other that if one was injured the other would save him. When Jerry was wounded charging after fleeing Federals, Larry threw him over his shoulder and carried him to the rear. As they left the battlefield, without Larry's knowledge, a cannon ball took off Jerry's head. When he reached the doctors, Larry was surprised when he was asked why he was carrying a dead man. Larry turned and looked at the corpse with a wondering expression and said with great gravity, "Begorrah, but he told me he was wounded in the leg!"

Looking to the Future

When a soldier in W. H. T. Walker's division applied for a furlough to go see his wife in 1863, General Walker disapproved the request but forwarded it to General D. H. Hill for review. General Hill approved the request, endorsing it as follows: "Approved for the reason that a brave soldier ought to be allowed to go home whenever practicable, else all the children born during the war or within the usual period afterwards will be the offspring of the cowards who remain at home by reason of substitutes or other exemption."

Hard to Be a Beau Brummell

Many of Hood's soldiers lost everything, including clothing, in the retreat from Nashville in December 1861. One day General Hood noticed Martin Brown of Company I, Texas, striding along wearing a long coffee sack in lieu of a shirt. Holes had been cut for Brown's head and arms. Hood asked Brown if he had no better uniform. With blood rushing to his cheeks, Brown looked Hood straight in the face and said indignantly, "Look here, General Hood, do you expect a man to have a thousand shirts?"

Don't Push Me!

As the Confederates were taking leave of Appomattox to begin their dreary tramp homeward, many of the Federals bade them a cordial farewell. One good-naturedly told a Southerner, "Well, Johnny, I guess you fellows will go home now to stay." The tired Confederate, who clearly did not understand the spirit in which those words were spoken, replied coldly, "Look here, Yank; you *guess*, do you, that we fellows are going home to stay? Maybe we are. But don't be giving us any of your impudence. If you do, we'll come back and lick you again."

A Different Reason

Captain John Y. Beall, CSA, was a college classmate of John Wilkes Booth, who was a devoted friend of the young officer. Beall caused consternation among Federal commanders by his bold and effective service to the South. It has been estimated that he and his followers caused enough problems to draw off 20,000 men from the Union Army of the Potomac.

When Beall was captured, he was tried by court-martial at Fort Columbus (in New York harbor) and sentenced to be hanged as a spy. Efforts to save his life were made by many persons, including Governor Andrew of Massachusetts, but to no avail. John Wilkes Booth tried in every way to secure Beall's release and managed to secretly stay in touch with the condemned officer. News reached authorities of efforts under way to help Beall escape and he was ordered executed without delay.

Booth learned of the expedited execution and hurried to Washington. There, on his knees, he implored President Lincoln and Secretary Seward to pardon Beall or at least suspend the sentence. Lincoln agreed to suspend the sentence. Booth was elated and wired the joyful news to Beall's mother in Brooklyn. That very night, the prison commandant received an order by wire to hang Beall. At 10:00 a.m. on the following morning, Beall was executed. Booth arrived in New York on the morning of Beall's execution and was so disappointed at what had happened that he went out of his mind. For what he termed the perfidy of Lincoln, Booth at once swore to avenge his friend's death by killing both Lincoln and Seward. He did not intend to slay Lincoln in the theatre, but found no other opportunity. He only told one man what he intended to do, and then only an hour before the assassination. The man to whom he revealed his plan begged Booth not to carry it out; when Booth could not be swayed, the other man left town.

Neither the war nor its results had anything to do with Lincoln's death. Booth knew the slaying could not help matters. Had Beall been pardoned or simply imprisoned, Booth would not have killed Lincoln. (Dr. Foote, Surgeon CSA, Library of Congress, reference RA807, N8W3; *Alexander Beall, 1649–1744, of Maryland*, compiled by Wm. Hunter McLean.)

Double Dippers

Two hundred fifty-three Union soldiers (primarily members of the 19th Massachusetts) obtained release from Andersonville by enlisting in a unit designated as the 10th Tennessee Infantry Regiment of Volunteers (Irish), CSA, which definitely was not the Sons of Erin regiment organized in Tennessee. When these troops were sent to the TransMississippi Department, they surrendered and re-enlisted in the Union army. Years later some of these men in blue-turned-gray-turned-blue applied for and legally received pensions from both Tennessee and Massachusetts for service on both sides of the war.

Man of War

Marching into position atop a ridge at Chickamauga, Texan George Cagle picked up four or five muskets dropped by slain or injured soldiers. After the Southerners had taken their position, while Yankee bullets flew around them, Cagle kept his guns at work. For four hours his unit was in battle, Cagle issued and obeyed orders to himself: "Attention, Cagle's Battery, make ready, load, take aim, fire."

Unforgiving

At one time, the Confederacy allowed the men in the ranks to elect their officers. Private Henry Robinson of Athens, Georgia, was a candidate in an election in the spring of 1862. He was not a "good loser." He wrote, "The lieutenant done tricked me out of being elected a sergeant. One thing is certain—I will be a tick on his stern and keep him scratching for the balance of this war, for I never forget and damned seldom ever forgive."

Heroic Young Men

The North Carolina Junior Reserves were 17-year-old conscripts who performed heroically in battle. In December of 1864, the Junior Reserves were on duty at Poplar Point on the Roanoke River. These 17-year-old conscripts had proven they could learn and accept discipline. However, with their youthful vitality and exuberance, they often acted foolishly, without thinking.

A Confederate officer inspecting his lines after a shelling by Union gunboats found one of the boys trying to extract the powder from an unexploded shell he was holding between his knees. Reprimanded for endangering himself and his associates, the boy answered, "I ain't skeered of the damn things when they're coming at me through the air and I know I ain't skeered of 'em when I got 'em in my hands."

In 1865, when news reached the young soldiers that Johnston had surrendered to Sherman, there was talk of going en masse to join Maximilian in Mexico. As the discouraged youths crossed the swollen Haw River, one of the smaller boys went under the water three times, being rescued each time by friends who thought he was attempting suicide. He finally explained, "My gun's down there and I been trying to git it!"

Lacked Understanding

When not in battle, Confederates and Federals often traded words as well as goods. After one conversational exchange with Southerners, a young Federal returned to his camp shaking his head in wonderment. He told his associates he had just learned the Southerners were fighting to keep rodents, explaining, "They said the reason they was up here fighting was because we're trying to take away their rats." (Some Northerners just don't know how to pronounce R-I-G-H-T-S!)

A Little Known Plan

William Clarke Quantrill, guerilla leader, developed a plan in early 1865 that would have eclipsed anything else he ever did. He decided to ride to Washington and assassinate Lincoln. With thirty followers disguised in blue uniforms as the 4th Missouri Cavalry and carrying forged papers, Quantrill mounted up and rode eastward. The guerillas, in their disguise as Federal cavalry, were welcomed and entertained all along the way until the news of Lincoln's death ended their mission. Shortly thereafter Quantrill's horse was injured while being shod. Quantrill pronounced the mishap an omen. True to his premonition, Quantrill was fatally wounded a few days later on 10 May 1865 in a skirmish with Federals in Kentucky, about fifty miles southeast of Louisville.

Loyalty Remained Southern

Holly Springs, Mississippi, stood squarely in the path of Union attempts to invade the state from the north. This location resulted in some 61 raids by both armies during the course of the war. The town changed hands so frequently that the citizens made a daily practice of checking to see which flag was flying overhead.

The Noble Cause

On July 17, 1861, Reverend Dr. Robert Ryland, longtime president of Richmond College, wrote a letter to his son who had enlisted in the Confederate army:

My Dear Son:

It may have seemed strange to you that a professing Christian father so freely gave you, a Christian son, to enlist in the volunteer service. My reason was that I regarded this as a purely defensive war. Not only did the Southern Confederacy propose to adjust the pending difficulties by peaceful and equitable negotiations, but Virginia used again and again the most earnest and noble efforts to prevent a resort to the sword. These overtures having been proudly spurned, and our beloved South having been threatened with invasion and subjugation, it seemed to me that nothing was left us but stern resistance or abject submission to unconstitutional power. A brave and generous people could not for a minute hesitate between such alternatives. A war in defence of our homes and firesides—of our wives and children—of all that makes life worth possessing is the result...We pray for a speedy, just, and honorable peace and for the safe return of all the volunteers to their loved homes.—your loving father Ro.Ryland

Such Immodesty

The cool water of a nearby river tempted the young men of a Confederate regiment camped in Pennsylvania on a hot summer day just before the battle of Gettysburg. The nearest house was a half-mile away, so the men didn't hesitate to strip and plunge into the water. They were greatly enjoying the swimming when a young boy trudged into camp with a note for the commanding officer. It came from the old spinster resident of the distant house and read, "Dear sir, I wish you would order your men out of the river. I can see them plainly through my brother's field glasses."

Too Demanding

On July 3, 1863, the Confederate troops and the civilian population within the besieged Vicksburg were starving and supplies were dwindling. Confederate General John C. Pemberton met with Union General U. S. Grant to discuss terms of surrender, asking that the Confederate troops be paroled rather than imprisoned. Grant demanded "unconditional surrender." Pemberton replied to that demand, "Sir, it is unnecessary that you and I hold any further conversation. We will go to fighting again at once. I can assure you, you will bury many more of your men before you will enter Vicksburg." Grant relented and Pemberton formally surrendered the city on July 4, 1863.

Preached to the Choir

Just before the 6th New York left for war, its colonel gave his men a pep talk. Holding up his gold watch, he proclaimed that Southern plantation owners all had such luxuries that awaited confiscation by Union soldiers. A few moments later he reached into his pocket to check the time and found his watch gone.

A Free Election

Early in the war, field grade officers were elected by company officers who were elected by the men of each company. A member of the 3rd North Carolina reported on how a lieutenant in his company "honored" the procedure. After having the men of the company fall into ranks at attention, the officer shouted: "Men, there are two candidates for office and there is but one of them worth a damn, and I nominate him. All who are in favor of electing Sergeant ——— come to shoulder arms. Company, shoulder arms!" With the election over, he then dismissed the company.

Less Than Admirers

Many in the Confederate infantry held the cavalry in open contempt. General D. H. Hill reportedly offered a five dollar reward to anyone who could find a dead man wearing spurs. General Jubal Early once was impatient with the conduct of certain cavalry units and threatened that if they didn't do better, he would *put them in the army*!

An Inspiration

Lieutenant General Dick Ewell looked on as Stonewall Jackson knelt hatless before his tent on the morning of one of his great victories, praying to his Lord. Aware of the great faith and military talent before him, Ewell commented, "If that is religion, I must have it."

Close Order Drill

The captain of a Georgia home guard unit took advantage of the temporary presence of a Confederate general to show off his company's outstanding abilities in executing various drills. As the company was going through its paces outside the general's quarters, the captain's shouted orders attracted the general's attention and he came out to watch. The marching troops did quite nicely until the captain attempted some complex maneuvers at the double-quick. Immediately the neat formation disintegrated into a churning mob. Fearing a withering blast from the attentive general, the captain cried, "Halt!" and despondently eyed the mess he had created. Suddenly his face brightened as he conceived and issued an order which earned the general's compliments for the best command he had ever heard given. In seconds the company returned to proper formation after the captain ordered, "Company, disentangle to the front, march!"

Lincoln Miscellany

Abraham Lincoln was the first U.S. president to wear a beard. Often speaking of God and quoting the Bible, he is the only U.S. president who never was baptized or joined a church. His Emancipation Proclamation freed no slaves in the states that had not seceded nor in those portions of seceded states which were under control of the U.S. Army.

Official Reasoning

The first Confederate balloon ascension was made by Lieutenant John Randolph Bryan on the peninsula below Richmond. Yankee fire rapidly caused Bryan to return to earth. There he promptly submitted his resignation. General Joseph Johnston refused the resignation on the ground that Bryan was the only Confederate with any experience in balloons.

Mistakes Do Happen

Erstwhile guerilla and head of "The Comanches," Elijah White, went on to become a successful Virginia businessman, a banker, and a preacher. Once in his later years, he and a granddaughter were riding near Leesburg one evening. "Lige" drew rein, pointed to a rock, and told the girl how he once lay badly wounded behind it, how the Union officer who shot Lige had asked if there was anything he could do for him, gave him a drink of water and then said, "I hope you will forgive me." Lige paused in his story, drew himself erect, and said, "Betsy, I thought I was going to die and, do you know, I forgave that damn yankee!"

Battlefield Consideration

Seventeen-year-old Private William F. Jenkins of the 12th Georgia was wounded and left on the field during a day of bitter fighting at Second Manassas. After nightfall two of his buddies searched him out and carried him toward a field hospital. From out of the night rang out a challenge: "Who goes there?" They replied, "Two men of the 12th Georgia, carrying a wounded comrade." Suddenly there appeared a Yankee sentry who said, "Don't you know you're in the Union lines?" "No," said the startled Georgians. "Well you are. Go to the right," said the bluecoat, fading into the darkness. The Georgians continued on their way as one of them called out, "Man, you've got a heart in you."

There Had to Be a Reason

One evening Generals Stephen D. Lee and Nathan Bedford Forrest were discussing the day's events. General Lee wondered aloud why he and other Southern generals had not met with the success in battle that Forrest usually experienced. Forrest responded, "Well, General, I suppose it's because I'm not handicapped by a West Point education."

Not To Worry!

When General William B. Bate succeeded to General John C. Breckinridge's division command, there was a great deal of dissatisfaction among members of the Orphan Brigade who opposed serving under any non-Kentuckian. Many were not careful to conceal their displeasure. Bate complained to General Joseph H. Lewis, brigade commander, about his men's behavior. Lewis replied, "General, I think I wouldn't pay any attention to that if I were you. My boys are always pestering some damned fool!"

Taking No Chances

A soldier detailed for picket duty was observed pulling off a new shirt and donning an old and tattered one. His explanation was, "I'm not going to let the Yankees shoot my new shirt!"

Couldn't Trust Dem Yankees

Unscrupulous recruiters played some scurvy tricks on foreigners to entice them into the ranks of the Northern army. Obviously new to the country and speaking little English, a sullen and angry German was among the Federals captured at Pittsburg Landing. One Confederate said to him, "Hans, what are you doing here, anyhow? What do you want to fight the South for?" "Py Himmel, I vish I didn't!" blurted the German, showing how he had been taken in. "Zey dell me to zay boo! at the Southern man unt he runs off. I zay boo! and shoots; but py tam! Southern man he runs the wrong vay!"

Loose Orders Dangerous

Braxton Bragg once directed General William Hardee to send his own regiment and that of Colonel Thomas Hunt's Kentuckians toward the Yankees at

Murfreesboro, wording the orders "to proceed as far as he possibly could." Hardee dutifully transmitted the order, but knowing the ardor of the Kentuckians, he then immediately rode to Bragg's headquarters. There he told Bragg it would never do to start the Kentuckians toward Murfreesboro with such an order as that because "they wouldn't stop this side of Hell!" Bragg agreed and amended his order to provide specific goals.

Homesick

As panic-stricken Union troops fled Winchester, Virginia, ahead of advancing troops of Stonewall Jackson on May 25, 1862, General Nathaniel Banks attempted to stop them and restore order. To a mob of running soldiers, Banks shouted, "My God, don't you love your company?" "Yes," came a reply from an unknown soldier, "and I'm trying to get back to it as fast as I can!"

First Manassas

As jokingly reported by the *Winchester Republican*, August 16, 1861

> To take Manassas Junction
> The Yankees thought was fun,
> But greatly were mistaken,
> For they only took the Run.

Six Heads Better Than One?

Late one day in May of 1862 Stonewall Jackson was about to order a night attack on the Federals in Winchester. He summoned the five regimental commanders of the Stonewall Brigade for a council of war. He then issued orders incorporating their advice. When the desired assault failed to work out, Jackson was furious. "That is the last council of war I will ever hold." He kept his word!

Lines from "The Texas Bible"

(Biblical parody sung by Southern infantrymen)
The race is not to them that's got the longest legs to run,
Nor the battle to the people that shoots the biggest gun.
(Editor's note: Maybe not, but that's still the way I'd lay my bets.)

Ball's Bluff

On October 21, 1861, the Battle of Ball's Bluff was fought about thirty-five miles west of Washington, D.C., on the Virginia bank of the Potomac River. Confederates scored probably the most complete victory by either side in the war. Union soldiers were driven in a panic off the high bluff into the river where many drowned. The Confederates captured more than 550 Union soldiers; the Federals captured one Confederate.

After the battle several people from the area came out onto the battlefield. One was Murphy Schumater who lived five miles south of the battle site. Schumater heard that his son's unit was in the battle and came seeking him. Encountering a soldier covered with grime and the powder of battle, Schumater drew in his horse and asked if the man knew anything of Private Lewis Schumater of Captain Berkley's Company C, 8th Virginia. When the soldier broke into laughter, Schumater bent down and peered into the smiling powder-stained face of the son he sought.

How Lincoln Won Re-Election

In August of 1864 Lincoln appeared to have little chance for re-election. Only the Radical Republicans wanted to continue the war and they nominated John C. Fremont to be their presidential candidate. Powerful publisher Horace Greeley supported the peace movement and the popular Democratic candidate, General George B. McClellan. Greeley told his readers Lincoln was already beaten and could not be elected. Lincoln shrewdly went to work on his problem. Learning that Fremont hated the postmaster general, Montgomery Blair, Lincoln secured Fremont's withdrawal as a candidate by making Blair resign his post. Knowing his own popularity with Federal troops, Lincoln then moved to overcome that of McClellan. While some states allowed soldiers to vote absentee, several crucial ones did not. Lincoln sent messengers to Generals Meade, commanding the Army of the Potomac, and Sheridan, commanding the Army of the Shenandoah, requesting furloughs from men from vital states. The generals acted promptly. From Meade's command, 10,000 men went home to Pennsylvania. Lincoln won that state. Sherman furloughed 29 regiments and two batteries, many to Indiana, which had been seen as a sure win for McClellan. With the return of the troops, Lincoln carried the state by 1,500 votes. Philip Sheridan was made a brigadier general of the regulars. The delivery of the soldier vote turned the tide for Lincoln. McClellan won only 3 states and 21 electoral votes.

Gone with the Cook

From *The Confederate Veteran*, July 1898:

"On a Sabbath after the Battle of Chickamauga, the men of a certain regiment were gathered just beyond the top of Missionary Ridge for religious services. A good congregation of the soldiers were seated on the ground. In the early part of the service a battery belonging to 'our friend the enemy' sent a shell, which exploded some two or three hundred yards below our position. A cook who had his belongings just outside of the place occupied by the congregation put them over his shoulder with the remark that he was going to get out of there. That caused a ripple of laughter in the congregation but all sat still. During the longer prayer of our service another shell came much nearer. When the prayer was finished and the chaplain's eyes were opened, he saw that the congregation, with the exception of five or six men, had followed the cook."

Slight Problem

Following a fight near Groveton, Virginia, on 29 August 1862, panic-stricken Federals fled from attacking Confederates. Some of their officers rode among the disorganized Yankees, trying to rally them. Major Charles Livingston, of the 76th New York, finally came across a regiment marching in tolerable order. Waving his sword to emphasize his orders, Livingston ordered the men to halt and turn about. An officer of the regiment, annoyed that a stranger would usurp his command, challenged the major: "Who are you, sir?" "Major Livingston of the 76th New York." "76th what?" "76th New York." "Well then, you are my prisoner, for you are attempting to rally the 2nd Mississippi!"

Someone Was Listening!

During an engagement at Kingston, Kentucky, on August 30, 1862, U.S. Brigadier General "Bull" Nelson propelled his vast bulk along in front of a line of his soldiers who were faltering under the attack of Confederates. Seeking to stir his men to action, he called out, "If they can't hit me, they can't hit anything!" He did get immediate action. Two Confederates shot him!

A Bet's a Bet

While occupying a home in Warrenton in August 1862, a Union quartermaster boasted he would enter Richmond before the month ended. The lady of the house bet him a bottle of champagne he wouldn't. Shortly thereafter he was taken prisoner by Jeb Stuart's troops. As he started off to Libby Prison under guard, the lady stepped forward and gracefully paid her wager.

Establishing Priorities

Captain W. W. Parker, battery commander under Colonel Stephen D. Lee, glared after the Yankees retreating toward Groveton Woods. An exuberant young man from his battery gushed, "Captain, the Yankees are running. Let us give thanks!" Parker growled that thanks could come later, "Give them a few more shots first!"

A Difference

Two elderly ladies were discussing the raging war. One remarked, "I think President Davis is a praying man." To that the other replied, "But so is Abraham Lincoln." "Yes," the first admitted, "but the Lord will think Abraham is joking."

From the Ultimate Authority

In July of 1864, an army correspondent of the *Augusta Constitutionalist* reported as fact: "A soldier on the mountain was struck a few days ago by a minié ball in the breast. The ball penetrated a pocket Bible which saved his life. But the most singular part of the incident is that the tip of the ball indented the following line and penetrated no further: 'Thou shalt not fall in the pit.' "

Bourland's Border Regiment

The 2nd Frontier Regiment, Texas Cavalry, CSA, was organized in October of 1863. Headquartered in Gainesville, it guarded Red River counties against outlaws, Indians, and deserters. Colonel James Bourland was appointed commander. The unit became known as "Bourland's Border Regiment." The regiment patrolled and maintained posts along the river and in Indian Territory. Federal invasion from north of the Red River was a constant threat. Confederate Seminole troops served along with the regiment, as did General Stand Watie and his Cherokee Brigade. Bourland also worked with frontier regiments of state troops that maintained lineposts 100 miles west, a day's horseback ride apart, from the Red River to the Rio Grande, and with a state militia line 30 miles west.

At one point during the war, Federal scouts seeking Colonel Bourland stopped in Glen Eden (now under Lake Texoma) at the home of Sophia Porter. Learning of their aim, she distracted them by a fine meal. While they were busy, she slipped out, swam her horse across the icy Red River, and warned Colonel Bourland. Failure to capture Bourland prevented a planned Federal invasion of North Texas.

Practical

Stonewall Jackson's practicality was not as recognized as his religiousness. In discussing preparations for battle in one campaign, one of Jackson's officers stated he was planning on praying. Jackson agreed that praying would be a very good idea, adding, "But, colonel, don't forget to drill."

Proper Commands

In one of the preliminary skirmishes at Perryville, General Abraham Buford ordered a captain to oblique his company to the right. The officer misunderstood the order and led his men to the left. General Buford, a horse breeder, yelled out to the captain, "If you don't know what I mean by 'right oblique,' sir, then gee them, sir, gee them, gee them!"

Proud of the Name

Captain Robert Emory Park of Alabama wrote in December of 1864 that he exulted in being called a "Rebel." After writing that George Washington, Thomas

Jefferson, Patrick Henry, and "Light Horse Harry" Lee were all Rebels, Park added that even our martyred Savior was called "seditious." He modestly asked pardon if he should rejoice in being a "Rebel."

As Needed

Stonewall Jackson's chief commissary of subsistence was Major Wells J. Hawks. In March of 1861, after Jackson had halted his troops for the night, Hawks moved his wagon train off the road and into a field. Wanting to waste neither time nor resources, the conscientious Hawks sought to organize the train to be ready to move promptly when morning came. He asked Jackson which way the troops would go the next morning so that he would know which way to head the train. Jackson knew the importance of keeping his plans from the enemy and was secretive even with his own staff. Jackson told Hawks to arrange the train with the horses' heads toward the pike. Hawks persisted, asking whether to head up the pike or down it. "I said *towards* the pike, sir," Jackson fumed, refusing to divulge even the least bit of intelligence.

The Not-So-Solid North

Following Lincoln's issuing his so-called Emancipation Proclamation, Northern opposition to the war increased and spread across the Midwest, from Ohio to Michigan. The Illinois and Indiana legislatures called for an armistice and repeal of the proclamation. State conventions pledged to oppose the "wicked abolition crusade against the South" and "resist to the death all attempts to draft any of our citizens into the army." Newspapers called for soldiers to desert, and all but 35 men of the 128th Illinois *did* desert, declaring they would lie in the woods until moss grew on their backs rather than help free the slaves. One Union soldier received a letter from his father telling him, "I am sorry you are engaged in this unholy, unconstitutional and hellish war ...which has no other purpose but to free the negroes and enslave the whites. Come home. If you have to desert, you will be protected." Lincoln's imposition of martial law across the Union prevented outright revolt but made obvious his disregard for the Constitution.

Could Start a Man on a Diet

On 17 December 1861, Confederate gunner Private George Neese went on a mission to destroy the Chesapeake & Ohio Canal Lock No. 5 near Martinsburg, Virginia. During that mission he came under enemy shelling for the first time. Later he described his reaction: "I laid so close to the ground that it seemed to me I flattened out a little."

Anyone Have a Map?

A trooper who was fording a stream flanked by miles of swamp on either side commented, "Blowed if I don't think we have struck this stream lengthwise."

Unjustly Accused

Union General "Beast" Butler once complained that Father James Mullon, pastor of St. Patrick's in New Orleans, had refused to bury a Union soldier. A true Confederate, peppery Father Mullon denied this, stating, "I'm ready to bury the whole Union army!"

Had Weighed Alternatives

Stonewall Jackson believed that he and the other Confederates had left their homes to do a job and the sooner they did their work, the sooner they would return home. To him speed was a weapon that could save lives and he suffered no qualms about asking his men to make long, fast marches. When a Valley woman berated Jackson for driving his men too hard on a strenuous march, Jackson tersely replied, "Legs are cheaper than heads, madam."

Robert E. Lee's Definition of a Gentleman

Original in the Virginia Historical Museum, Richmond

"The forebearing use of power does not only form a touchstone; but the manner in which an individual enjoys certain advantage over others, is a test of a true gentleman. The power which the strong have over the weak, the magistrate over the citizen, the employer over the employed, the educated over the unlettered, the experienced over the confiding, even the clever over the silly; the forebearing and inoffensive use of all this power or authority, or a total abstinence from it when the case admits it, will show the gentleman in a plain light. The gentleman does not needlessly and unnecessarily remind an offender of a wrong he may have committed against him. He cannot only forgive, he can forget; and he strives for that nobleness of self and mildness of character, which imparts sufficient strength to let the past be but the past. A true man of honor feels humbled himself when he cannot help humbling others."

By the Numbers

A private in General Bragg's army wrote his parents:

Dear Mother and Dad,

Here I am in Louisiana where it's summer all winter and hot as hell all summer. I must tell you that I no longer bear our proud family name. I am just a number. My number is 97. I am always 97. They take me out on the drill grounds marching me from sunup to sundown. Last Sunday I went to a religious service for what I thought would be spiritual nourishment and I had hardly sat down before the chaplain took his songbook in hand and said, "We will now turn to number 97, 'Art Thou Footsore, Art Thou Weary?' " and folks, I'm doing five days in the stockade just because I stood up and replied, "You're darn tootin' I'm tired."

Love,

your son Robert

Plans not the Highest Priority

One evening Stonewall Jackson called in Captain Myers, one of his veteran officers, and pointed out the urgency of building a bridge over a small creek. Jackson told Myers he would send plans for the bridge as soon as they were completed by his colonel of engineers. The next morning Jackson asked Myers if the plans had arrived. "Well," said the captain, "the bridge is built, but I don't know whether the picture is done or not!"

Dead Certain

In passing to the lower part of an encampment of the 12th Tennessee, a soldier passed two others from his company making a rude coffin. When he asked who it was for, he was told "Johnny Bunce." He told the two, "Why, John is not dead yet! It is too bad to make a man's coffin when you don't know if he is going to die or not." "Don't trouble yourself," said one of the men, "Dr. Coe told us to make his coffin, and I guess he knows what he gave him!"

Doesn't Time Fly!

A hungry Confederate was out foraging when he spotted a likely farm. Approaching the door, he told the lady there, "Madam, will you please give me something to eat? I haven't had a mouthful for three days—today, tomorrow, and the next day!"

Honest Men, All

As one of his recruits entered the camp with a fine turkey, the colonel of a Texas regiment asked him where he got it. "Stole it," came the laconic reply. "Ah," said the colonel to a bystander, "you see my boys may steal, but they won't lie!"

Detached Service

A Methodist circuit rider met a Texas soldier and asked him to what army he belonged. "I belong to Van Dorn's Army," replied the soldier, "What army do you belong to?" "I belong to the Army of the Lord," was the solemn response. "Well, then, my friend," commented the soldier drily, "you've got a long way from headquarters!"

A Helpless Target

On 7 May 1862, General John Bell Hood neared Eltham's Landing with troops who had never been in combat. Fearing that indiscriminate firing by the untried troops might alert the foe of his presence, Hood ordered that rifles be carried unloaded. Coming over a crest of a ridge that had a steep slope toward the York River, Hood was suddenly confronted with a long line of Federal skirmishers whose approach had been hidden by the ridge. The skirmishers immediately fired on the Southerners as the brigade stood helpless with unloaded guns. A Federal corporal standing close to Hood selected the general as his target. Hood was about to lose his life when the corporal was slain by a sudden shot from Private John Deal. Orders or not, Deal didn't believe in going into battle with an unloaded gun!

Jackson Had a Different Opinion

Stonewall Jackson was shot in the hand at First Manassas. After the fighting was over, he sought out a surgeon. The surgeon examined Jackson's hand and said a damaged finger would have to be amputated. He turned to find his instruments and when he turned back again, Jackson had ridden away.

A Most Incorrigible Rebel

From *The Confederate Veteran*, October 1909:

During the occupation of Frederick City, Virginia, by the Federal forces, there was residing there a young lady, Miss Eliza Putnam, who was a most incorrigible Rebel. Whenever she saw the provost guard coming on the street upon which she lived, she would immediately go to the parlor, seat herself at the piano, and play "Dixie" and "The Bonnie Blue Flag." Upon one occasion, having refused to pass under the Stars and Stripes, she was arrested and ordered to report to the provost marshal every morning. After several calls, she noticed one morning the flag draped over and above the marshal's office, whereupon she stepped outside and refused to enter. The marshal requested her to enter, but she pointedly refused. He then told her that if she did not come in he would order two of his men to bring her in. "Under those circumstances, Captain Ellett," she replied, "I am forced to enter." She then took from her pocket a small Confederate flag, and holding it with both hands over her head, she walked into the marshal's office. The captain then said to her, "Miss Eliza, go home. I give up."

To Each His Own

In addition to his other abilities, General Henry Wise was noted for his proclivity for profanity. Once after General Robert E. Lee gently took him to task for his language, he responded, "I am perfectly willing that Jackson and yourself shall do the praying for the whole Army of Northern Virginia, but in Heaven's name let me do the cussin' for one small brigade!"

Partisans

Many authorities believe the partisan forces did not receive full credit for their contribution to Southern efforts. One of their main achievements was the diversion of thousands of Union troops to guard duties who otherwise would have been available for battle. As stated by General Hooker, the planks on the Chain Bridge into Washington were taken up nightly to keep Mosby from invading the city. At the time, Mosby could not have mustered twenty men.

An Essential Amendment

General Leonidas Polk and his staff met with Union officers under a flag of truce in November 1861. After disposing of matters of business, the men adjourned for a simple luncheon. A Union colonel raised his glass and proposed a toast, "George Washington, the Father of His Country." To that toast General Polk quickly added, "And the First Rebel!" All officers drank the amended toast!

Batter Up

After Jeb Stuart took his troopers around McClellan's army for the second time, Abraham Lincoln said in reference to McClellan, "Three times and out!"

Why the War Lasted Four Years

The process by which a soldier loaded and fired a regulation Springfield muzzle-loading rifle started with the man reaching into his cartridge pouch for a paper cartridge containing the powder charge and bullet. He then tore the cartridge open with his teeth. Next he emptied the powder into the barrel and disengaged the bullet with his right hand and thumb and two fingers of the left. Holding the ball with its point up, he pressed it down into the bore with his right thumb. He drew his ramrod halfway out, steadied it, grasped it again, and pulled it clear. Using the ramrod, he pushed the ball halfway down, grasped the ramrod higher, and drove the ball home. He removed the ramrod and returned it to its tube, with each movement again in two stages. He primed his piece by raising it, half cocking it, taking off the old cap, getting a new one out of his pouch, and pressing the new cap on the nipple. At last he cocked the gun, aimed it, and fired. And if he had a particular target in mind (highly unlikely in all the excitement), he probably missed it clean.

Onward, Christian Soldiers

Stonewall Jackson was noted for the rapid movements of his "foot cavalry." One struggling veteran was heard to avow that Jackson was bound to have been a better general than Moses. It took Moses forty years to lead the Israelites through the wilderness and Old Jack would have double-quicked them through it in three days!

Taking the Oath

After the fall of Richmond, a modest young Rebel maiden, on applying for rations was asked if she had ever "taken the oath." This resulted in the following dialogue: "No, indeed, sir, I never swore in my entire life." "But you must take the oath, my good girl, or I can not give you the rations." "No, indeed I can't, sir. Mother always taught me not to swear." The Federal agent mildly persisted and the young girl was finally overcome by dire necessity and stammered out, "Well, sir, if you will make me do such a dreadful thing, then...Damn the Yankees!"

Arming the South

To a large extent, the North helped arm the South, albeit unintentionally. Southern troops collected Federal arms on every battlefield on which they fought. After Southerners collected 100,000 Union rifles in 1862 alone, *the Macon (Georgia) Daily Telegraph* boasted:

> Want a weapon? Why, capture one!
> Every Doodle has got a gun!
> Belt and bayonet, bright and new,
> Kill a Doodle and capture two!

Song of the South

"The Bonnie Blue Flag" once rivalled "Dixie" as a Southern favorite. The flag was a symbol of secessionists and when "Beast" Butler occupied New Orleans he made it a penal offense to hum, sing, whistle or perform the song or to be in possession of a copy of it.

General Observation

At a council of generals early in the war, one remarked that a certain officer was wounded and would not be able to perform a duty that had been proposed for him. Said Stonewall Jackson in surprise, "Wounded? If it is really so, I think it must have been by an accidental discharge of his duty!"

Supply Problem

On Christmas Day, 1862, Jeb Stuart took 1,800 men on one of his famous raids through Federally held territory. Capturing a Federal telegraph operator at one point, Stuart had the following message tapped out to the Union army's quartermaster general, Montgomery Meigs: "Quality of the mules furnished me very poor. Interferes seriously with movement of captured wagons. J.E.B. Stuart."

Balance of Power

One evening in February 1861, two councilmen of New Orleans were reeling down the city hall steps, discussing politics as well as their cups and hiccups would allow. One said solemnly, "The South's true balance must not be overthrown." To which the other replied, "Confound the South's balance; try to keep your own."

Earned

A Confederate soldier buried a Federal who had been killed in one of the many battles for Richmond. Over the grave he then fixed a shingle with the inscription:

> The Yankee hosts with bloodstained hands
> Came Southward to divide our lands.
> This narrow and contracted spot
> Is all that this poor Yankee got!

Beating the Odds

General John B. Magruder once issued a general order that whenever any of his command met the enemy, they were to engage them at once and stay there, even if the odds were fifty to one or more. Although this was slightly in excess of the number of live Yankees his men thought they could eat before breakfast, he came close when he saved Richmond in the spring of 1862. For nine days he defended a line stretching ten miles from the York to the James River with a total force not exceeding 7,000 men against McClellan's Army of the Potomac consisting of 121,500.

When Duty Calls

During the engagement at Farmville, Robert E. Lee often exposed himself to great danger from shells and bullets. In answer to protests he responded that he had to see for himself what was going on. As he sat on his horse watching the effects of the fire from one of his batteries, a staff officer rode up to him with a message. Lee noticed that the young man had exposed himself unnecessarily in approaching him. Lee reprimanded him for not riding on the side of the hill where he could have been protected from the enemy's fire. The officer replied that he would be ashamed to seek protection while the commanding general was so exposed himself. Sharply Lee told him, "It is my duty to be here. Go back the way I told you, sir."

Well...

The colonel of an Alabama regiment was famous for his military strictness. Once, while he was field officer of the day, he came on a sentinel from the 11th

Mississippi Regiment sitting down on his post, with his weapon taken completely to pieces. Said the colonel, "Don't you know that a sentinel while on duty should always be on his feet?" Without looking up, the sentinel replied, "That's the way we used to do it when the war first began, but that's played out long ago." Beginning to doubt that the man was on duty, the colonel asked, "Are you the sentinel here?" "Well, I'm sort of a sentinel." "Well, I'm sort of officer of the day." "Well, if you'll hold on 'til I sort of get my gun together, I'll give you a sort of salute."

Some Men Became Beasts in War

While Generals Sherman and Joseph Johnston were working out surrender terms, Sherman got up from the table, walked to his saddlebags, found a bottle, and helped himself to a swig. Deep in thought, he replaced the bottle and returned to the task of drafting something that both sides could sign. After the agreement had been signed, Johnston and Secretary of War Breckinridge, who had also signed the document, rode back to camp together. Breckinridge sized up Sherman in this way: "Sherman is a bright man, and a man of great force, but, General Johnston, General Sherman is a hog. Yes sir, a hog. Did you see him take that drink by himself? No Kentucky gentleman would ever have taken away that bottle."

A Critic in the Crowd

John B. Hood was once addressing the 19th Tennessee when he asked for a show of confidence, remarking, "The cards were fairly dealt at Nashville, boys, but they beat the game." A private in E company promptly answered, "Yes, General, the cards were fairly dealt, but they were mighty badly shuffled!"

Lost Opportunity

As General Jubal Early approached the thick of the battle at Fredericksburg in December 1862, he met one of his chaplains "advancing to the rear" as fast as his legs could carry him. Halting the chaplain, Early asked him where he was going. The chaplain replied that he was going to a place of safety in the rear. Early commented, "Chaplain, I have known you for the past thirty years and all of that time you have been trying to get to Heaven, and now that the opportunity is offered, you are fleeing from it!"

Different

Union General Don Carlos Buell drew the following comparison to illustrate the confidence with which Southern soldiers followed their leaders: "At Cold Harbor when ordered to another sacrifice, the Northern troops answered the demand as one man, with silent and solid inertia. At Gettysburg, when Pickett received the signal which Longstreet dreaded to repeat, saluted and said as he turned to his ready column, 'I shall move forward, sir.' "

Drinking Man

Coffee was a precious commodity to our beleaguered Southerners. At Chancellorsville, when the Confederates charged through the camps of the Union 11th Army Corps, Lieutenant E. M. Perry of the 6th Georgia snatched a bucket of coffee from a camp fire. He fought the rest of the ferocious fight with the coffee in his left hand and his sword in his right.

Opposing Force

At Donelson, when viewing the Confederate prisoners marching out, Union General U. S. Grant exclaimed, "Where are all the men who have been opposing me?" When told that they were before him, Grant burst forth involuntarily, "Men, you were not whipped, you were overpowered!"

He Knew

Illiterate but to the point was the following letter from a Confederate soldier in Virginia: "I say agen deer malindy weer fitin for our liburtis to dew gest as we pleas, and we will fite fur them as long as goddlemity give us breth."

Looking on the Bright Side

After fleeing from Nashville, a soldier of Major General W. B. Bate's division had thrown away his gun and accoutrements and sat dejectedly in the woods. Finally he arose and sighed, "I am whipped, badly whipped, and somewhat demoralized, but no man can say I am scattered."

Stonewalling It

News of the First Battle of Manassas spread throughout a jubilant South and Stonewall Jackson was mentioned prominently. Having received garbled reports, the people of Lexington awaited reliable news. Finally the minister of Jackson's church received a letter from Jackson, written the morning after the battle. Telling his eager parishioners, "Now we shall know all the facts," the minister opened the letter to read the following: "My dear pastor, in my tent last night, after a fatiguing day's service, I remembered that I had failed to send you my contribution for our colored Sunday School. Enclosed you will find my check for that object, which please acknowledge at your earliest convenience, and oblige yours faithfully, T. J. Jackson."

Only One Thing in His Favor

A critique of Nathan Bedford Forrest: "He exposed his command to piecemeal destruction. Once battle was opened, he could not exercise control because he himself was in the thick of the fighting. The mounted pursuit he led after the field was won was inexcusable since he had no idea where most of his men were. He was completely unprepared for a Union attack. The only thing he did right was win."

Forrestry

During a raid on Memphis by General Nathan Bedford Forrest, Union General Washburn fled his sleeping quarters in his night clothes. The next day Washburn's predecessor, General Stephen Hurlbut, remarked, "They removed me from command because I couldn't keep Forrest out of West Tennessee, but apparently Washburn can't keep him out of his bedroom!"

Truth Unchanging

William Howard, Company H, 4th Arkansas: "When I enlisted in July 15, 1861, I felt the South was being imposed upon and that we had the right to secede and form a Confederacy of our own, and the longer I live, the more I am confirmed in that belief."

Inborn

Conspicuously demonstrated by the rank and file Confederate soldier was an acute sense of duty. After Chancellorsville, one soldier wrote to his wife, saying, "I was very near not going into the fight; I had been sick so long; but when I got to thinking about it, I could not stay behind if it killed me. I do not think I could have kept out of the fight."

Point of View

After years of combat with little opportunity for obtaining fresh uniforms, the vaunted Texans of Hood's Brigade once passed in review for General Robert E. Lee. A visiting foreign officer remarked on the ragtag condition of the seats of their pants. Lee replied that they might not look good from the back, but their enemies never saw them from that viewpoint.

Miscellany

Confederate General George Pickett received his appointment to West Point through John Todd Stuart, Abraham Lincoln's law partner.

Our Military

In the *Southern Historical Society Papers* I (January–June 1876), General D. H. Hill said that "the Southern soldiers united the elan of the Frenchman with the dogged determination of the Englishman, the careless gaiety of the Italian with the uncomplaining fortitude of the Russian." Southern soldiers came out of the war unrepentant and as convinced as before that there are things worse than war.

Even When Desperate

The February 1890, *Century* Magazine reported that near the end of the war an inventor designed a hollow container that looked like a lump of coal. Its purpose was to be filled with explosives and put in fuel yards of U.S. Naval Stations. President Jefferson Davis rejected the proposal as "an unjustified mode of warfare," unworthy of Christian soldiery.

Quaker Guns

Never overly equipped with cannons, the South in the early days of the war painted logs to look like cannons. These logs were then placed in embankments where they deceived Yankee scouts. McClellan's attack on Confederate forces at Yorktown was withheld as a result of his falling victim to this type of ruse.

The Wrath of the Lord

Chaplains varied greatly in ability and attitudes in our Southern army. Leonidas Polk was both a bishop and a lieutenant general. In the heat of battle some chaplains could not resist joining their flocks. At Chancellorsville one chaplain not only stayed at the forefront with his musket, but also directed the movement of skirmisher units. In an action near Columbus, Kentucky, another chaplain shot two Yankees, slashed the throat of a third, then ran after the foe shouting, "Go to Hell, you damned S.O.B.'s." (Only he didn't use the initials!)

Passed On

An incident near Chambersburg indicates the tender memory and sense of duty Stonewall Jackson left behind him. The assistant quartermaster of the Second Corps had spent the evening in town and was returning late at night when he was halted by a sentry. Having neither pass nor countersign, he finally produced an old pass signed by General Jackson. After reading the pass and lingering over the signature, the sentinel handed it back, looked up at the stars for a moment, then said sadly and firmly, "Captain, you can go to heaven on that paper but you can't pass this post."

For a Cause

Following the two-day bloody battle at Fort Robinett, some Union troops were burying the valiant Confederate dead. As one soldier removed a haversack from the body of a Rogers Texan, another soldier remarked, "Empty, isn't it?" The first put his hand into the haversack and drew forth a handful of roasted acorns. "That's all," he said. "And he has been fighting two days on that forage," commented the second, "...this is what I call patriotism."

Another Way of Saying It

Following his defeat at New Market by General John C. Breckinridge, Major General Franz Sigel reported to the Union's adjutant general: "The retrograde movement was effected in perfect order. The troops are in very good spirits and will fight another battle if the enemy should advance against us." General Halleck translated this when he reported to General Grant, "Sigel is in full retreat on Strasburg. He will do nothing but run: never did anything else."

Lending His Strength

At the Battle of Sayler's Creek, General John B. Gordon was inspecting his lines when he noticed a soldier with his arms hanging limp and bloody by his side. Both had been shattered by minié balls. When General Gordon asked him why he didn't go to the rear since he could not even shoulder a rifle, the soldier replied, "No, sir, but I can still yell!"

Trained

As the war wore on, travel by train became slower, with numerous delays in addition to being unpleasant, expensive, and hazardous. *The Daily Southern Crisis* of Jackson, Mississippi, published the following dialogue in the spring of 1863:

First person: "Have you heard of the railroad accident?"

Second person: "No, where was it?"

First person: "The Western train left Meridian and arrived in Jackson on time!"

Decorum a Must!

During a battle General Sterling Price once had a spyglass shot out of his hands while he was reconnoitering the enemy. His son, Colonel Ed Price, rode up and exclaimed, "Are you hurt, Pa?" The reply came sharply, " '*General*' on the battlefield, sir!"

Tall Tale

In 1861 a Texan named Henry C. Thruston enlisted in the Morgan County Rangers. Henry was seven feet seven and one-half inches tall. Enlisting at the same time were his four brothers, the shortest of whom stood six feet six inches in height. Although Henry took an active part in battles and raids, he was wounded only one time. Surprisingly enough, that was by a bullet that grazed the top of his head. After the surrender of his command in June 1865, he returned to Texas where he lived until his death in 1909.

Now That's Quick!

A Texas veteran said once that Texas has the quickest climate in the world. He told of an old farmer driving two oxen along the road. It was so hot that one of the oxen fell dead. While the farmer was skinning him, the other one froze to death.

He Took a Positive View

Abraham Lincoln denied the Southern victory at Chickamauga in a letter to his wife dated September 24, 1863. He stated that Union forces were only worsted in that after the battle was over they yielded the ground and left considerable artillery and their wounded to fall into Confederate hands.

Write On!

From a patriotic envelope printed in 1861:

> Stand freely by your cannon
> Let ball and grapeshot fly,
> And trust in God and Davis,
> But keep your powder dry.

Even

A wounded Confederate on his deathbed comforted himself with the reflection, "I reckon I killed as many of them as they did of me!"

Proper Spirit

John B. Gordon, in preparing for battle: "With me is Right, before me is Duty, behind me is home."

Finding a Spot

While the Confederate capital was located in Montgomery, a small town packed to overflowing, even the highest officials were forced to scramble for room in which to operate their departments. Robert Toombs was approached at that time with a request for a post in the State Department. Whipping off his hat and pointing to it, he roared, "There is the State Department of the Confederacy! Jump in!"

Proper Response

An officer once asked a picket what he would do if he saw a body of men coming. "Halt 'em and demand the countersign, sir." "But suppose they wouldn't halt?" "Then I'd shoot." "Suppose that didn't stop them?" "I reckon I'd form a line, sir." "A line? What kind of a line?" "A beeline straight for camp, and run like thunder!"

Spirit

In the early days of the war there was much equality between the officers and the enlisted men. Many of the latter were both socially and intellectually superior to the former. Irritated by a private's remarks, a Southern captain exclaimed, "If you repeat that, I'll lay down my rank and fight you." "Lay down your rank?" was the indignant response. "That won't make you a gentleman. A coward can fight with straps on his shoulders, but it takes a gentleman to fight for eleven dollars a month."

Ethics

While serving as a U.S. Senator, Jefferson Davis was once severely ill. Among his visitors was William Seward, senator from New York. During their conversation, Seward frankly admitted that many of his anti-Southern utterances were expedient, calculated for their effect on the Northern voter. Davis was aghast. "But Mr. Seward," he said, "do you never speak from conviction?" "Never!" replied Seward cheerfully. Davis was so astounded that he tried to sit up, stating straight from the heart, "As God is my judge, I never speak from any other motive."

Our Ladies

The devotion of Southern women to the Confederacy has often been noted. A Union officer with Sherman on his "march to the sea" stated that in two thousand miles of tramping through the South he saw many Southern men who were loyal to the Union and regretted the secession of their respective states, but only one woman whom he ever suspected to be Union in sentiment.

Philosophy

Shortly before the fall of Atlanta, the *Daily Intelligencer* left the city and moved its presses down to Macon. In its last Atlanta issue, it published a bit of a chin-up farewell:

Hoot away despair,
Never yield to sorrow,
The blackest day may wear
A sunny face tomorrow.

Bit Off a Bit Too Much

Due to his slight stature, Alexander Stephens, vice president of the Confederacy, was known to his friends as "Little Aleck." His mind, however, was neither small nor stunted. A Congressional opponent once spoke sneeringly of Stephens' size, saying, "I could swallow him whole and never know the difference." On hearing of the remark, Stephens promptly commented, "If Judge Colquitt should swallow me whole, there would be more brains in his stomach than there ever were in his head!"

May I?

Reports from detective Allan Pinkerton that Joe Johnston was defending Richmond with 250,000 men resulted in extreme caution by Union General George

McClellan. McClellan drilled his troops for six exhausting months, drawing an exasperated growl from Lincoln that "If he doesn't intend to use his army, I would like to borrow it!"

Properly Drawn Requisition

A lieutenant protested an order to take a squad of men across a swamp where he knew the depth was enough to drown them. His superiors sternly rebuked him, ordered him to make the crossing, and told him his requisition would be honored for whatever might be required for the purpose. He thereupon requisitioned "twenty men eighteen feet long to cross a swamp fifteen feet deep."

Tough

George B. Zimpleman of Terry's Texas Rangers may have been the fightingest soldier in the war. He went through more than four hundred battles and skirmishes, led his regiment in the number of horses shot out from under him, and suffered two wounds.

The Rifled Musket

The rifled musket was the most commonly used infantry weapon on both sides of the War for Southern Independence. Equipped with a rifled musket, a good marksman could fire two shots per minute and hit an 8'x8' target two times out of four at one thousand yards. From this distance the bullet had sufficient power to go through four inches of soft pine.

Might Not Be Good

When asked for a pass to go through the lines to go into Richmond, Abraham Lincoln replied, "I don't know about that; I have given passes to about two hundred and fifty thousand men to go there during the last two years, and not one of them has got there yet."

Names

Northern armies were generally named for rivers, such as the Army of the Cumberland, the Army of the Ohio, the Army of the Potomac. Southern armies were named for states or regions, such as the Army of Northern Virginia. This becomes especially confusing when reading of two similarly designated armies meeting in an engagement or campaign. For example, in 1864, before Atlanta, the Confederate *Army of Tennessee* was fighting the Union *Army of the Tennessee*. (Incidentally, the 7th Tennessee Regiment, CSA, once captured the entire 7th Tennessee Regiment, USA.) Further confusion resulted from the Confederates naming battles for towns while Federals often used the names of nearby streams. The Confederate

Manassas was the Union *Bull Run*. The Confederate *Pittsburg Landing* was *Shiloh* to the Yankees. The Confederate *Sharpsburg* was the Union *Antietam*. *Murfreesboro* to the Confederates was *Stone's River* to the Yankees. Confederate *Seven Pines* was the Federal *Fair Oaks*.

Post Script

A drunken Confederate soldier met Jefferson Davis on a Richmond street and stared at him before asking, "Are you Mister Davis?" "I am." "Ain't you president of the Confederate States?" "I am, sir." "Well, by God, I thought you looked like a postage stamp."

Swift and Sure

In the early days of the war, military usages were not yet established and ideas of frontier justice often prevailed. For instance, a Texas cavalryman was once apprehended in the act of rape. While his officers debated his disposition, the man was removed from the guardhouse by his comrades, hanged, buried, and his belongings were distributed among the needy of the company.

Change

At First Manassas the 2nd U.S. Cavalry was officered by Captain Frank C. Armstrong and Lieutenant Manning M. Kimmel. The following month Armstrong resigned and went south to become a Confederate brigadier general. He was shortly followed by Lieutenant Kimmel who became assistant adjutant general to General Earl Van Dorn.

Going into Battle

From a diary of Private W. R. Howell, Company C, 5th Regiment, Texas Mounted Volunteers:

"The CS soldier goes to battle with the belief that our cause is just and right and that if he live or die the God of battles will not suffer him to pass unnoticed or unattended in his dying moments."

Rebels

From a poem in the *Richmond Daily Dispatch* of May 12, 1862:

> Then call us Rebels if you will,
> We glory in the name,
> For bending under unjust laws
> And swearing faith to an unjust cause
> We count as greater shame.

Just Jottings

When Colonel John S. Mosby slipped into Alexandria and captured Union Colonel D. H. Dulaney, his guide was well qualified for the task. The guide, a member of Mosby's Rangers, was French Dulaney, the son of Colonel Dulaney.

One of the most despicable Union generals, Ben "Beast" Butler, was once a pro-slavery Democrat who repeatedly tried to nominate Jefferson Davis for the presidency of the United States.

Troops both Southern and Federal studied tactics from the same book, written by Confederate General William J. Hardee.

After a valiant charge by his Florida company that overran the opposing Federal guns, Captain John L. Inglis accepted the surrender of the Union commander, his brother.

In 1863, when an army private's pay was $11 per month, it cost $30 per month to hire a slave.

General Nathan Bedford Forrest had twenty-nine horses shot out from under him in the course of the war.

Missouri furnished 39 regiments for the siege of Vicksburg. Seventeen were Confederate, twenty-two were Union.

Abraham Lincoln was a Confederate private in Company F, First Virginia Cavalry, from Jefferson County. He deserted in 1864.

To the Point

Nathan Bedford Forrest was a man of direct action and direct thought. A subordinate officer once sent a message stating, "I'm facing superior force in my front, on my right and my left flank. What shall I do?" Forrest's reply, written on a hand shingle: "Fitem."

Amazing!

With comparatively few armories Southerners often fought with captured Yankee weapons. A North Carolinian who was made prisoner at Sharpsburg was being marched to the rear when he paused to read aloud the "US" markings on a number of fieldpieces. With surprise he said to his captor, "Mister, you all got as many of these US guns as we has!"

A Close Shave

In 1861 the word went out to Federal units to "Bring in Mosby, dead or alive!" Knowing John Mosby's wife was living just south of Warrenton, Virginia, the Yanks concentrated on that little town, twenty miles inside the Union lines. Men in blue questioned everyone, including loafers on the square and customers in the barbershop. No one would talk except a little sandy-haired man being shaved who said he had not seen Mosby. As the soldiers clattered away, the barber wiped the lather off and sighed, "I sure wish you wouldn't take such chances, Major Mosby!"

Better Not Ask

A South Carolina soldier, writing home in 1862, told his wife he was cooking dinner while writing. The meat was either pig or mule and he didn't know which.

Stalwart

At Seven Pines, Colonel (later General) Wade Hampton outdid the famed Bunker Hill injunction of "Don't shoot 'til you can see the whites of their eyes." Hampton's orders were: "Don't fire until you can feel the enemy on your bayonet!" During that battle, Hampton received a shot in his foot that left blood pouring from his boot. Hampton refused a surgeon's order to dismount, saying, "If I get off this horse, I can't get back on with that wound. Take off the boot and dig for the bullet." The doctor did so and Hampton rode back into battle.

Spirited Discussion

From a Southern newspaper during the "late hostilities" came the story of some Yankee officers who started to go through the gate of a Virginia home but were stopped by the daughter of the house. Confronting them from the porch of the house, she demanded to know their business. They informed her they were looking for Southern flags to take up. The young lady scornfully informed them, "Brave men take flags on the field of battle—cowards hunt them at the houses of defenseless women. Mine is in the hands of our brave volunteers; go and take it from them!"

Saying It Properly

While in command of the James River defenses, General Henry Wise was camped on the plantation of one of Richmond's wealthiest and most influential citizens. That citizen annoyed Wise with complaints of depradations committed by Wise's men. Wise ordered the man out of his tent. Before leaving, the man told Wise that Wise owed him an apology. Wise said, "My apology is that having on my slippers, I could not possibly do you justice. I ought to have kicked you out of my tent, and will do so now if you will wait 'til I put on my boots!"

Spirited

At Malvern Hill in 1862 a Confederate colonel running ahead of his regiment discovered his men were not following as closely as he wished. Uttering a fierce oath he exclaimed, "Come on! Do you wish to live forever?"

By the Numbers

The Southern belief that one Confederate could whip any number of Yankees was bolstered by the actions of such men as General Adam R. Johnson. Early in the war, with only two men, he demanded and received the surrender of the home guard at the town of Henderson, Kentucky. When his force had grown to seven, he made a midnight attack on 350 Pennsylvania cavalrymen, scattering and routing them. Following the flight of the Union force and swollen with the addition of twenty reinforcements, he accepted the surrender of Henderson, guarded 180 prisoners, and carried away several hundred stands of arms while the Union gunboat *Brilliant* lay opposite the town.

An Example

In September of 1862, General D. H. Hill sat astride his horse with field glasses to his eyes, watching the battle of Sharpsburg from the front line. A Union shell struck his horse, killing it instantly. Without removing his glasses from his eyes, he calmly disengaged his feet from the stirrups and continued to watch the battle until his adjutant brought him another horse. When he was later asked why he did not evidence surprise or nervousness, he explained that had he done so his men might have panicked and given way.

Fair Is Fair

In the midst of confusion of a raid on Kilpatrick's camp, General Calbraith Butler stopped for a moment to watch a duel on horseback taking place a few yards away. Unable to see who the Confederate was, but deeming the man to be evenly matched with the Yank, Butler saw no reason to interfere. The two fired and missed from ten paces, then fired again. This time the Yank fell. Butler rode on, not learning until that night that the unknown fellow Confederate was his own brother.

Insurance

As Maryland was considered a Southern state, it was believed that she would follow Virginia out of the Union, leaving Washington, D.C., as an isolated island within the South. To abort such action, Lincoln jailed the leading legislators until he was sure there would be no secession.

An Even Fight

Separated from his men in Northern Virginia, Jeb Stuart suddenly faced an enemy company in position behind a rail fence. Boldly riding up to them, he trumpeted, "Take down those bars!" Riding in, he shouted, "Throw down your arms or you are all dead men!" Unable to imagine such boldness if they were not surrounded, the Federals dropped their weapons and surrendered. Stuart was a merry man as he single-handedly captured an entire company of forty-nine Pennsylvania volunteers.

Looky There!

At the head of fifty troopers on a scouting mission, Nathan Bedford Forrest turned a sharp bend to find himself in the middle of a Yankee camp and outnumbered twenty to one. With a fight hopeless and too late to retreat, Forrest motioned for his men to do as he did, then screamed loudly and pointed to the sky. When his troopers did likewise, the Yankees reacted just as Forrest expected. While they gaped skyward, Forrest and his men raced out of range, leaving the Yankees cursing themselves for falling for the ruse.

Contentious

While still a young company commander, Braxton Bragg once had to double as post quartermaster. Day after day, as company commander he conscientiously filled out requisitions to meet his company's needs. Then as quartermaster and unable to fill the requisitions due to a lack of supplies, he would refuse to honor them. His superior finally heard of these actions and told him, "Mr. Bragg, you have quarreled with every officer in the army, and now you are even quarreling with yourself."

And Pass the Ammunition

While Leonidas Polk was probably the most widely known minister in the Confederate service, many others contributed in non-religious roles. Charles T. Quintard of the 1st Tennessee Regiment was a trained doctor and served as such. T. L. Duke of the 19th Mississippi directed skirmishes and carried a musket. William N. Pendleton was Lee's chief of staff. Dabney Ball was commissary officer for Jeb Stuart and famed as the "Foraging Parson" in whose territory no chicken was safe. Thomas N. Conrad of Wickham's Brigade served as a daring scout. Many won official commendation for heroism on the battlefield, while others gave their lives in line of duty.

Always Pious

On July 1, 1861, bluecoat brigades beyond counting advanced against the troops of Colonel Thomas J. Jackson, near a small settlement in Virginia called Falling Waters. Jackson's artilleryman was the Reverend William N. Pendleton, in charge of four guns named Matthew, Mark, Luke, and John. As a pell-mell charge carried the Union troops down a crowded roadway toward Jackson, Pendleton gave the order which cleared the road: "Aim low, men, and may the Lord have mercy on their souls!"

A Lesson in Negotiations

Smarting from John S. Mosby's raids against George Custer, U. S. Grant ordered Philip Sheridan to hang without trial any of Mosby's men he captured. In September when six of the Rangers were captured at Fort Royal, four of them were shot and two were hanged. Three weeks later another captured Ranger was hanged. Mosby promptly captured six of Custer's men, shot two, hung four, and sent Sheridan written details of their deaths. This brought the executions to an end.

Unchanged

During the war, the following letter was received by General Robert E. Lee from a newspaper in England. It shows that the often shallow intelligence of the press is nothing new:

General Robert E. Lee, Commanding
Army of Northern Virginia
Richmond, Virginia

Dear General Lee:

In order for our reports on your movements to be as accurate as possible, we need to have your position title, the army that you represent, and your complete address. We would appreciate a prompt response.

Quickly Healed

A colonel on Robert E. Lee's staff suffered a wound to his dignity when Lee gently rebuked him for an obvious error. He thereafter acted politely but coldly when in Lee's presence, rejecting Lee's overtures to return to familiarity. The coolness ended one morning when the colonel awoke to find that it had rained during the night and he had slept through the night protected by Lee's own cloak while Lee himself lay unprotected.

Duty

During the invasion of Maryland, Wade Hampton was in a grim fighting mood at Burkittsville. Snatching off his overcoat, he threw it to his son who was riding with him. "Take care of my overcoat, Preston," he said, drawing his sword and spurring into the fight. Flinging the coat into a fence corner, his high-spirited son followed him into battle with the comment, "I've come to Maryland to fight Yankees, not to carry Father's overcoat!"

In Command

During the opening moments of Second Manassas, with shells bursting nearby, President Davis and an entourage appeared on the road approaching General Lee, with the evident purpose of watching the battle. General Lee was annoyed at what he considered a foolhardy exposure of the head of the government. He faced the cavalcade indignantly, saluted Davis, and asked quickly, "Who are all this army of people and what are they doing here?" The president was taken aback at such a greeting and replied, "It is not my army, General." Lee said without hesitation, "It is certainly not *my* army, Mr. President, and this is no place for it!" When Davis recovered his composure, he withdrew to where he could still watch the battle but where Lee could not see him.

Equal Rights, 1862

Many Federals were brought into Jeb Stuart's camp after a raid by his troopers on Catlett's Station in 1862. One of those women was found to be a pretty woman in a Union private's uniform. She begged for a release on the basis that she was a woman. Stuart refused her plea, stating, "If you're man enough to enlist, you ought to be man enough to go to prison."

Proof Positive

During the Georgia campaign General (and Bishop) Leonidas Polk was inspecting the lines. Nearby was another general, a cavalry officer noted not only for his daring and bravery but also for his use of vigorous language and strong expletives. A Union shell exploded nearby and stunned both officers momentarily. The other man awoke first and soon satisfied himself that Polk was safe, although unconscious. When he heard Polk say, "Oh Lord, where am I?" he replied with grim humor, "In hell, General." "Impossible," murmured Polk. "Who is it that tells me so?" When the practical joker identified himself, the good bishop groaned, "Oh Lord, have mercy on me! If he is here I know it must be true!"

Defiance

When Union soldiers occupied Williamsburg in 1862, they hung Union flags over the sidewalks to make townfolk pass under the Stars and Stripes. Victoria King, a sixteen-year-old girl, regularly walked up the street, avoiding the sidewalks on her way to bring biscuits and buttermilk to the Confederate wounded housed in the Baptist church. A Yankee guard tried to make her walk under the flag one day, whereupon she broke a crock of buttermilk over his head. Thereafter the guards only stared as she daily made her way down the center of the street.

A Steed in Need

The air was thick with shot and shell as Adams' Cavalry Brigade valiantly resisted the advance of the strong Union force at the Battle of Baker's Creek. One member of the brigade finally lost his nerve, wheeled his horse, and dashed to the rear, shouting, "I can't hold my horse." Munford Bacon of Madison County, Mississippi, rose up in his saddle and yelled in reply, "Boy, I'll give you $1,000 for one of them horses you can't hold."

Tourism

Several years after the war, General John B. Gordon explained the 1863 Confederate invasion of Pennsylvania as, in part, a "recruiting expedition" for beeves for the Southern commissary. His account: "For more than two years the effort to fill the ranks of the Southern armies had alarmingly reduced the ranks of Southern producers, with no appreciable diminution in the number of consumers. Indeed the consumers had materially increased; for while we were not then seeking to encourage Northern immigration, we had a large number of visitors from that and other sections who were exploring the country under such efficient guides as McClellan, Hooker, Grant, Sherman, Thomas, and others. We had, therefore, much need of borrowing supplies from our neighbors beyond the Potomac."

Quick Thinking

A Georgian in command of the Banks County Guards, Captain Candler was marching his men in a column when they approached a narrow gate. Unable to think of a proper command to get them through the gate, he halted them and then said, "Gentlemen, we will now take a recess of ten minutes. Break ranks, and when you fall in, will you please reform on the other side of the fence."

Well Said

Major R. E. Wilson, First North Carolina Battalion Sharpshooters, CSA, spoke for all good Southerners when he said, "If ever I disown, repudiate, or apologize for the cause for which Lee fought and Jackson died, let the scorn of all good men and true women be my portion. Sun, moon, stars all fall on me when I cease to love the Confederacy. 'Tis the Cause, not the fate of the Cause, that is glorious."

No Appetite

The 1st Tennessee was advancing to the attack at Chickamauga, exhorted to bravery by an accompanying chaplain who stated that if only he had a gun he too would go to fight. As a shell screamed through the air, the chaplain exclaimed, "Remember, boys, that he who is killed will sup tonight in Paradise." Just then a shell burst near him and he immediately spurred his horse to the rear, prompting the laconic comment from one observer, "The parson isn't hungry!"

Popular Beliefs

After receiving many complaints from civilians about the foraging of General Jo Shelby's troops, General Theophilus Holmes ordered Shelby arrested without investigating the charges. When the dashing Shelby appeared before him, Holmes opened up on Shelby with invectives, charging him with being a robber and his men with being thieves. When Shelby asked who had made the charges, Holmes told him, "Everybody, sir, everybody!" "And you believe them, do you, General Holmes?" "Certainly I do, sir. How can I help believing them?" Proud of his command and deeply indignant, General Shelby quietly replied, "Well, General Holmes, I will be more just to you than you have been to me and my men. Everybody says that you are a damned old fool, but I do not believe it!" That ended the interview and nothing more was heard of the arrest and charges.

A Vital Difference

It was in the night's darkness at the battle for Lookout Mountain that brave little Billy Bethune of Georgia made his debut as a fighting soldier. Shortly thereafter he made his exit on an Irishman's shoulder. As Billy was being carried off the field of battle, his major asked, "Who is that you're carrying to the rear?" "Billy Bethune, sir." "Is he wounded?" "Yes, sir, he's shot in the back, sir." This was more than Billy could endure and he indignantly shouted, "Major, he's an infernal liar; I am shot *across* the back, sir!"

Take Care, Brazil!

A Confederate recipe: Take sound, ripe acorns, wash them while in the shell and dry them. Parch until they open, take the shell off, roast with a little bacon fat, and you can make a splendid cup of coffee.

Limitations to Authority

A former surgeon on duty as a line officer in the U.S. Army complained to General George Meade that some soldiers called out "Old Pills" after he passed. He asked Meade to make them stop. Not in the best of moods Meade seized the large eyeglasses he habitually wore, clapped them into position on his nose, glared at the officer, and exclaimed, "Well, what of that? I hear that when I rode out the other day some of the men called me a 'damned old goggle-eyed snapping turtle' and I can't even stop that!"

Linguists

Two slaves were discussing the meaning of the name "Manassas." While not certain of the derivation they finally decided that it must be because "....we is de man and dem Yankees is de asses."

Only under Proper Conditions

A Massachusetts man called on former U.S. Senator James S. Mason at his Virginia home early in 1861. Recalling a visit to Boston a few years earlier, the visitor remarked, "I hope, Mr. Mason, we shall see you again at Bunker Hill." Mason quickly responded, "Not unless I come as an ambassador."

Good Idea

One Sunday while General Richard Ewell's troops were occupying Carlisle, Pennsylvania, a committee waited on him to ascertain whether or not he had any objections to a prayer for the president of the United States. "Certainly not," said Old Dick bluntly, "pray for him, I'm sure he needs it!"

Talk About Being a Pain

Few housewives have been such a pain in the side as that of Confederate Brigadier General Clement A. Evans. On July 9, 1864, Evans was hit by a minié ball that drove his housewife into his side. Evans survived but doctors picked pins out of the wound for years. (A soldier's "housewife" was his sewing kit.)

Unfortunately Skilled

During a battle at Belmont, Missouri, a Federal officer took note of a Confederate soldier who was conspicuous for his daring and gallantry. Aiming carefully at the Southerner, the Federal shot and killed him. Returning the next day with a party sent to bury the Union dead, he sought out the body of his target. Turning the man over, he found he had killed his brother.

Critique

Both during and since the Second American Revolution many detractors have attacked Jefferson Davis' management and administration of his responsibilities as president. However, since so many of these same people are ardent admirers of Robert E. Lee, it might be well for them to consider General Lee's opinion: "You can always say few people could have done better than Mr. Davis. I know of none that could have done as well."

Disheartened

Stolidly stacking his arms and falling back into line after Lee's surrender at Appomattox, a tall gaunt North Carolinian had quit fighting, not because he wanted to, but because he had been so ordered. Worn, hungry, and dirty, he had still been willing to continue. Suddenly realizing the full effects of what was happening, he drawled to his neighbor, "Damn me if I ever love another country!"

Not the Time

A deeply religious man, Jeb Stuart neither smoke nor drank. Offered brandy to deaden the pain of his dying moments, he refused, saying he had promised his mother never to drink and saw no reason to break his promise at that late date.

Keeping the Faith

Heros von Borcke, who served the South so well under Stuart, never forgot the Confederacy and the cause for which he fought and nearly died. When Colonel Charles Venable visited Prussia after the war, he found von Borcke flying the Confederate flag on one tower of his castle and the Prussian flag on the other.

Good Reason

From the *Confederate Veteran* for October 1913:

"Lincoln once asked General Winfield Scott the question, 'Why is it that you were able to take the City of Mexico in three months with five thousand men, and we have been unable to take Richmond with one hundred thousand men?' 'I will tell you, sir,' said General Scott. 'The men who took us into the City of Mexico then are the same men who are keeping us out of Richmond now.' "

Don't Spread Rumors

Stonewall Jackson was unshakably calm even in the excitement of battle. During one battle an officer rode up to him from another part of the field and exclaimed, "General, I think the day is going against us!" In his usual curt manner Jackson responded, "If you think so, sir, you had better not say anything about it!"

Timing

Just before the Battle of the Wilderness a Southern sergeant received a letter from his wife. She said she had heard there was going to be a big battle and her greatest wish was to see him before it was fought. He wrote back stating that he would be happier seeing her after it was over!

In Keeping

After the Catholic priest Father Mullen stated in New Orleans that he would cheerfully bury the whole Yankee army, General Ben "Beast" Butler took him to task for his statement. Said Butler, "Do you know, sir, that I can send you to Fort St. Phillip and keep you there?" Undaunted, Father Mullen promptly shot back, "And do you know, General Butler, that I can send your soul to hell and keep it there?" With many Irish Catholics in his army and fearful of offending them, Butler immediately released the gallant priest.

A Justified Action

A Georgia colonel who had charged the enemy furiously and successfully drew a reprimand for making the charge without orders. He had a good excuse, though. His ammunition was low and was about to give out.

Franking Privilege

An old North Carolina soldier told of how he sent letters home during the war when he couldn't afford postage. He would write across the corner of the envelope:

> In camp without a red;
> Hard-tack instead of bread.
> Postmaster, please push this through;
> When old Jeff pays me, I'll pay you.

He said his letters always went through.

A Modest Request

During the summer of 1864 the hospitals of Richmond were crowded with the wounded. The ladies of the city visited the wounded daily, carrying with them delicacies of every kind and vied with each other to comfort and cheer the wounded. On one occasion a bright-eyed damsel of about seventeen summers was distributing flowers and speaking tender words of comfort to those around her. When she heard a young officer exclaim from the pain of his wounds, "O, my Lord!" she approached him timidly. In order to rebuke his profanity, she said, "I think I heard you call upon the name of the Lord. I am one of his daughters. Is there anything I can ask him for you?" A hasty glance at her lovely face and perfect form caused his countenance to brighten as he instantly replied, "Yes, please ask him to make me his son-in-law!"

Learned Well

At one time officers were elected by their company. Active in raising a company, John W. Dean failed to be elected an officer when elections were held. Later he helped to form another company and administered the following oath to the incoming recruits: "You solemnly swear to obey, fight for and maintain the laws of the Confederate Government and Constitution, and support John W. Dean for captain of this company."

Terminology

Stonewall Jackson instantly corrected an officer's reference to his men as "poor devils," stating that they were "suffering angels."

Interpretation

A Presbyterian minister who served on Stonewall Jackson's staff, Dr. Dabney ducked quickly behind a stone pillar when bullets suddenly began flying toward him. A comrade gently chided him about the strength of his convictions, asking if he didn't feel guilty about letting the pillar stand between him and Direct Providence. The minister replied he did not, because he felt the presence of the pillar *was* Direct Providence.

Even Up

During the Battle of the Wilderness, the lines were very mixed up. Colonel Davidson of the 7th North Carolina and Colonel Baldwin of the 1st Massachusetts each crept up to a stream to get a drink of water, only a few yards apart. Baldwin was promptly captured by Southerners. At the same time Davidson was captured by Federals.

Daddy's Little Darlin'

Rebecca, aged eight, was very proud of her Confederate father's rank as a first lieutenant and grew quite indignant when a neighbor boy called him "Captain." "I'll have you understand that my daddy is not a captain, he's a lieutenant," she said. The boy replied, "Oh, it doesn't matter, he is an officer." "Indeed he is not an officer," Rebecca protested. "Yes, dear, a lieutenant is an officer," interrupted her mother. "Well," persisted Rebecca, still determined to maintain her daddy's dignity at all cost, "he's not much of an officer."

Diplomatic

A slave serving as body servant to his master often developed an intense family pride, always guarding his master's honor. One of General Floyd's slaves had been sent far to the rear following a defeat in Virginia. When asked how Floyd's troops were doing, he didn't want to admit defeat. He replied, "When I lef'em, our men wuz advancing backwards on dem Yankees, and dey wuz retreatin' on us."

A Remarkable Distance

City Point, on the James River, was the landing for transports with soldiers released from Northern prisons for parole. As a woebegone and emaciated Confederate sat waiting his turn, a pompous Union major remarked to no one in particular about how close Richmond was. The Southerner drawled weakly that it must be about three thousand miles. "Nonsense, you must be crazy!" replied the major. "Well, I ent a-recknin' edzact, just thought so, kinder," was the slow reply. "Oh, you did? And why, pray?" "'Cause it took'n youens nigh on to foore years to git thar from Washington!"

Stonewall's Type of Humor

Stonewall Jackson was not always grim. He laughed loudly at a story told by Major Wells Hawks: "In the early days a Pilgrim father was going out in the woods with his gun. He met a man who asked, 'Where are you going?' 'Out in the woods,' he replied. 'I thought you were a Calvinist.' 'I am a Calvinist.' 'Don't you believe you can't die till your time comes?' 'I know I can't die till my time comes.' 'Then why carry a gun?' 'Because I might meet an Indian whose time had come!' "

A Brave Man

In one of the battles around Richmond an Alabama regiment was fiercely attacked by a whole brigade. Unable to withstand such great odds, the Alabamans were forced to fall back about thirty or forty yards. To the utter mortification of the Alabamans their flag was lost, remaining in the hands of the enemy. Suddenly a tall Alabama private in the color company rushed across the vacant ground and attacked the squad of Yankees who had possession of the flag. He felled several of them, snatched the flag from them, and returned safely to his regiment. He was immediately surrounded by his jubilant comrades and praised highly for his gallantry. His captain appointed him sergeant on the spot, but the hero cut everything short, saying, "Oh never mind, Captain. Say no more about it. I dropped my whiskey flask among the Yankees and fetched that back, and I thought I might just as well bring the flag along!"

Dress Right

In the spring of 1861, before adoption of the Confederate uniform, officers dressed as fancy as they desired. A procession of officers was being formed for a ceremony near Pensacola, with the men being placed in order by rank. One man was moved several times before the officer of the day told him, "You must really excuse me; but you will appreciate the difficulties under which I labor when you remember that you have on a commodore's hat, a major general's epaulettes, a captain's coat, and a sergeant's sword."

The Right Tactic

An Irish follower of General John Hunt Morgan came back from an expedition against the enemy with three Union soldiers as prisoners. When he delivered the Yankees, General Morgan complimented him for his feat. "How on earth did you capture three men single-handed?" inquired the admiring cavalry leader. "Oi surrounded 'em, sir!" was the explanation.

For a Friend

During a lull in fighting at Chickamauga, Private Robert Shields of the 7th Texas Infantry went out on the field of battle and brought his wounded companion back to the company lines. However, his friend was dead by the time Shields got back and Shields himself had received a wound that would prove fatal. His commanding officer chided Shields, saying, "I lost one man and now it looks like I've lost you. It was not worth it, soldier." "Oh, but it was, sir, because when I got to him he whispered to me, 'I knew you would come, Bob.' "

Hidden Treasure

After the battle of Spotsylvania, a surgeon probed and probed, cutting a bit here and there as he examined a wound in the leg of Private Bill Calhoun of the 4th Texas Infantry. When he could stand the pain no longer, Calhoun asked the doctor why he was carving him up. The surgeon replied that he was searching for the ball. Reaching into his pocket, Calhoun handed a lead ball to the doctor, saying, "Here it is, if that's all you want." He had gouged it out with his finger before limping to the rear after the battle.

The Obvious Solution

Stonewall Jackson usually thought only in terms of attack. This attitude was exemplified on December 14, 1862, at Fredericksburg, Virginia. Vastly outnumbered by the Federals, Jackson was asked by a staff member, "How shall we ever cope with the overwhelming numbers of the enemy?" Jackson's reply was to the point, "Kill them, sir, kill every man!"

Properly Attired

To a Yank's taunting shout of "Hant you got no better clothes than those?" the ill-clad Private Tom Martin replied, "You are a set of damned fools—do you suppose we put on our good clothes to go out to kill damned dogs?"

Humanity for a Gallant Opponent

The Stonewall Brigade once defended a railroad cut against a bayonet charge by the 52nd New York Infantry Regiment. The brigade exhausted all ammunition then threw rocks. The major of the New York unit bravely led their charge and was forcing the brigade back until Jeb Stuart's cavalry arrived and saved the day for the Southerners. In Stuart's attack the major fell with a severe wound and was left on the field when his men retreated. Jackson immediately sent his surgeons to care for the Federal officer and do all they could for him. The news of Jackson's kind treatment shortly reached the New Yorkers, and you can bet other Union troops were amazed to hear the 52nd shouting, "Three cheers for Stonewall Jackson!"

Standard Bearers

The courageous actions of standard-bearers were mentioned in report after report of regimental commanders. Keeping the flag flying was a matter of pride; its loss was a great disgrace. Many, many heroes who carried and guarded the flags paid with their lives for the honor of holding the cherished emblems aloft. Colonel Jenkins of the Palmetto Sharpshooters reported that out of eighty men in his two color companies, forty were killed or wounded in one battle. Out of eleven in the color guard ten were shot down. Once his colors were pierced by nine shots and passed through four hands without touching the ground. At Antietam the 1st Texas Infantry lost eight standard-bearers in rapid succession. At Gettysburg the 26th North Carolina lost fourteen.

Support

Some ladies living near the site of an impending battle rushed from their house to ask Nathan Bedford Forrest what they could do to help. According to George Cary Eggleston, Forrest told them, "I really don't see that you can do much except to stand on stumps, wave your bonnets, and shout 'Hurrah, boys!'"

Odds

One Yank was discussing Hood's Texas Brigade with another: "Those Texans aren't as tough as everyone says. Last night me and the sergeant and the two Dooleys ran into one, jumped him and would have licked him if one of his friends hadn't come up and butted in."

Of Course Not!

First Southern lady: "I'm sure I do not hate our enemies. I earnestly hope their souls may go to heaven, but I would like to blow all their mortal bodies away as fast as they come on our soil." Second Southern lady: "Why, you shock me, my dear; I don't see why you want the Yankees to go to heaven! I hope to go there myself someday, and I'm sure I shouldn't want to go if I thought I should find any of them there."

One Round

While trading tobacco and coffee during a temporary truce, some Rebels started bragging about how tough one of their men was, which led the Yanks to produce their own champion for a fight. Bets were placed and the troops gathered about the two men. It was agreed that the two men would fight until one said "Sufficient," which would mean the other won. At a signal the two began their fight. After an hour of heavy and painful scrapping, the Yank gasped "Sufficient!" whereupon the Rebel sighed, "Damn! That's the word I've been trying to think of for the last half hour!"

Masters of Their Craft

Thomas Maguire, an Irish immigrant living on his plantation in Gwinett County, Georgia, described the Federal soldiers who visited him on July 21, 1864:

"At 12 or 1 o'clock at night the Yankees came here in force…Robbed us of nearly everything they could carry off, broke open all our trunks, drawers, etc., and carried off the keys. They must have practiced roguery from their childhood up, so well they appeared to know the act."

A Simple Truth

A private in Company D, 49th Tennessee Infantry, was taken prisoner at Port Hudson and sent to Camp Douglas near Chicago. One day a civilian visitor engaged him in conversation: "Did you have plenty to eat down South?" "Yes." "Well, did you have houses to live in?" "Oh, yes." "Then what in the world were you fighting for?" "Sir, there is something more to live for than victuals, clothes, and a roof over your head. We are fighting for the same thing our fathers fought for in the Revolution. The right to our destiny!"

His Little Visitors Came First

As Generals Lee and Ewell and their staffs rode through a camp, a North Carolina soldier standing nude to the waist showed no sign he even knew they existed. His attention was focused on the dingy shirt he held over a smoldering fire, trying to smoke out the lice. A general's aide spurred up and queried him sharply, "Didn't you see the generals, soldier? What in thunder are you doing?" Drawled the unmoved warrior, "Skirmishing! And I ain't taken no prisoners nuther!"

Sick Joke

Confederate soldiers often joked about even their serious injuries. At a hospital in Dalton, Georgia, one soldier asked another, "How is your wounded leg coming on, Bob?" "Well," Bob replied, "it isn't coming on. It's coming off."

True Grits

Having been dumped several times into the muddy waters when the mule on which he was riding fell into another hole in the depths of the swamps around the Chickahominy River, a Yankee prisoner was heard to mutter, "How many are there of these damned Chickahominies?"

Doughboys

Although the term "doughboys" was applied to the American Expeditionary Forces of 1918, it was originally used in reference to Confederate soldiers. In the spring when the sap was up, the soldiers would peel the bark off trees and make trays to bread their dough. They then wrapped the dough around their ramrods and cooked it over their fires.

No Sleeping on Post

William H. Lessing of Waco, Texas, was barely fifteen when he managed to get himself recruited into service under Hood. On guard early one morning near Hood's headquarters in Virginia, the young private drowsily leaned against a tree, allowed his musket butt to touch the ground, strictly against orders. He must have had a feeling of terrible apprehension as a great hulk of a man suddenly appeared, seized his arm, and said, "Come with me, soldier." The colossus was Hood. He half-dragged the awakening youth to his tent and ordered him to sit down. In a few minutes the commander was handing him a cup of steaming coffee and some hard, sweetened bread. When the snack was consumed, General Hood arose and said, "Texans don't sleep at their posts, do they, son? You may return to yours."

Deafened by Fury in Battle

With most of the Union troops who had erupted from the Crater at Petersburg pushed back into the Crater, the surrounding Confederates rained death upon them. Shells and cannisters were lobbed into the pit to the accompaniment of withering rifle fire. Inflamed by the black troops who had stormed the Confederates yelling, "No quarter to the Rebels!" the Southerners felt little sympathy for the cowering Federals. Pleas for mercy were drowned out by the roar of explosives, rifles, and combat. Finally, a Confederate officer screamed at a Federal colonel, "Why the hell don't you fellows surrender?" When the Federal quickly screamed back, "Why the hell don't you let us?" sanity returned and the battle ended.

Hard at Work

Two young Yankees were looking up at Buzzard's Roost, dreading the coming attack they were to make against Joe Johnston's Confederates. Noting a bird flying overhead, one expressed hope it was a hawk. The other man replied it was a buzzard. "But why does he stay so quiet and so motionless?" "He's counting us!"

Right Tune, Wrong Verse

Just prior to the Battle of Franklin, an officer in A. P. Stewart's corps addressed a Confederate regiment, attempting to inspire them with determination. He called upon them to respond as Lord Nelson's crew had responded at the battle at Trafalgar, when Nelson said, "England expects every man to do his duty." The solidly Irish immigrant regiment roared with laughter when Sergeant Denny Callahan commented, "It's damned little duty England would get out of this crowd."

No Quitter

Mary Boykin Chesnut, noted Confederate diarist, recorded the story of a determined old veteran on his way to join the crippled General John Bell Hood and his Army of Tennessee en route to Chattanooga. The man had hair as long as any woman's, due to his pledge not to cut his hair until the war was over and the South free. Of the four men who had made that pledge one was killed in Missouri, one in Virginia, and one in Georgia. This man, the sole survivor, had lost one arm at the socket. When Mrs. Chesnut remarked that he was disabled and ought not to be with the army, the man responded, "I am First Texas. If old Hood can go with one foot, I can go with one arm!"

Not Likely Candidates

Federal recruiters were not the most welcome wartime visitors in Maryland. Two who visited the home of Charles Howard received a somewhat hostile response. When they asked Mrs. Howard the names and location of all males in the family capable of bearing arms, she informed them there was her husband and six sons: Husband Charles was a prisoner in Fort Warren, along with eldest son Frank Key Howard. Son John was a captain in the Confederate army. Next son, Charles, was a major in the Confederate army. Next son, James, was a lieutenant colonel in the Confederate army. Next son, Edward, was a surgeon in the Confederate army. When the flustered men finally asked about her youngest, she replied, "McHenry Howard, he is also in the Southern army and with Stonewall Jackson and I expect he will be here soon!" and she slammed the door in their faces!

Personal Protection

After Shiloh, Federals in pursuit of Confederates were met by Nathan Bedford Forrest and his troops who turned on the Federals and drove them back. At one point, Forrest on horseback outraced his own men to charge a line of Federal infantry and found himself surrounded. The bluecoats closed in on him, shouting, "Kill him!" Forrest struck out with his saber in one hand and a blazing pistol in the other. One enemy soldier stuck his rifle right against Forrest and pulled the trigger, sending a bullet tearing into Forrest's back. The infuriated Forrest reached down, grabbed a bluecoat by his collar and hoisted him up behind him on the horse. Employing the Federal as a shield, he galloped through a mass of guns and bayonets back to his own lines where he dumped the amazed man on the ground.

What a Blow-Up!

General Nathan Bedford Forrest was travelling down a narrow, muddy road in September of 1864. Coming upon a captured Federal caisson stuck in the mud and blocking the road, Forrest asked, "Who has charge here?" "I have, sir," spoke up Captain Andrew McGregor. "Then why in hell don't you do something?" Forrest asked, following his question with profanity. McGregor promptly responded, "I'll not be cursed by anyone, even a superior officer!" He seized a lighted torch and rammed it into the ammunition chest. This apparently suicidal act sent Forrest spurring his horse away. He reined up at a safe distance and angrily demanded what that lunatic was doing in charge of anything. This drew a laugh from his staff who already knew that the caisson had been unloaded in the effort to move it; the ammunition chest was empty!

He's Not Heavy

On May 6, 1864, at the Wilderness, the sharpshooters of Company K, 11th Mississippi, had advanced so far that the enemy was about to cut them off. The order came to fall back. Eager to get in a few more shots, brothers Jimmy and Tommy Kimbrough were slow to draw back. When they turned to do so, a bullet struck Jimmy in the back, temporarily paralyzing him. Believing the wound to be fatal, Jimmy begged Tommy to leave him. Tommy refused. In the face of withering fire, Tommy held the enemy in check by rapidly loading and firing while he pushed Jimmy along in front of him until both were safe within their own lines.

Our Lads Were Ever Considerate

A lady once asked Brigadier General Thomas Moore Scott of Louisiana if soldiers regarded petty pilfering as among the "accomplishments" of camp life. He replied, "A base libel, madam, a calumny. True, they never left a friendless chicken to nod on its uncomfortable roost; never suffered an overburdened apple tree to break down from its load of fruit; never removed a bee-gum until the shades of night made the removal more to the comfort of the bee; never permitted the lacteal fluid to sour in badly ventilated milkhouses; and never, no never, left a wounded shoat to bleed its young life away by the roadside."

Seemed Like a Good Idea

When asked if he were going to attend the funeral of longtime foe of the South, Senator Sumner, a Southern senator replied no, but he approved of it!

For the Books

Major Roberdeau Wheat, commander of the Louisiana Tigers at Manassas, former lawyer and soldier of fortune, took a Union bullet through both lungs and was told by his surgeon that he must die. Wheat disagreed, saying he didn't feel like dying yet. The doctor said, "There is no instance on record of recovery from such a wound." "Well, then," commented Wheat, "I will put my case on record." He lived!

Overconfident

Joseph E. Johnston was never on the best of terms with Jefferson Davis. Informed that the president had expressed the opinion that in Johnston's place he could whip Sherman, Johnston responded, "Yes, I know Mr. Davis thinks that he can do many things that other men would hesitate to attempt. For instance, he tried to do what God had failed to do—he tried to make a soldier of Braxton Bragg!"

Hard to Distinguish

At Yorktown in 1861, a pompous colonel was loudly upbraiding his regiment when a nearby tethered donkey began braying. With one voice, the men of the regiment shouted, "One at a time, colonel, one at a time!"

A Well-Known Officer

After his first ride around McClellan, Jeb Stuart joked to Longstreet that he had left one general behind. "Who's that, Jeb?" "General Consternation!"

Not Moving Day

Judge N. B. Green's wife was alone in her home at Marietta, Georgia, when it was surrounded by Yankee troops who demanded she leave. She refused. The Yankees told her, "Get out of there, we're going to burn the house." She replied defiantly, "When you do, you'll burn a woman with it." The house was not burned.

A Ruse by Any Other Name

Young John B. Johnson tried several times to run away from his Virginia home and join the Confederate army. Each time he was returned to his home. Finally he reached the ripe old age of sixteen and his father resignedly sent him off to war in the care of a family slave who devotedly served him as a body servant. Serving with the cavalry, John was wounded. Recuperating from the wound, he was awakened by his servant calling, "Young marster, the world is full of Yankees." Shortly thereafter the slave walked humbly through the surrounding Federal troops, leading his ebony young "son." The two grinned vacantly at everyone they met. Upon reaching freedom the "son's" ebony vanished with soap and water, but the grins remained because the faithful servant had outwitted a "world full of Yankees."

Had Enough

During a retreat a Southern artilleryman was approached by a Yankee cavalryman who shouted for him to surrender. The Southerner walked on. The indignant Yank shouted, "Halt, d——n you, halt!" The Southerner continued to walk. "Halt," the now furious Yank repeated, "halt, you d——n s.o.b.!" That did it. The Southerner halted and remarked that he allowed no man to talk to him that way. He seized a huge stick, turned to the cavalryman, knocked him out of the saddle, then proceeded on his way to the rear.

Not Available

When a rumor reached Richmond that Heros von Borcke had been killed at Chancellorsville, Governor Letcher wired Jeb Stuart instructions to bring the Prussian's body to Richmond for a state funeral. Stuart wired back, "Can't spare body of von Borcke. It is in pursuit of Stoneman."

No Way

Hearing of Union raiders approaching her plantation near Anderson, South Carolina, Mrs. Humphrey sent the horses and other livestock to be hidden by slaves. After hiding her valuables, she sat down with what composure she could muster to await the invaders. Dilcey, an alert little slave girl crouched by her side, wide eyed and terrified. Mrs. Humphrey told her to get up and get busy, that they must not let the Yankees know they were afraid. The girl grabbed a cloth and began dusting. As soldiers entered the room, Mrs. Humphrey glanced up and saw with dismay her prized gold watch on the mantel. The Yankee raiders made a thorough search of the house and after a seeming eternity finally left. Apprehensively Mrs. Humphrey looked at the mantel. The watch was gone! Sadly she told Dilcey of the theft. Dilcey came forward, thrust her small black hand into her bosom and drew out the dustcloth. In its folds lay the gleaming watch. "No Yankee mens is goin to git my Mistis' watch," she said with simple but stubborn loyalty.

A Terrible Fate

Mrs. Bryce Russel of Lenoir County, North Carolina, informed her old slave cook of Lee's surrender and added, "You are free now, Aunt Susan, to leave here and do what you please." Aunt Susan gave the idea a little time to register, then replied, "Mistis, Marse General Lee ought to be tarred and feathered for doing that."

One of Beauregard's Aides, Maybe?

Puzzled at first as to who Robert E. Lee was, an elderly Louisiana gentleman finally recalled something of him and commented, "Oh, yes, Lee. General Beauregard always spoke well of him."

Sign of the Times

During the great battle raging around Cemetery Hill at Gettysburg, the sign posted near the gate to the cemetery must have brought grim smiles to those who noticed it: "All persons found using firearms in these grounds will be prosecuted with the utmost rigor of the law."

Yea Though We Walk through the Valley

One evening in 1862 Jed Hotchkiss was given an assignment by Stonewall Jackson to locate some needed wagons that had become separated. Hotchkiss told

Jackson, "I fear we will not find our wagons tonight." Jackson replied earnestly, "Never take counsel of your fears."

The Best Man for the Job

Freedom of the press was unlimited in the Confederacy. Many of the newspapers carried violent attacks on the president, the different generals, and the activities of all. These attacks provoked Robert E. Lee to comment: "We put all our worst generals to commanding our armies and all our best generals to editing newspapers! If some of these better generals will come and take my place, I am willing to do my best to serve my country editing a newspaper!"

Motivation

One evening two Johnny Rebs slipped out of camp to visit the saloon of a nearby town. After a few hours there one noticed the approach of a storm and decided to hurry back to camp. The shortest route was through the town cemetery. In the dark he stumbled into an open gravesite. Luckily he wasn't hurt but he found himself unable to scramble up the steep sides of the open pit. He finally gave up and seated himself in one corner to await daylight and possible help. It began to rain. Shortly thereafter the second soldier, sodden both internally and externally, stumbled into the same grave. Not seeing the first man he began his own frantic efforts to get out. When he paused for a moment, the first man spoke to him from the darkness, saying, "You'll never get out." But he did!

Capable of It

Stonewall Jackson was known to keep his plans to himself. Those plans often came as complete surprises to his subordinates. Major General Richard Ewell, Jackson's second in command, said he never saw a courier from Jackson approaching without anticipating orders to attack the North Pole.

A Restful Visit

Stonewall Jackson was a regular visitor to Dr. Moses Hoge's Second Presbyterian Church in Richmond, but Jackson quite regularly went to sleep when Dr. Hoge started his sermon. It was once suggested that a tablet should be erected at the church to say: "Stonewall Jackson slept here."

Effective If not Formal

Untrained though many of them were, Southern officers knew how to communicate their intent to their men. With a line of blue cavalry fast approaching him, Captain John Winfield rallied his men and ordered them to hold their fire. At the last second he told them, "Boys, pick your man like a squirrel up a tree and FIRE!" The enemy dead piled up in front of them.

Even the Children Were Inspired

Confederate children played soldiers and sang songs about their idolized Confederate leaders, such as the following:

> I want to be a soldier, and with the soldiers stand,
> A knapsack on my shoulder, a musket in my hand.
> And there beside Jeff Davis, so glorious and brave,
> I'll whip the cussed Yankee and drive him to his grave.

Not the Only Way to Fight

Bringing up the reserves for the fighting near Kernstown, Stonewall encountered men going to the rear. He asked why they were leaving the fight. When he was told because they had fired all their cartridges and didn't know where to get any more, Jackson shouted, "Then go back and give them the bayonet!"

Opinion Unchanged

After the battle at Fredericksburg, Generals Lee, Hampton, and Early sat conversing about the Federals. Early remarked that he wished all the Federals were dead. Lee rebuked Early, saying that he did not wish them dead, just that they were back home minding their own business. Early didn't argue with Lee, but when Lee left he told Hampton, "I not only wish they were dead, but I wish them all in hell!"

An Equal Trade

Spying a fine Union horse drinking from a river, a Confederate picket lured it into crossing to him. Federal General Patrick sent a demand for the return of the horse, as it was not taken in battle. The Southerner responded he would do so with pleasure if the Yankees would return the slaves and other Southern property not taken in battle.

Appreciative of Beauty

Even in the press of battle a soldier's thoughts can stray. At Sharpsburg, a Southern soldier, a musician of considerable merit, crouched beneath the flying bullets. After a few minutes he surprised his companion at his side with the comment, "I caught the pitch of the minié that just passed. It was a swell from E flat to F and as it retrograded in the distance receded to D, a very pretty change."

Libby Prison

Libby Prison in Richmond was a large brick tobacco factory, three stories high, owned and used by the manufacturer whose name it bore. It was opened by the Confederate authorities as a hotel for the reception of Federal troops who persisted in "marching on to Richmond" after First Manassas and who were generously allowed to make the trip in railway cars instead of being required wearily to tramp there. The accommodations furnished these gentlemen were not equal to those ordinarily found in a first-class hotel. However, it must be remembered that they had made no reservations, they were not expected in such numbers, and consequently due preparation had not been made for their reception.

Rubbing It In

John Hunt Morgan always made good use of Union telegraph systems. Returning from a raid, he halted long enough to send a wire to Union General Boyle: "Good morning, Jerry. The telegraph is a great institution. You should destroy it as it keeps me posted too well. My friend Ellsworth has all your dispatches since July 10 on file. Do you want copies?"

Equals

In the early days of the war, every private thought himself as good as the highest officer. At Piedmont, General Kirby Smith was supervising the loading of troops onto a train when a private asked him a question. Preoccupied, the general gave him a rough reply. The soldier straightened himself up and said, "I asked you a civil question, sir, and if you were disposed to act the gentleman, you would give me a civil answer." Kirby Smith at once grasped the hilt of his sword, whereupon the private drew his pistol and quietly said, "If you don't put up that sword, I'll shoot you." The private was arrested, but his colonel interceded for him and General Smith generously consented to his release.

Growing Numbers

Jubal Early once remarked to D. H. Hill that Union General "Commissary" Banks overestimated the numbers of Southern troops because he saw them through a magnifying glass whenever Stonewall Jackson was about.

Into the Fray

The famed gallantry of Confederate infantry in charges involved more than sheer courage. Sometimes it was hunger! Colonel Len T. von Zincken overheard a wounded Southerner cry out in the midst of battle, "Charge 'em, boys! They have cheese in their haversacks."

When Properly Motivated

Private Black, a Scot with Southern kin, joined the Union army hoping to cross the lines. One day while on guard duty on the Potomac River, he struck out for the Southern lines, shouting back, "Goodbye, boys, I'm bound for Dixie!" and escaped under fire. Later he was serving in the Confederate army when he was called upon to guard newly captured Federals from his old unit. He explained to their captain, "I hope you and the boys are alright, Captain. It's not because I didn't want to fight that I left you. I like to fight in the right cause!"

Ought to Work

A courier galloped up in haste to Major General Matthew Galbraith Butler with a message from his colonel saying the colonel's men were being flanked by the enemy. The general's laconic response was, "Tell him to flank them back."

Children of the Confederacy

George S. Lamkin of Winona, Mississippi, joined Stanford's Mississippi Battery at the age of 11 and was wounded at Shiloh before he was 12. E. G. Baxter of Clark County, Kentucky, enlisted in Company A, 7th Kentucky Cavalry, when not quite 13 and was a second lieutenant when he was 14. John B. Tyler of D Troop, First Maryland Cavalry, was 12 when he enlisted; he served until the war's end. T. G. Bean of Pickensville, Alabama, organized two companies at the University of Alabama when he was 13, although he was not accepted himself until he was 15. M. W. Jewett of Ivanhoe, Virginia, was a private in the 59th Virginia at 13. Billings Steele, grandson of Francis Scott Key, joined Mosby's Rangers at 16. W. D. Peak of Company A, 26th Tennessee, Matthew J. McDonald of Company I, First Georgia Cavalry, and John T. Mason of the 17th Virginia, were all 14.

Dis-Union

In Illinois over two thousand U.S. deserters were arrested in the last six months of 1863. Two draft officers were killed in Indiana; in Pennsylvania one was shot, while others were wounded, burned out and driven from their homes. In January of 1863, Governor Morton wired Lincoln that he expected the Indiana legislature to recognize the Confederacy. In the summer of 1863 mobs ran through Chicago streets after Burnside's troops seized the newspaper plant of the *Times*, with the crowds threatening to sack the loyalist *Tribune* in retaliation. A bloody draft riot in New York City in July 1863 left almost two thousand casualties.

The Best Reason

The young recruit watched as his grizzled sergeant repeatedly and vigorously applied his fingernails to various parts of his body. Finally the young man asked, "Why do you scratch yourself so much?" "Because I'm the only one who knows where I itch!"

Ever Kind

Southern soldiers watched General Robert E. Lee as he dismounted under fire at Petersburg to pick something from the ground and place it in a tree. Curious, the men afterward found that Lee had replaced a fallen baby bird in its nest.

Le Difference

After the war U. S. Grant remarked to an English acquaintance, "Some of our generals failed because they worked out everything by rule. They knew what Frederick did at one place and Napoleon at another. They were always thinking about what Napoleon would do. Unfortunately for their plans the Rebels would be thinking about something else!"

A Stinging Reply

Seeing that the advancing enemy was unaware of his presence, the officer decided to keep his troops hidden until the last minute. He ordered them to get behind a nearby hillock and not to move nor make a sound. A few minutes later he was irritated to see someone wriggling behind the small mound. He said angrily, "Do you know that you are giving our position away to the enemy?" "Yes, sir," came back a voice filled with anguish, "and do you know this is an ant hill?"

Sam Houston

Many people have the impression that Sam Houston was removed from his position as governor of Texas for being anti-secession. Actually, Houston had no problem with the secession, but would have preferred for Texas to once more become a republic. While he agreed that the proper steps had been taken for secession, he believed that following the secession convention's completion of its functions any exchange of emissaries with other states and uniting with the Confederacy were properly in the domain of the Texas government and the legislature. Since he believed the union with the Confederacy was illegal, as governor he could not swear allegiance to the Confederate States. Even after his removal from office, Houston helped sell Confederate bonds, raised troops, and saw his own sons off to Confederate military service.

Religious to the Core

A young soldier was leaving his camp in Virginia when he was stopped by a friend who asked where he was going. He replied that he had heard that Richmond was filled with loose women, liqueur, and gamblers and so he was taking advantage of a short leave to go in and check out the rumors. Asked why he was carrying his Bible along, he responded that if all the tales he had heard were true, he would probably have so much fun that he might just stay over for church Sunday.

Unchanging

French Emperor Louis Napoleon first allowed Confederate Commissioner Slidell to have vessels built in France and then refused to allow them to leave. President Jefferson Davis never forgave him. When the president visited France after the war, the Emperor sent word that if Davis desired an interview, he would be glad to grant it. Davis promptly sent word back that he did *not* desire it.

Commiseration

On the way back to Virginia after Gettysburg, General James Longstreet stopped to eat at a Yankee farmhouse where General McLaws and his officers were just finishing eating. General Longstreet had more food procured and was enjoying a good meal when some women of the house came rushing in to exclaim that the soldiers had killed their hogs and were going after the cows. Longstreet shook his head and replied in a melancholy tone, "Yes, madam, it's very, very sad, and this sort of thing has been going on in Virginia more than two years, very sad!"

R.H.I.P.

Brigadier General Abraham Buford's troops had captured a heavily laden transport. Buford discovered a two-gallon jug of choice Kentucky bourbon. He was striding the deck of the ship, enjoying the contents of the jug, when some of his men called out, "Hold on, General, save some of the whiskey for us." His full-voiced reply was, "Plenty of shoes and blankets for the boys, but just enough whiskey for the general!"

Men of Letters

The typical common soldier was not well educated. His letters, rich in humor, courage, pathos, and description, were mostly poor in spelling, handwriting, and grammar. For instance, one man wrote, "They are dividing the Army up into Corpses." One Confederate noted that the Yankees were "thicker than lice on a hen and dam site ornier." Another reported his comrades "in fine spirits pitching around like a blind dog in a meat house." A storm was described as "raining like poring peas on a rawhide." A Mississippi soldier wrote, "Our General is a vain, stuck-up illiterate ass," while an Alabamian described his colonel as an ignoramus "fit for nothing higher than the cultivation of corn." A Floridian opined his officers were "not fit to tote grits to a bear." Thomas Taylor, 6th Alabama Volunteers, wrote to his wife, "You know that my heart is with you but I never could stay home when my country is invaded by a thieving foe, by a set of cowardly Skunks whose motto is *BOOTY.*"

Equal Treatment

The schooner *Savannah*, a privateer fitted out by authority of the Confederate governor, was captured by the U.S. brig *Perry*. Its captain and fourteen of the crew were sent in irons to New York. Lincoln had proclaimed privateers to be pirates and it was proposed that the Southerners be hung. The Confederate authorities sent word that an equal number of the highest-ranking Union officers would be hung the day following execution of the Southern sailors. The message gave the name of each officer. None of the privateers were executed and all were subsequently exchanged.

An Inquiring Mind

Federal General Boyle, commanding at Louisville, Kentucky, received a telegraphed message signed by General Granger, in charge of Federal troops at Bowling Green. The wire asked for aid and stated that John Hunt Morgan was in the vicinity of Bowling Green and threatening the town. Boyle replied he could give no aid. Back came a message asking if there were at least some troops in Louisville that could be sent. Boyle replied that there were no troops in Louisville at all. He was then asked if they were not in Louisville, where were his troops. Boyle responded with the numbers and locations of the various units of his men. The final transmission was a polite thanks from John Hunt Morgan who had sent all the previous messages.

Food for Thought

Artillerymen, having tender consciences (and no muskets), seldom shot any stray pigs. However, they occasionally in a disinterested way pointed out to an infantryman a pig that seemed to need shooting. It was not unknown for such infantryman to share with them a choice part of the deceased. A visiting civilian once remarked to an artillery mess upon the fine pig being served for dinner. He was assured that while stealing corn, the pig had been kicked by one of the battery horses. (The "head of a horseshoe nail" upon which the visitor had bitten looked remarkably like a pistol bullet.)

Just What It Took

Lincoln's call for troops to invade the South was the major catalyst that converted many Southerners to Secessionists. Senator Vance of North Carolina was making a speech against secession when a man rushed into the hall and announced Lincoln's proclamation. Senator Vance had just raised his arm in a gesture to emphasize a point when the man entered. Vance said later that "the arm I had raised to emphasize my point against secession fell by the side of the most convinced secessionist in America."

Against All Odds

When the wagons carrying Confederate wounded from Gettysburg reached the Potomac, the army was not there, but the Union cavalry was, and in strength! The wagons formed themselves into a stockade and the wagoners fired through the spokes of the wheels. They could not have held out except for the arrival of two slim units that made their way across from Virginia. One was a relic of Richmond's "corps d'elite" with only eight men. The other contained forty-four conscripts and paid substitutes. The fifty-two men charged what turned out to be twelve Union cavalry regiments with twelve guns, holding the Union forces at bay for half an hour until Jeb Stuart's troopers came to the rescue.

Faithful Troopers

A Confederate soldier in camp near Shelbyville, Tennessee, wrote: "There are two sorts of bodyguards. Some are men and the others are lice, and the lice are the most numerous. They are in for the duration and they don't desert their command."

Morale Builder

Southern women tried to keep up the morale of their soldier husbands. A stalwart Georgia woman received a letter from her husband saying he could not send her any money owing to failure to receive his army pay. She wrote back, "John, don't disfurnish your self to send me mony for I will make out som way. I hope you will chire up and not study too much for it onle mak bad wors. Don't be unese about me." This consoling response did not disclose that she had been forced to sell her home and small farm and was having great difficulty in supporting herself and their baby.

Simple Eloquence

After Gettysburg, young Jere Gage of the University Greys of Mississippi lay dying but he found strength to scrawl a note:

"My dear Mother, this is the last you may hear from me. I have time to tell you that I died like a man. Bear my loss the best you can. Remember that I am true to my country and that my greatest regret at dying is that she is not free and that you and my sisters are robbed of my worth whatever that may be."

Origin of the Quote

Nathan Bedford Forrest's most famous quote arose during a conversation with John Hunt Morgan. Asked by Morgan how he had been so successful at Murfreesboro, capturing garrison and stores although Union forces filled the countryside, Forrest said, "Oh, I just took the shortcut and got there first with the most men."

Power of the Pen

In the summer of 1862 General Thomas Hindman in Little Rock, Arkansas, was faced with the advance of Union troops under General Samuel R. Curtis. Hindman had no troops and no arms. He had only two assets: his intellect, and the slow advance of the Federals due to their search for cotton to steal. Hindman approached over a hundred men, women, and young people and had them write letters to sons, husbands, friends, etc., serving with troops across the South. The letters, all different, told of the arrival of thousands of Texas and Louisiana troops, splendidly armed. Hindman then arranged for a courier to take the letters in a pouch and lose the pouch in an "accidental" encounter with Union troops. The letters were soon in Curtis' hands. Curtis halted his troops and pleaded for reinforcements. While Curtis waited, Hindman secured troops with which he soon drove out the Union forces.

Knew How It Felt

Zebulon Vance's North Carolina brigade lay awaiting the final advance at Malvern Hill. As the Union cannons roared, a panic-stricken rabbit came running through the Confederate lines. The troops laughed and yelled, "Run, run, run!" A staff officer asked Vance if he could shoot it. Vance shook his head and called out, "Run, little cottontail! I'd run too, if I wasn't governor of North Carolina!"

No Chance

A Southerner had hired Confederate veterans after the war. He divided them into work groups according to their ranks in the army. A neighbor asked about the way the different groups worked. The first group, he said, were privates and were first-rate workers. The next group was made up of lieutenants and captains and worked fairly well, but not as good as the privates. The neighbor asked about the last group and was told, "Them is colonels." "Well, how about the colonels? How do they work?" "Now, neighbor, you'll never hear me say one word agin any man who fit in the Southern army, but I ain't agwine to hire no generals!"

Don't Rile 'Em

A Confederate cavalry colonel was leading his regiment in a gallant advance to the rear, with the Federals pressing close behind. The colonel noted some of his men turning and firing at the pursuers and he shouted back to them, "Boys, stop that shooting. It just makes them madder!"

A Soldier's Prayer

Now I lay me down to sleep
The graybacks o'er my body creep;
If they should bite before I wake
I pray the Lord their jaws to break.

Mirror Images

Thomas Owens was a sergeant in Company I, 4th Kentucky Regiment, CSA. His brother was a sergeant in Company I, 4th Kentucky Regiment, USA.

Not Quite

Union General A. J. Smith, with 20,000 men, was ordered to rid Mississippi of "that devil Forrest." Smith moved cautiously, usually in battle formation, against Forrest. Nathan Bedford Forrest, who had only 3,200 men, devised a daring plan. He left part of his army under General Chalmers to delay Smith and took the rest on a 100-mile detour to attack Memphis. On August 21, 1864, Smith wired Sherman, "I have thoroughly defeated Forrest." Sherman ended Smith's invasion of Mississippi when he wired back, "Forrest occupied your headquarters today."

Not Old Bob!

After Robert E. Lee's surrender at Appomattox, General Fitzhugh Lee was riding away from there when he met an old North Carolina soldier and asked him where he was going. The soldier replied that he had been off on a furlough and was going back to join "General Bob Lee." The general told him that he need not go back because Lee had surrendered. The soldier was shocked. He walked off with a look of contempt on his face, saying, "It must have been that damned Fitz Lee, then. Bob Lee would never surrender."

Mutual Feelings

Robert E. Lee's concern for his men was reciprocated. Once when he fell asleep while attending outdoor church services conducted by General W. N. Pendleton on a hot Sunday morning at Petersburg, no one disturbed him (nor did enemy shells bursting nearby).

In Perspective

At First Manassas a soldier was startled when his companion on his left had his head knocked completely off by a cannonball. A few minutes later, the man on his right had his fingers broken by another ball. As the injured man screamed with pain, the man in the center reproached him, saying, "Blast your soul, old woman, stop crying. You make more noise about it than the man who lost his head."

It Might Be Expected

This story circulated among Stonewall Jackson's men after his death: "Two angels came to carry Stonewall back to Heaven with them. They searched all through his camp but couldn't find him. They went to the prayer meeting, to the hospital, every place they thought he might be, all to no avail. They finally returned to Heaven to find Stonewall had executed a splendid flanking movement and gotten to Heaven before them."

Time To Leave

A black ambulance driver, reporting on a battlefield experience: "Ye see, massa, I was drivin' an ambulance when a musket ball come and kill my horse; and den, pretty soon, the shell comes along and he blows my wagon all in pieces, and den I got off!"

Unswerving

A Southern girl wrote to her cousin who was a prisoner at Camp Morton, Indianapolis:

"I will be for Jeffdavis til the tenisee river freezes over and then be for him and scratch it on the ice."

Hoss Loss

General Nathan Bedford Forrest had twenty-nine horses shot from under him in the course of the War. On the other extreme, one horse outlived four masters. Four brothers of the Guillet family were shot and killed in separate incidents while riding the horse in battle.

For His Mother

A Virginia lass approached a building near her home. It was used to quarter soldiers, and word had reached the village that the body of a young Southern officer lay there. Halted by a guard, the young lady told him that she had heard of the lad's death and that, although she did not know him, she wished to kiss him for his mother. Allowed to enter, she walked through sleeping men 'til she saw what she took to be the body. Exclaiming, "Let me kiss him for his mother!" she ran and pressed her lips to his forehead. To her amazement the "corpse" clasped his arms around her and exclaimed, "Never mind the old lady, miss; go it on your own account."

Force of Habit

Formerly a railroad conductor, a captain was drilling a squad. While marching them on a right flank, he turned to speak to a friend for a moment. On looking again toward his squad he saw them just about to butt up against a fence. In his hurry to halt them, he cried out, "Down brakes! Down brakes!"

Specific

An Arkansas colonel had the following orders for mounting his men: "Prepare fer tuh git onto your critters." "Git!"

Homecoming

Many know the story of Wilmer McLean who moved his family after the First Battle of Manassas was fought over his farmland so he could get away from the war and then had his home used as the site for the surrender of the Army of Northern Virginia. Almost as ironic was the tale of Sergeant Henderson Virden of the 2nd Arkansas. After he left for war he had no news of his wife and child for a year. In March 1862, he found himself in familiar country. He was soon fighting across his own farm in the Battle of Elkhorn Tavern. Wounded, he was carried into his own home where his wife tended him until he could return to his regiment.

Rapid Planning

The night after the Battle of Fredericksburg, General Robert E. Lee held a council of war and invited all his generals. General Jackson slept throughout the proceedings. Upon being awakened and asked his opinion, Stonewall Jackson curtly said, "Drive 'em into the river; drive 'em into the river!"

Do It Right!

A Confederate colonel was dining with some of his fellow officers and imbibing apple brandy freely with his meal. At the start of the meal he reported that his regiment had met the enemy the preceding day and had killed 50, wounded 100, and captured 200. After a few rounds he once more discussed the late engagement in which his men killed 500, wounded 1,000, and captured 1,500. After still more brandy he made it to his feet to tell of the wonderful victory in which his command killed 10,000, wounded 20,000, and captured 25,000. One of his audience held up a jug toward him and exclaimed, "Here, Colonel, for God's sake, take another drink and kill the whole Yankee army!"

Oops!

One Confederate, seeking to cure an ailing mule, was told by a veterinarian that if he would put a tube in the mule's mouth, insert a certain pill in the tube, and then blow hard, the mule would be cured. A few days later the veterinarian met the man looking "poorly." Asked the reason for his appearance, the soldier replied, "The mule blew first."

Caught Him

On the night of March 8, 1863, U.S. Brigadier General Edwin H. Stoughton was asleep in his bedroom at Fairfax Court House. Someone awoke him by slapping him on the rear and asking, "General, did you ever hear of Mosby?" "Yes, have you caught him?" "No," replied the daring John Mosby, "he has caught you!"

A Proper Evaluation

Mules have long been noted for their abilities to withstand extreme temperatures and to carry heavy loads longer than horses could. Obviously these were important during the war. It was reported that when Lincoln was informed of the capture by Confederates of a Union general and forty mules, he said, "I'm sorry to lose those mules."

Revenge Is Sweet

Sometimes sorely tried Southern soldiers took upon themselves the responsibility of putting offensive superiors in their places. Privates of the 53rd Georgia Regiment rode their colonel on a rail and extracted from him a promise to treat them more civilly, and the colonel did so. A North Carolinian wrote in 1862 regarding his captain, "He put me in the guardhouse one time and he got drunk agoin' from Wilmington to Golesboro on the train and we put him in the sh——t house, so we are even."

Rank

The finery of the uniforms of the early days of the war did not last. Soldiers sewed, patched, and did whatever they could to keep clothes on their backs. In June of 1864 a Texan near Atlanta summed up the clothing situation: "In this army, one hole in the seat of the breeches indicates a captain, two holes a lieutenant, and the seat of the pants out indicates that individual is a private."

Victuals

For most of the war cornbread and meat were the mainstays of the diet of the Southern soldier. The quality of the meat may be judged from one private's observation that the "beef is so poor it is sticky and blue. If a quarter was thrown against the wall it would stick." A Louisianan gave his opinion of the cornbread by stating, "If any person offers me cornbread after this war comes to a close I shall probably tell him to go to hell!" Suffering from the failure of Bragg's commissariat, a Texan said that if he ever got back home he intended "to take a hundred biscuits and two large hams, call it three days rations, then go down to Goat Island and eat it all at ONE MEAL!"

Hot Property

Winchester, Virginia, changed hands 72 times during the war, including 13 times in one day!

Raphael Semmes

Admiral Semmes was once described as an old seadog whose barque was unseen by the Yankees, but whose bite was often felt by them.

A Logical Explanation

Stonewall Jackson once demanded an explanation from Jubal Early of why he had seen so many stragglers behind Early's division. Early replied that Jackson had seen so many stragglers because he rode behind the division. Contrary to the general expectation, Jackson only smiled and dismissed the subject.

Making Do

In 1863 the First Kentucky Cavalry had turned in their weapons for repair. When ordered to return to the field they were without guns. Issued Belgian rifles, which were long and heavy and had a horrible recoil, the men took them without a murmur. They knew the clumsy weapons would enable them to get what they wanted. A few days later, the battle of Chickamauga was fought. At its conclusion the entire regiment was armed with new Enfields bearing the U.S. brand.

Prepared for It

While posted near Suffolk, Virginia, a six-foot Georgian attempted to cross a little stream when the tide was in. Encumbered with his clothes he had to swim for his life and narrowly escaped being drowned. That afternoon, as he returned, the regiment watched him sit down on the bank of the creek, remove his shoes and clothing and tie them carefully into a bundle, then resolutely plunged into the water. The regiment cheered as he discovered the water was barely calf deep; the tide had gone out!

Not the Usual Picture

President Davis often is portrayed as cool and aloof. However, in speaking of the president, George Davis, the former attorney general of the Confederacy, said, "It was the most difficult thing in the world to keep Mr. Davis up to the measure of justice. He wanted to pardon everybody. If ever a wife, a mother, or a sister got into his presence, it took but a little while for their tears to wash out the record."

A Lesson in Leadership

According to one of Jeb Stuart's troopers, one of the main reasons for the devotion of his men to Stuart was that he never said, "Go get them, men!" He always said, "Follow me!"

Outnumbered

John Lake of Company F, 17th Mississippi, once captured an entire Federal company with only the aid of his slave, Sandy. When the two discovered the encamped Federals, Lake gave instruction to Sandy, who flanked the enemy. Lake drew his sword, then strode into the camp and demanded its surrender. As the Yankees sprang for their arms, Sandy yelled, "Shall we open fire, Captain?" Thinking they were surrounded, the Yankees laid down their arms and became prisoners.

Quick Change

Early in the War a Louisiana regiment advanced into battle wearing their unit's blue uniforms. Misled by the color, other Confederates poured a volley of minié balls into them. In short order they were all wearing new uniforms: their old ones turned inside out!

Honorable

With the war just ended, Andrew Johnson urged the "halter and gallows" for President Davis and all other "conscious, intelligent, leading traitors." He and Secretary of War Edwin M. Stanton proposed the arrest of all Confederate colonels and generals, including those surrendered at Appomattox. Opposed to this policy, U. S. Grant declared, "You will have to whip me and my army before one hair of one head of the men whom we captured, and to whom we promised protection, shall perish."

Bragg-Ing

Captured and carried into Chattanooga, a Confederate soldier escaped in the confusion following the defeat of the Federals at Chickamauga. He made his way back to his unit where he told of the Yankee demoralization and the apparent intentions to retreat. His story led to his being asked to repeat it to General Braxton Bragg. Doubtful of the man's judgment, the dour Bragg asked him, "Do you know what a retreat looks like?" Stung by Bragg's attitude, the soldier replied, "I ought to know, General, I've been with you during your whole campaign!"

Just Two Men

General U. S. Grant was inspecting the Federal lines near Chattanooga when he reached a spring that soldiers of both sides used at various times. Resting on a log with his musket by his side was a young private dressed in blue. The man rose and saluted respectfully. When Grant asked him to what corps he belonged, the soldier replied he was one of Longstreet's men. Neither man seemed alarmed. They simply paused and talked a while before going their separate ways, the Union commander and the Confederate private.

Relative Value

Willis Cutchen was a slave and cook for Reverend Jesse H. Page, a regimental chaplain. Somehow and somewhere Willis obtained some real coffee, which he prepared for dinner for the chaplain and his guests one night. As the chaplain was saying grace over the meal, he accidentally knocked over one of the cups of coffee. Willis' aggrieved cry rang out, "La, Mr. Page, I wouldn't a-give that cup of coffee for *three* graces!"

Worth

Frank, a young visitor to a plantation, was playing with Sharper, a little slave boy, when a second little slave came by. In banter between the little slaves, Sharper told the other boy he wasn't even worth a hundred dollars. Curious, Frank asked Sharper how much Sharper was worth. "$500," was the reply. Not wishing to be outdone, Frank asked, "How much am I worth?" "Lord, Marse Frank," said Sharper in a tone of disdain, "you's white. You ain't worth nothing!"

Why Davis Wasn't Tried

Supreme Court Chief Justice Salmon P. Chase wrote to Edwin Stanton urging him to forget any attempt to bring President Davis and other Southern leaders to trial: "If you bring these leaders to trial, it will condemn the North, for by the Constitution, secession is not rebellion...Lincoln wanted Jefferson Davis to escape. And he was right. His capture was a mistake. His trial will be a greater one. We can not convict him of treason."

Meet the Press

A Southern editor wished to compliment General Pillow and wrote a notice in which the general was referred to as "battle-scarred hero." Due to a typographical flub the phrase was printed as "battle-scared hero." The irate soldier demanded a correction, to which the editor agreed. The next day's paper spoke of the general as a "bottle-scarred hero." It is not believed any further correction was requested.

Surely a Sincere Conversion

During the 1863–64 winter there was intense rivalry between an Alabama and a Georgia regiment attached to the same brigade. Each colonel tried to excel all efforts of the other. During the famous revivals the Georgia colonel discovered there was an impending baptism of 13 Alabama soldiers. Calling in his adjutant, he ordered him to detail 15 men for immediate baptism. He thundered, "These ___ Alabamans can't crow over Georgia!"

A Noble Name

When the 18th Virginia was encamped at Centerville, one of the privates fell asleep too close to a campfire and caught fire. All of his clothing on one side was burned off. Thereafter his comrades always referred to him as "General Burnside."

Effective Writing

President Jefferson Davis received the following letter:

Dear Mr. President,

I want you to let Jeems C. of company oneth, 5th South Carolina Regiment, come home and get married. Jeems is willin, I is willin, his mammy is willin, but Jeems's captin he ain't willin. Now when we are all willin ceptin Jeems's captin, I think you might let up and let Jeems come. I'll make him come stright back when he's done got married and fight just as hard as ever.

Your affectionate friend,

Mr. Davis wrote on the letter "Let Jeems go." Jeems went home, married, returned to his regiment, and *did* fight as promised.

Aplomb

Federal troops prepared to bivouac on the grounds of an estate in Rappahannock County, Virginia. Their commander, General Franz Sigel, arrived at the house with his staff. The aristocratic lady of the mansion eyed them calmly, rang for her servant, and told him, "John, tea for fourteen."

Description

Gules, on a saltire azure, fimbriated argent, thirteen stars of the last. *(For those of us unfamiliar with such matters, that is a heraldic description of the Confederate battle flag.)*

Quite a Performance

Colonel Charles Marshall of General Robert E. Lee's staff took part in one of the battles near Petersburg shortly after buying a horse. Riding the horse through a field under fire, he found his horse capering about in an odd manner. When they came to a large stump the horse placed his forefeet on it and kept them there while moving about in a sort of waltz. The hotter the fire, the faster the waltz. When a lull in the battle came, Marshall was able to guide the horse away. Shortly later, the colonel discovered he had bought a horse trained to perform in a circus.

Proper Choice

The attention of Lieutenant Colonel J. C. Upton was drawn to where some of his men of the 5th Texas were trying to keep some of the Yankees taken prisoner at Gaines Mill from escaping. Upton roared, "Let them go, let them go! We'd a damned sight rather fight 'em than feed 'em!"

Self-Defense

When it was pointed out to one Confederate officer that fresh sheepskins had been found where his men had camped, he replied sternly that no sheep could attack his men without getting hurt.

Quite a Catch

Occupied Nashville was agog one morning with the information that John Hunt Morgan had arrived at a well-known boarding house during the night. The

Federal provost marshal surrounded the house with a large force and demanded Morgan's surrender. He was greatly chagrined to discover that the John Hunt Morgan on the premises was six hours old, the newborn son of a patriotic Southern lady.

Wrong Interpretation

Near Chattanooga CSA Colonel William Gates came upon a fifteen-year-old Confederate lagging in the rear and crying. Gates told him not to cry, that he had not been hurt and he should not be so unmanly as to become frightened and cry. The boy replied, "Afraid, hell! That ain't it. I was so damned tired I can't keep up with my company."

A Striking Pet

Somber in his portraits, Robert E. Lee did have a sense of humor. In a letter to his wife he teasingly informed her that after first growing sick and then refusing to eat its frogs, his only pet, a rattlesnake, died.

Mighty Numbers

In June of 1862, Southern pickets were meeting with pickets from McClellan's forces for a moment of trading during a lull in battles. A Southerner called out, "Hello, Yank! What regiment do you belong to?" "To the Ninety-ninth Rhode Island," came the reply. "Good heavens," cried the astonished Southerner, "how many regiments must New York have if Rhode Island has ninety-nine?"

Had Clean Hands in the Matter

Jo Shelby had issued stern orders to his half-starved troops against looting. Coming back from a raid on Yankee forces, Shelby encountered a young trooper named Dick Gentry. Across Gentry's saddle was a carefully tied sack from which blood was seeping. When Shelby asked what was in the sack, Gentry said he'd been having his clothes washed. Shelby ordered Gentry to return to camp before his clothes bled to death and he had Gentry put in the guardhouse. That night a portion of fresh pork found its way to Shelby's quarters. Shelby looked at it and said, "I haven't any idea where this comes from but go round to the guardhouse, orderly, and tell 'em to turn Gentry loose. No use keeping a man shut up all his life for a little laundry."

No Time for Games

A teamster with the army in Virginia got stuck in the mud and let fly a stream of profane epithets that were astonishing in their broadness and intensity. A chaplain passing at the time was greatly shocked and said, "My friend, do you know who died for sinners?" "Damn your conundrums," yelled the teamster, "don't you see I'm stuck in the mud?"

A Beautiful Scene

The names of three milestones in President Jefferson Davis' life all had the same meaning: Fairview (his birthplace), Buena Vista (where he won undying fame), and Beauvoir (haven of his final years).

Ready and Waiting

One of his commanders galloped up to Stonewall Jackson at Malvern Hill. He asked, "Did you send me an order to advance over that field?" "I did, sir," was the cold reply. "Impossible, sir!" exclaimed the officer. "My men will be annihilated! Annihilated, I tell you, sir!" With his voice showing repressed anger, Jackson told the officer, "I always endeavor to take care of my wounded and bury my dead. Obey that order, sir!"

Strict Orders

A captain sternly lectured his men against *any* raiding of nearby orchards, and then told them, "Boys, if you will go, bring your captain a few."

Mosby

Union General Joseph Hooker commented on Confederate Colonel John Singleton Mosby:

"I may state here that while at Fairfax Court House my cavalry was reinforced by Major General Stahel...the force opposing to them was Mosby's guerillas, numbering about 200 and, if the reports of the newspapers were to be believed, this whole party was killed two or three times during the winter."

Go Where Needed

A chaplain of the Federal army was taken prisoner and brought to the headquarters of General Nathan Bedford Forrest. His first surprise came when he was asked to share General Forrest's meal and to say the blessing. The next came on the following morning when Forrest gave him an escort to return him safely through the lines. Forrest sent him away with the humorous comment, "Parson, I would keep you here to preach for us if you were not needed so much more by the sinners on the other side."

Change in Viewpoint

Henry Benning of Georgia was rallying his men to assist the Texas Brigade. "G—— d—— you men, get from behind those trees and rocks and give 'em hell!" screamed Benning. Just then a shell burst close to the general, killing his horse and tumbling him to the ground. Scrambling to his feet he made an instant conversion, shouting to his men, "G—— d—— you men, stay behind those trees and rocks and give 'em hell!"

Unshakeable

At Chancellorsville, General McLaws stood under a tree observing the fighting. He was joined by General Robert E. Lee. Shortly thereafter a Union shell cut the tree off about a yard above the heads of the two officers. Lee did not even indicate he noticed it. Completing his conference, Lee remounted and rode a few paces toward a nearby artillery battery. A shell burst immediately in front of Traveller, Lee's horse. The horse reared almost straight up, but Lee sat serenely until the horse's feet came down. The battery commander ran to Lee, saying, "General, we can't spare you; go back under the hill." Lee turned and rode away. In a few minutes a lull in the fighting came to the area in front of the battery. Heavy fighting was taking place about three hundred yards from the battery. The attention of the artillerymen was soon drawn to a man on horseback who sat calmly watching the fighting as bullet after bullet flew by him. General Lee was right where he could see, back in the thick of the attack.

Like Inventing *Six*-Up

Pascal Plant was a Washington inventor who tried to sell the U.S. Navy a rocket-driven torpedo. In December 1862, tests were conducted that seemed to critical officers to hold little promise. One torpedo blew up a mud bank. A second became the first driven torpedo to sink a ship when it veered from its course to sink a small schooner moored nearby. A month later in another test the torpedo leaped from the water and soared into the air to fall back a hundred yards away. That caused the navy to drop testing the weapon. After all, nobody would be interested in a flying missile.

Green and His Texans

General Richard Taylor described General Tom Green and his Texas cavalrymen at the Battle of Mansfield, Louisiana:

"Upright, modest, and with the simplicity of a child, danger seemed to be his element, and he rejoiced in combat. His men adored him and would follow wherever he led, but they did not fear him for, though he scolded them in action, he was too kind-hearted to punish breaches of discipline. The men, hardy frontiersmen, excellent riders and skilled riflemen, were fearless and self-reliant, but discharged their duty as they liked and when they liked. On the march they wandered about at will, as they did about camp, and could be kept together only when a fight was impending...Yet, with these faults, they were admirable fighters."

Each for His Own

A long stream of Federals marched along the streets of Nashville. A bright young boy looked on dolefully and finally screamed out, "Hurrah for Jeff Davis!" A passing Yankee said loudly, "Pshaw, hurrah for the devil!" "Alright," said the boy, "you hurrah for your captain and I'll hurrah for mine."

Letters

Letters from home were exceptional joys to all soldiers. They pleaded for letters. An Alabama soldier wrote to his wife, "Martha, I waunt you to write often and send me all the nuse for I am one of the Glades fellowes that you ever seen when I git a letter from you. You dont no how much good it dus me." Although mainly the men wanted frequency of correspondence, they really preferred long letters. One soldier wrote teasingly to his spouse, "Yore leter was short and sweet jist like a rosted maget."

The Last Confederate Warship

The Confederate States Navy really had to work to get its last warship from Europe. A light-draft ironclad ram, the CSS *Stonewall* was intended for the Confederacy when its construction was started in Bordeaux. The sale to the Confederacy was halted by the French bowing to pressure from the United States. Denmark, then at war with Prussia, agreed to purchase the ship. When construction was completed in early 1865, the Danish-Prussian war had ended and the Danes refused to accept the ship. Learning of the Danes' refusal, the Southerners promptly purchased the ship and took it to sea. Off the coast of Spain, the *Stonewall* encountered two U.S. warships but the U.S. ships deemed the C.S. ship too powerful for just the two of them and left the area. Continuing across the Atlantic the *Stonewall* arrived in Cuba in July 1865 to find the war over. Destined to complete its Confederate service without engaging in combat, the ship was surrendered to Spanish officials who later turned it over to the United States. The ship was later sold to the Japanese. After several sea battles in the Imperial Navy service, the ship was lost during a violent storm in the Pacific.

What Was He Doing?

Near Culpeper one day a Confederate signalman was waving his flag to the right and to the left as required for transmission of his message. A Southern soldier who had never seen nor heard of this means of communication gazed with wonder upon this action for a while. Finally he drawled, "I say, stranger, are the flies a-pestering you?"

Lost Family, Not Dedication

At the outbreak of the war, young Edward C. Wilson, of Electra, Texas, enlisted in the same Louisiana regiment as his father and three brothers. Later, disguised as a black female produce vendor, he was successful as a spy and brought back much valuable information. Clad in a bandana, calico dress, and apron, he ventured into a Yankee officer's tent where a Union soldier slapped him for his audacity. The blow brushed off some of the charcoal used to darken his skin. He was arrested and put into prison from which he escaped and rejoined his regiment. After being captured at Gettysburg he obtained a parole to search on the field for a brother he had seen fall. Sadly he discovered the bodies of all three brothers and his father. The hearts of the Union officers were touched by this tragedy. His parole was extended to allow him to take the bodies home for burial. Honoring his word, he returned, surrendered, then escaped again.

Simply Reacting

Captain William Downs Farley, "Farley the Scout," was a favorite of Jeb Stuart. Farley was credited with killing one hundred or more of the invaders before finally losing his life in combat at the Battle of Fleetwood on June 3, 1863. Contemptuous of danger, Farley went after Yankees as he had hunted wild animals in the mountains of his native South Carolina. More than once he said he did not feel like he was killing humans; he considered them to be wolves that had come to attack Southern homes. As such, they were to be hunted down and destroyed. He stated his premise: "My principle is to kill a Yankee wherever I find him. If they don't like that, let them stay home."

Cogent Comment

In March 1865, inflation was rampant and food was in short supply in Richmond. With grim humor a Georgia woman visiting there commented, "Close time in this beleaguered city. You can carry your money in your market basket and bring home your provisions in your purse."

No Enthusiasm for the War

Oliver P. Morton, wartime governor of Indiana, earned the name "Dictator" for his successful efforts to suppress representative government in his state. Morton caused the Republican minority in the Indiana legislature to absent themselves to prevent assembly of a quorum. He had good reason to fear an assembly of his legislature. He informed the malevolent Edwin M. Stanton, "I am advised that it is contemplated when the legislature meets in this State to pass a joint resolution acknowledging the Southern Confederacy and urging the states of the Northwest to dissolve all Constitutional relations with the New England States. The same thing is on foot in Illinois."

In Illinois, Governor Yates described his legislature as "a wild, rampant, revolutionary body." He prevented his legislature from meeting for two years by using a technicality that provided that the governor could adjourn the legislature when the two houses could not agree on a date themselves. To protest Yates' actions 40,000 Democrats met in a mass rally in Springfield. They adopted resolutions asserting that Constitutional liberties continued in force in wartime and declared that "further offensive prosecution of this war tends to subvert the Constitution and the government, and shall entail upon this nation all the disastrous consequences of misrule and anarchy."

Yankees?

The Union enlistment bounty brought half a million foreigners into the Union army, with the majority of them German and Irish. One Confederate veteran was asked how many Yankees he had killed. He replied, "I don't remember killing any, but I shot eighteen Germans trying to get at the Yankees."

Small Wonders

As Sherman advanced through Georgia, a wild tale spread ahead of him that the Federals would slay all male children. At the coming of the enemy, many anxious mothers sought to disguise their young sons by dressing them in the clothing of girls. One youth so attired was engaged in the unfeminine pastime of sliding down a stair rail in the presence of some Yankee soldiers. His mother, fearful for his safety, called out, "Bessie, my son, come down from there!" Smiling, one of the Federal troopers said, "Oho, I thought it strange that the children of this neighborhood were all girls."

Made Them "Beehive" Themselves

A Georgia lady had numerous beehives in the yard around her home. She tied cords to the beehives and ran the cords up to her door. Whenever Yankee "bummers" came toward her home, she turned over a beehive by pulling the cord through a hole in her door. At times the thieves were stung badly, while at other times their horses would throw their riders and hurt them. The raiders always left without bothering the lady or her precious food supply.

Not from a Mold

George St. Leger Grenfel, a British soldier of fortune, provided invaluable assistance in the training of John Hunt Morgan's 2nd Kentucky Cavalry, and the men developed a respectful affection for him. However, he was never able to instill discipline in them. He commented, "I never encountered such men who would fight like the devil, but would do as they pleased like these damned Rebel cavalrymen."

Time for a Break

Among prisoners being transferred to a Confederate prison camp in Salisbury, North Carolina, were a number who spent the journey speaking the dialect of their native Swiss canton and plotting their escape. When they made their bid for freedom at a way station, they found themselves encircled by the waiting bayonets of their entire guard. Unfortunately for those Union soldiers, one of their guards may have been the only man in the Confederate army who could understand their language. That man, Beverly Tucker, had gone to school in their native canton.

Welcome Supplies

In the fall of 1864, the Federal quartermaster in Washington wired U. S. Grant at City Point, requesting a guard to meet a shipment of 2,486 cattle where they would be landed. The cattle were met by a guard, *almost* as requested. A Southern telegraph operator named Gaston had intercepted the request. The welcoming guard was Wade Hampton and a body of Southern cavalry who convoyed the 40-day supply of food-on-the-hoof to the Confederate army.

As Seen from Abroad

From the October 3, 1863, issue of the *Preston Chronicle* of Preston, England:

"Grievances, great, deep, and lasting, had existed for years between the North and the South. The Confederates did not wish to secede for having suffered one wrong, nor in consequence of the election of this or that individual to the presidential office; it was because wrongs had been heaped upon them, and because they could stand the wrongs no longer, that they deemed separation a necessity. They had borne silently the insults and tyranny of the North; but they could bear them no longer; and they had resolved to fight and die rather than sacrifice their liberty and independence."

Well Loaded

In battle men were often so keyed up that they failed to load and cap their cap and ball weapons properly after the first time they fired. Even though they went through the repetitive loading, aiming, and firing they were doing the enemy no harm. Instead they were simply piling ball on ball until the gun barrels were gorged with unexploded charges. Of approximately 28,000 guns that were picked up after Gettysburg, 12,000 had two charges, 6,000 had from three to ten, and one had *twenty-three* charges!

School Daze

A young Union officer on his way to his first assignment was captured and brought before Colonel John S. Mosby. The man was very neatly attired with a fine beaver cloth coat, high boots, a new hat, etc. When he learned that the man was from Germany, Mosby inquired as to why he had come to fight the South when the South had done him no harm. The German replied that he had come to learn the art of war. Shortly thereafter the German, now shabbily clad, complained to Mosby that he had been forced by one of Mosby's men to exchange clothing. Asked by Mosby if he had not come to learn the art of war, the German said, "Yes." Mosby responded, "Very well, this is your first lesson!"

Not Responsible for Their Brother-In-Law

Three brothers died in the service of the South. Samuel was killed at Pittsburg Landing while serving in a Louisiana regiment. Alexander, a member of the First Kentucky Cavalry, was killed near Baton Rouge. David was a Confederate artillery battery commander who died at Vicksburg. Another Todd brother who was not killed was a surgeon in a South Carolina regiment. Their brother-in-law died in Washington, D.C.—Abraham Lincoln!

Money's Worth

Ordered to protect an artillery battery, troopers under Tom Rosser did so under increasing enemy fire. Their situation rapidly became more and more hazardous. The officer in charge exhorted them to keep their position or the enemy would capture the Southern cannons. Finally, one man asked what the guns cost. The officer replied that he didn't know but he supposed a thousand dollars. Said the trooper, "Well, let's take up a collection and pay for the guns and let the Yankee have 'em."

Female of the Species

The ladies of Tazewell County, Virginia, were as devoted to the Confederacy as the men were. For instance, in 1863, some one thousand Federals under a Colonel Toland camped there while en route to attack a Southern railroad, lead mines, and salt works. Molly Tynes, who was visiting her parents there, realized the importance of warning those in the paths of the invaders. Although she was primarily a city girl, she rode forty-four miles across four mountains and along rough mountain roads, shouting, "The Yankees are coming at dawn!" to every home she passed. Warned, the Confederates gathered their forces and defeated the Federals, with Colonel Toland killed in the fighting.

Another lady of the area, Mattie Hendrickson, was forced by a Federal to prepare a meal for him. After she did so, she used his own rifle to make him a prisoner. Nearby, as a group of Federal officers dined, young Louisa Bowen carried off their pistols and hid them so well they were never found again.

Knew What He'd Done

Army language was baffling to many of our Southern boys. Upon returning from the commissary with potatoes that had not been listed on his requisition, a private explained, "I went to the conesary to draw some visions and seein' these taters I consecrated them."

Yankee Cowardice, Southern Chivalry

For the severely wounded Confederates on their way home after Gettysburg the trip was pure agony. They lay upon the naked boards of wagons pressed into service as ambulances, drenched by a blinding rainstorm. As the wagons filled with helpless men reached Greencastle, Pennsylvania, about forty axe-wielding men hacked spokes from the passing wagons, toppling them into the mud. When Confederate soldiers arrived to stop their villainy, the cowardly Yankees sought mercy on the grounds that they were civilians. The Southerners showed restraint and freed them.

He "Lost" It

In the very early days of the war, many young Texans outfitted themselves with huge homemade knives, called "side-knives" in lieu of the sabers and swords available elsewhere in the Confederacy. Although of doubtful tactical value they helped the untrained soldiers attain a ferocious look, and the budding warriors undoubtedly dreamed of lopping off the heads of their foes. One young man honed his knife to razor sharpness and then rode off into the woods to practice using the blade against imaginary Yanks. With his first swing he chopped off the right ear of his horse. His second swing sliced flesh from his own leg. His third and final swing was off his horse so that he could hide the dangerous weapon in a hollow log and ride off and leave it!

If You Are Going to Be Shot

As Richard S. Ewell rode into Gettysburg with John B. Gordon at his side in 1863, Ewell reeled in his saddle immediately after the ominous sound of a bullet hitting home. Anxiously, Gordon asked, "Are you hurt, sir?" General Ewell replied unconcernedly, "No, no, it doesn't hurt a bit to be shot in a wooden leg!"

A Man to Count On

John C. Breckinridge needed to send some information through the Union lines in May of 1862. The data was too important to send enciphered or on paper. Adam R. Johnson, later a Confederate general, memorized the message after it was enciphered into a series of unrelated numbers and delivered it. He made a two-day trip through enemy-occupied territory, was twice in the hands of enemy pickets, and delivered the message without error. The message: "Number 7 to 11. Number 21 back to 11 except 13. From 21 to 77 except 33, 41, and 56. Also figure 3 to 177 except 140, 50, and 60." *(Editor's Note: Not only is that amazing, but we have not an inkling of its meaning.)*

Little Charlie

Five-year-old Charlie Reigh was one of three small children of a Confederate navy officer who died at Orangeburg. The mother, a gentlelady unused to poverty, was reduced to being the sole support of her family by sewing. One day Charlie came up to a neighbor in Charleston to ask her advice on how to make some money, saying that his mother had not been paid and the family needed food. The neighbor was inspired to gather roses and lilies from her garden and make bouquets for the boy to sell. Charlie trudged off down King Street with his wares. No luck, then to the Charleston Hotel. No luck, then to the Mills House. No luck. Darkness came. The little boy began to despair and to sob softly to himself. A gentleman walking by asked if his flowers were for sale. The boy answered yes, but he hadn't sold any. The man asked about the boy's parents and Charlie told him his mother was home sewing and his father was a Confederate naval officer in heaven. The man led the boy into the hotel and approached a group of ladies in the lobby. He explained that this was Charlie's first day as a salesman and that Charlie's father was a Confederate naval officer in heaven. The ladies all agreed that they had a Confederate army and navy in heaven, bought all of Charlie's flowers, and then joined Charlie and his escort, General P. G. T. Beauregard, for dinner.

Sufficiently Tested

In 1864 the Confederacy needed a railway locomotive. A band of one hundred men were selected from Lee's army and put under the command of a 6'4" Georgian, formerly a foreman of a stone quarry. The men went into Maryland and tore up a section of B&O Railway tracks, enabling them to capture the next train. With nothing except rope, those one hundred men carried the locomotive fifty-two miles across streams, over hills, through bogs, into and out of woods. When they struck a line heading south, they ran the engine down to Virginia. President Garrett of the B&O could not believe the feat until he personally inspected the route taken with the locomotive. He declared the feat the most wonderful engineering ever accomplished. After the war he searched for and located the Georgian leader of the band. On the basis of that single action, Garrett made him road master of his entire system of railroads, saying, "Any man that can pick up an engine with fishing lines and carry it over a mountain has passed his examination with me."

Dutiful

A lady in the parish of Claiborne was telling a neighbor how Captain Slack and his men surrounded her home searching for her son, John, who had hidden to escape conscription. The troops had found him hiding in the chimney and ordered him to come down. The neighbor asked the mother what John had done then. "Do? Why, he came down and 'listed like a man."

Terribly Wounded

On the first day of battle at Gettysburg a fragment of a Federal shell scratched a captain's head, drawing blood. The officer ran away, excitedly screaming, "I'm dead! I'm dead!" Beckoning two stretcher-bearers, the colonel calmly told them, "Go and take that dead man off, if you can catch him."

Overpowering

Leonidas Polk, Episcopal bishop of prewar Louisiana and later a Confederate general, owned hundreds of slaves who worked on his large plantation. Faithful to his responsibilities, Polk regularly provided elaborate moral instructions for them. Although Polk was a kindly master and the slaves were not overworked, some slaves reportedly wished they would be sold, as they felt the burden of working in the cane fields was easier than listening to twelve hours of instruction per week.

Loyalty

The patriotism often exhibited by body servants who accompanied their masters to war is well exemplified by the statement of one, Robin, who was captured along with his master on Morgan's raid into Ohio. Imprisoned apart from his master, he was offered his liberty on condition he took an oath of allegiance to the United States. He responded, "I will never disgrace my family by such an oath." Other examples were the number of servants who surrendered with their masters at Vicksburg and could have had their freedom for the asking, with Federal protection. Instead they chose to share the hardships of a Yankee prison with those whom they had served in the Confederate army.

With Due Reverence

News of Lincoln's assassination caused the Union general in charge of Richmond to order all city churches to hold commemorative prayer services. On the day specified for such services, one Methodist minister ascended his pulpit to address his congregation: "My friends, we have been ordered to meet here by those in authority for humiliation and prayer on account of the death of Lincoln. Having met we will now be dismissed with the doxology, *Praise God from whom all blessings flow.*"

A Veteran's View

Exhausted after the defeat at Nashville, an old soldier trudged wearily southward, his garments of rags covered with mud, powder covering his face. All he wanted to do was to get to safety; the battle was lost and over. A young staff officer, fresh from a furlough home, stopped before him, calling, "Where are you going? Halt and form a line here, there is no danger down there." The veteran grimly responded, "You go to hell. I've been there."

All Southern

In the nine companies of the Shreveport Rifles, formally the First Louisiana Infantry Regiment, there were men of thirty-seven national origins. There were so many men of French nativity that French was almost an official language. Shortening a French oath commonly used by these men, General P. G. T. Beauregard referred to these men as "sacredams."

Crowded

In an 1862 letter to her aunt a young Mississippi lady said that Satan sent a note to General Beauregard requesting him to stop killing Yankees for a while since hell was so full of them that he didn't have room for any more until he stewed down the ones he already had.

Sensitive

When the busy quartermaster was told that the waiting soldier needed quite a few items, the quartermaster asked the man if he had a list. The soldier appeared startled, then replied, "Yes, ever since being shot in the leg at Sharpsburg."

They Understood

Nathan Bedford Forrest was master of many crafts, including communications. His phrasing was sometimes unusual but his meaning was always clear. At Johnsonville he ordered a gun crew to "elevate the breach of that gun a little lower."

Poorly Located

Before Second Manassas Union General John Pope allegedly reported his headquarters to be in the saddle. Stonewall Jackson was amused to hear the report and remarked that he could whip any man who didn't know his headquarters from his hindquarters.

The Rockbridge Artillery

The Rockbridge Artillery was outstanding in both composition and performance. It was first commanded by an Episcopal minister, William Nelson Pendleton.

The battery's four cannons were nicknamed *Matthew*, *Mark*, *Luke*, and *John*. So many men applied to join that membership had to be restricted. Although 147 men were lost during the war, when the unit surrendered at Appomattox, it had 93 members, more than when it was originally mustered. Among its men were 7 MA degrees, 28 other college degrees, and 25 theology students.

Plenty of Targets

During one of the many occasions when the Federals placed General Zebulon York and his men in uncomfortably close quarters, one of York's colonels rode rapidly up to the general and exclaimed, "General, we are ruined; they are all around us!" "So much the better," replied the cool York, "for now we know it is impossible to shoot without killing some." He and his men made it out in good shape.

Language Masters

Before Confederate authorities ordered the use of English commands, Louisiana troops were objects of curiosity to non-French-speaking soldiers in Virginia. After one Georgian witnessed a Louisiana officer drill his battalion using French commands, he declared, "That thur furriner he calls out a bunch of gibberish, an them thur Dagoes jes maneuver-up like hell-beatin' tanbark! Jes like he was talkin' sense!"

Needed to Work on that Problem

General Robert E. Lee once encountered John Singleton Mosby walking with the aid of crutches as the result of a battle injury. Lee told Mosby that the daring ranger had one bad fault: He got wounded too often!

Biblical

Slight in build and weak in appearance, a young lieutenant was assigned to a company of rough recruits. His appearance evoked a shout from the rear ranks, "And a little child shall lead them!" With that a roar of laughter from the entire company arose. The lieutenant was apparently unfazed by the barb. When the men awoke the following morning they were greeted by a posted notice that the company would be going on a twenty-mile march in full gear. The notice ended with the comment, "And a little child shall lead them, ON A DAMNED BIG HORSE!"

Scorn

After one hard-fought battle, one shaken Yankee captive remarked to his Texan guard on the ferocity of the Texas troops. The Texan modestly replied that they were just living up to Texas traditions, citing 136 Texans at the Alamo holding off 15,000 Mexican troops for four days, Dick Dowling and less than 50 others defeating several thousand Federals at Aransas Pass, and other examples. The Yankee, defending his own heritage, remarked that Northerners also had heroes, such as Raul Revere. "Paul Revere?" questioned the Texan. "You mean that fella who had to ride for help?"

Not Hidden from Sight

While commanding a spearhead attack in the battle of White Oak Swamp, Colonel Micah Jenkins drew a lot of attention from the Yankees. His bridle was shot in two. One shot went through his saddle blanket. His overcoat, tied behind his saddle, showed fifteen ball and shell holes. His horse was wounded twice. The point and knob were shot off his sword that was then shot in half. He was wounded in the shoulder by grape and in the chest and leg by shell fragments. Unbelievably, he was still in action at the end of the battle.

Conditional Travel Time

During the 1864–65 winter, Colonel Hillary Herbert, a distinguished Alabama officer in the Army of Northern Virginia, met with a Union lieutenant between the picket lines near Orange Court House, Virginia. When the Yankee commented, "Well, we are on the way to Richmond again," the colonel replied, "Yes, but you will never get there." The lieutenant said quickly, "Oh yes we will after a while, and if you will swap generals with us, we'll be there in three weeks."

Someone Learned a Lesson

General George "Maryland" Steuart was a tough and nasty martinet. He soon showed his power to the militarily ignorant Confederates in his command. It was not uncommon in his camp to see two or three men tied up by their thumbs to a cross pole. His favorite trick was to sneak up on sentries and try to catch them unaware. One night his trick backfired. He startled a private who grabbed hold of the little officer and pummeled him mercilessly, after which he pretended not to have recognized the general.

An Alternative

On the third day at Gettysburg, General Pettigrew had been ordered to go up against the enemy again. He told General Longstreet, "General, I can't get my men up again." Longstreet answered curtly, "Very well then, General, just let them alone; the enemy is going to advance and will spare you the trouble."

It's Possible

Under the 1863 United States conscription act a man could obtain an exemption in one of two different ways: He could pay the government $300 or he could hire a substitute for some lesser amount. One Yankee housewife reportedly told a neighbor, "My husband ain't going to war. He sent a prostitute." There is always the chance that this was not a malapropism. A Union general commandeered the steamboat *Idahoe* and paid $5,316.04 for it to take more than one hundred prostitutes from Nashville, Tennessee, to Louisville, Kentucky.

Loyalty

Prior to the company leaving Austin, a little white fox terrier, "Candy," was given to Company B, 4th Texas Infantry, as a mascot. Candy went everywhere with the company, becoming the pet of the whole regiment. Candy disappeared at the battle of Gaines Mill after being seen charging Turkey Hill with his companions. The next day a burial party discovered Candy cuddled in the arms of Private John Summers who had acted as his keeper and had been killed in battle. Candy had been loyal to the end, and even thereafter.

Wanted the Right One

According to the chaplain of the 49th Tennessee, Mike's father was opposed to his enlisting in the Confederate army because the boy was too young. Sent out to bring a log for the fire one evening the boy continued on his way and "jined up" anyway. Four years later he returned home for the first time and passed by the woodpile. Bringing in a log and throwing it on the fire, he said, "It took a long time to find it."

Could Count On Their Running

After the war, General W. T. Sherman listened as an Army of the Potomac veteran described the fighting of Hooker's troops at Chancellorsville. When Sherman asked if the Rebels had run, the soldier said, "Did the rebels run? Great Scott, I should say they did run! Why, General, they run so like thunder that we had to run three miles to keep out of their way, and if we hadn't thrown away our guns they'd run all over us, sure."

Southern Soldier Stuff

A typical Southern soldier prized a piece of soap almost as much as his gun. He preferred a knife to a bayonet.

Nearly every man tried to grow a beard, not only because beards were fashionable but also because a beard helped keep the face warm. If a man had trouble growing a beard he would probably rub his skin with "Bellingham's Stimulating Unguent." Even the medical authorities did not realize the diseases caused by vermin in the hair and in the prized beards.

Some of the richest Confederate soldiers served in the ranks rather than as officers due to a belief that one gentleman should not give orders to another.

The uniforms of one New Orleans company cost $20,000; its flag cost $750.

Many Confederates did not like to wear caps, such as kepis, and insisted on felt hats; they could go barefooted without complaint but as a matter of dignity raised heck if they had to go bareheaded.

When talking among themselves, typical Confederates were more apt to refer to each other as "Boliver Ward" than as "Johnny Reb."

Any Harm Done?

After Sherman's troops went through the area, the mayor of a small Georgia town was asked if Sherman had injured the town much. "Injured? Why he took it with him!"

A Weighty Question

Father James B. Sheeran, chaplain of the 14th Louisiana, CSA, was never noted for tact. Visiting the headquarters of General Ewell, he was introduced to the general's staff. One corpulent officer playfully asked, "Father, do you think you could send me to heaven?" Sheeran shot back, "Captain, I fear you have too much beef. I think I would have hard work to get you as far as Purgatory."

A Uniformed Thief

On February 26, 1865, Lieutenant Thomas G. Meyers of Boston, Massachusetts, wrote to his wife from South Carolina:

> My dear wife: ...We have had a glorious time in this state. Unrestricted license to burn and plunder was the order of the day. The chivalry has been stript of most of their valuables. Gold watches, silver pitchers, cups, spoons, forks, etc., are as common in camp as blackberries...Officers are not allowed to join in these expeditions without disguising themselves as privates. One of our corps commanders borrowed a suit of rough clothes from one of my men and was successful at this place (*Camden*). He got a large quantity of silver (among other things an old-time silver milk pitcher), a very fine gold watch from a Mr. DeSaussure at this place, one of the F.F.V.'s of South Carolina...If I live to get home, I have at least a quart of jewelry for you and the girls, and some number one diamond rings and pins among them. Don't show this letter out of the family. Your affectionate husband. *(Editor's note: I hope the thief never made it home.)*

Too Much for an Honest Man

Charles Brown, a 21st Michigan clerk, was one of Sherman's soldiers who deplored the behavior of that army. By mail he tried to tell his family of the terrors of Sherman's infamous march across the South: "I saw property destroyed until I was perfectly sick of it...I have been thankful ever since I have been in the army that this was the South. You can never imagine a pillaged house, never—unless an army passes through your town and if this thing had been North I would bushwhack until every man was dead or I was. If such scenes should be enacted through Michigan I would never live as long as one of the invading army did. I do not blame the South and shall not if they go to guerilla warfare."

Not the Time for New Friends

It was night when General James Longstreet and two Virginia brigades arrived to assist General Bragg in the Battle of Chickamauga. With his staff he started through the woods to find Bragg. The group became lost in the woods in the darkness. Unexpectedly meeting some soldiers, Longstreet asked to what units they belonged. The darkness was a welcome cover for the rapid departure of the Southerners when the men answered with numeric designations. The Federals numbered their units while Confederate units usually went by the names of their commanders.

Not Outgeneraled

Union General Phil Sheridan is often viewed as an irresistible conqueror because of his victorious campaign as Confederate abilities to continue fighting dwindled. However, when Sheridan finally overcame Early in his Valley Campaign, Sherman commanded nearly 50,000 Union troops, superbly equipped and conditioned. To combat him, Early had only 10,000 underfed, physically weakened men. With that small force, Early outmaneuvered and outfought Sheridan for two months before numbers and supplies brought the inevitable end to the unequal contest.

Difficult Task

John Randolph of Virginia said that asking a state to surrender part of her sovereignty was like asking a lady to surrender part of her chastity.

Couldn't Fool Him

Following a period in which he felt that his troops were drinking too much whiskey, General Felix Zollicoffer issued an order that no one other than himself could pass the guard lines without a proper pass. A little later a young recruit was placed on guard duty. Zollicoffer approached Stevens and was halted. The general identified himself as Zollicoffer, explaining he had the right to pass. Stevens replied, "You can't play that game on me. If I should let you pass, in half an hour there would be forty Zollicoffers here to pass."

Name That Tune

As the band struck up the *Rogue's March* to accompany the drumming out of a soldier, a Confederate stopped them, crying out, "Stop, you have mistaken the tune. Play *Yankee Doodle*; a half million rogues march to that every day."

The Secret Six

John Brown's murderous attack at Harpers Ferry in October 1859 was financed by six men who shared two traits: wealth and mental problems. Thomas Wentworth Higginson was a minister who had narrowly escaped indictment for the murder of a U.S. deputy in 1854. Samuel Gridley Howe was a physician unhappily married to Julia Ward Howe. Gerrit Smith was one of the nation's wealthiest men, but from a family with a history of mental illness and later was committed to an insane asylum. George Luther Stearns was a wealthy mill owner who belonged to a number of humane organizations but funded Brown in his homicidal activities. Theodore Parker was a tubercular minister who had outraged the religious community by denying the sanctity of Christ. Franklin Sanborn was an educator who had become deranged due to his young wife's death. None was ever punished for his part in Brown's activities or ever expressed regrets over backing him. One, Higginson, even termed "the hastening of...civil war...good, healthy, positive."

Black Sailors

Unlike Confederate law forbidding enlistments of blacks in the Confederate States Army, Confederate law permitted the Confederate States Navy to recruit black seamen, limited to 5 percent of a ship's company. In February 1865, Stephen R. Mallory, secretary of the navy, expressed the need for 1,150 more. A well-known photograph of Raphael Semmes' CSS *Alabama* shows a black seaman between two lounging officers. When the last Confederate commerce raider, CSS *Shenandoah*, lowered her ensign for the final time in Liverpool, England, in November 1865, black crewman Edward Weeks was there.

Appropriate

Early in 1861 Robert E. Lee observed one of his soldiers riding a very fine-looking four-year-old horse named Jeff Davis. Attracted by the horse's appearance, Lee asked if the horse was for sale and was disappointed to find it was already promised. A few months later while on duty in South Carolina he once again saw the horse, now renamed Greenbriar. The officer who owned the horse had also been transferred to South Carolina. When asked by Lee if he would sell the horse, the man offered him to Lee as a gift. Instead, Lee paid him $200. The horse then received its final name, one known all across the South. Knowing he would be riding all over the state inspecting forts, Lee called the horse Traveller.

Uninvited Guest

The fire of Confederate artillery on Lookout Mountain was doing relatively little damage to the Federals below, and the Yankees became rather accustomed to it. Near where two soldiers of the 18th Ohio were standing, one shell entered the door of a tent and buried itself in the ground. One of the soldiers turned to the other and said, "There, see what you get by leaving your door open!"

Obedient to Orders

Hugh Mc——, an Irishman in the 6th South Carolina Infantry, was stationed on the beach of Sullivan's Island with strict orders to walk between two points and to let no one pass without the countersign, which was to be communicated in a whisper. Two hours later the corporal with the relief discovered Hugh up to his waist in water; the tide had come in. "Who goes there?" "Relief." "Halt, Relief. Advance and give the countersign." "I'm not going in there. Come out and let me relieve you." "Divil a bit of it. The leftenant told me not to leave me post." "Well then, I'll leave you in the water all night." The corporal started away. "Halt. I'll put a hole in ye if ye pass without the countersign." "Confound you, everybody will hear it if I bawl it out to you." "Yes, me darlin', and the leftenant said it must be given to me in a whisper. In with ye, me finger's on the trigger, and me gun may go off." The corporal yielded to the force of that argument and waded to the faithful sentinel who exclaimed, "Bejabbers, it's well ye've come; the bloody tide has most drowned me!"

A Good Deed

At a railroad station a clergyman was conversing with a group of Southern soldiers, giving them good wholesome advice and enjoying their attention. The train's whistle blew and the soldiers ran for their cars. Just as the train began to move, one soldier cried out to the clergyman, "Oh, parson, I have left my oven behind. We can't cook without it. Please throw it up here." The good minister picked up the oven, ran after the cars, and succeeded in pitching it aboard. Jaded by the race but beaming with satisfaction he turned to face an indignant old man who asked, "What for did you throw that oven to the soldier? That was *my* oven!"

Missed Opportunity

In 1872 at a White House reception, President U. S. Grant told an audience that included John S. Mosby that Colonel Mosby had almost changed the course of the war, although he doubted if Mosby knew it. He went on to explain that during the war Mosby had crossed a railroad in pursuit of Federal cavalry just a few minutes before Grant's unguarded train came by. Grant said he had breathed a sigh of relief when he learned that Mosby had left, knowing that if Mosby had seen the train he would have taken it. Mosby quipped, "Well, if I had got hold of that particular train, maybe I'd be president and General Grant here would be calling on me!"

It Was That or a 2x4

On Thursday, September 4, 1862, Lee's army was headed north, crossing the Potomac at White's Ford. A bottleneck developed in midstream when a wagon train became entangled. Stonewall Jackson's quartermaster, Major John Harman, got the train moving again with a spectacular exhibition of profanity. The pious Jackson reprimanded Harman for his profanity, then smiled and accepted his explanation: "Ther's only one language that will make a mule understand on a hot day that they *must* get out of the water."

Hard to Move

During the battle for Fort Donnelson, a Southern soldier saw the head of a Yankee peering above a stump. Pointing his gun at the Yankee, he fired. The Yankee remained. The Southerner reloaded and fired once, then again, then again, then again. Still no result. The Southerner was astounded and yelled to another Southerner, "Do you see that Yankee behind that stump? I have fired five shots at his head and can not make him remove it." Just then the line advanced and the Southerner made for the stump. The Yankee still held his post…with five holes in his head!

A Lady with Pluck

According to the *Confederate Veteran* of November 1893, a young lady of middle Tennessee was engaged to be married to a Confederate soldier. During a visit to her home he was captured by a group of Yankee soldiers and murdered. A few months later the same men returned to her home and she recognized the man who had killed her fiancé. She walked into the yard among 40–50 Yankees and shot him down. No one ever did anything to her for that act. Further, the Union captain in charge of the squad returned after the war to woo her and marry her.

Not a Mutual Feeling

Confederate Brigadier General James Jay Archer and a large part of his command were captured at Gettysburg on July 1, 1863. Shortly afterward, U.S. General Abner Doubleday saw Archer and remembered him from West Point. Doubleday approached Archer, extended his hand, and said pleasantly, "Good morning, Archer! How are you? I am glad to see you!" Archer refused the handshake, saying brusquely, "Well, I am not glad to see you, Doubleday."

In and On the Front

William B. Bate, a brigade commander in Stewart's division, was the junior brigadier in the Confederate Army of Tennessee. Bate was known for his aggressive leadership. A few weeks after the battle of Chickamauga, President Davis toured the battlefield with some of his officers. Coming across a dead horse that showed it had belonged to a general officer, Davis asked to whom it belonged. He was told it had been Bate's. A short distance farther he saw another dead horse that was also identified as Bate's. At the body of a third horse, an artillery horse, the president was told that Bate was riding the horse when it was killed. The president was deeply impressed with the daring of the Tennessean. When he returned to Richmond, he appointed Bate a major general.

Lived Up to His Duty

In the North Carolina Department of Archives and History is a handwritten note from Colonel Isaac E. Avery. Mortally wounded at Cemetery Hill at Gettysburg, Avery penned the note to his friend, Major Tate, just before passing away: "Major, tell my father I died with my face to the enemy. I. E. Avery."

Taking a Dig

Alexander's Bridge at Chickamauga was the site of a valiant delaying action by Federals under Colonel John T. Wilder, who destroyed the bridge before escaping with most of his men. After the war, Captain Joseph Cumming, a Confederate who had attacked Alexander's Bridge at Chickamauga, enjoyed needling his friend Wilder about the bridge. Cumming would "set off" Wilder by casually remarking, "...when you and I opened the battle of Chickamauga and we whipped you down there at Alexander's Bridge..." Wilder would reply heatedly, "I whipped you!" Captain Cumming would then innocently ask, "Why then did you run away and leave the bridge?" "I didn't run away. I destroyed the bridge and then moved off to whip some more of you at another place." About that time Wilder would realize he'd been joshed.

Permanently Impressed

Kansas "Jayhawkers" raided the Missouri farm of Harriet Young and forced Mrs. Young to bake for them until her hands were blistered. The thieving Yankee vandals then shot her hogs, took the hams, ransacked the house, and rode away after setting fire to her home and haystacks. Martha, the youngest daughter of the family, never forgot the terrifying assault on her defenseless family. She remained "unreconstructed" for the balance of her life and was called "Old Rebel" by her son, U.S. President Harry S. Truman.

Peculiar to Where?

Northern writers have often referred to slavery in the South as "that peculiar institution." Logically this term should be used only in reference to slavery in the North where slavery remained legal up to passage of the 13th Amendment to the U.S. Constitution, long after it ended in the South.

A Grave Matter

Jim Jones was a prisoner in the infamous Federal military prison at Elmira, New York. Jones learned the prison doctor was a fellow Mason and talked him into providing a coffin for Jones' use. With the help of friends, Jones was wrapped in a sheet and placed in the coffin on which the lid was then lightly fastened. When a dead wagon arrived, Jones' coffin was placed on the top. Once outside the prison walls, Jones pushed off the coffin lid and said in a sepulchral voice, "Come to judgment." The driver jumped from the wagon and ran away screaming, "Ghosties! Ghosties! Ghosties!" Jones then stripped off the sheet, freed and mounted one of the horses, and galloped to Lake Erie where he found a boat and was soon in Canada.

Special Order 191

On Saturday, September 13, 1862, a copy of Robert E. Lee's Special Order 191 was found and delivered to Federal General George McClellan. This was the infamous "lost order" that outlined Confederate troop deployments and Lee's instructions for them prior to the battle at Antietam. This document is blamed for Lee's failure to win that battle on September 17, 1862. Historian Stephen Sears quoted McClellan as saying, "Here is a paper with which if I can not lick Bobbie Lee, I will be willing to go home." The question that has intrigued historians ever since then is: When did Lee discover that the Federals had his plans? On Monday, September 15, 1862, the *Washington Star* published an account of the discovery of the order and its contents. The next day the *Baltimore Sun* published the same article. Newspapers of that time were vital sources of military information. It seems curious that readers of the two newspapers knew about an intelligence coup of which Lee, only a few miles away, was unaware when he went into battle two days after the article was first published.

Identification Believable

The sentry halted a newly commissioned lieutenant heading back to camp and asked the officer to identify himself. Irritated that the sentry did not recognize him, the lieutenant gruffly commented, "Ass!" The sentry immediately responded, "Advance, ass, and give the password!"

Didn't Buy Mules Very Often

When Philip Honey of Stafford, Virginia, entered the Confederate army he took with him a mule named Fannie. He rode her home after Appomattox, rode her in the procession at the dedication of the Lee monument, and again when President Davis was buried. The mule finally died in October of 1894 at the age of thirty-nine.

The Williams Gun

The first machine gun used in warfare was the invention of Captain R. S. Williams of Covington, Kentucky, and was manufactured at the Tredegar Iron Works in Richmond, Virginia, in 1861. It was taken into action by the Confederates at the Battle of Seven Pines, May 31, 1862, with results so satisfactory that six more were made and went into battle with Pickett's Brigade. The Williams gun was a steel, breech-loading, rifled gun, with an air-cooled barrel four feet long and a two-inch bore. It shot a one-pound ball. A crank revolved a huge cylinder at the breech while a sliding hammer struck a percussion cap for each discharge. The rate of fire was reported as eighteen to twenty balls per minute, with accuracy up to fifteen hundred yards.

Battle of Hardup

In 1864 seventy-five Federals were stationed in a blockhouse near Smyrna, guarding the railroad between Nashville and Franklin. With John Bell Hood and Nathan Bedford Forrest both in the area, the Federals left their blockhouse post to join their fellow soldiers at Murfreesboro. Four Confederates who had slipped away from Hood's army to visit their homes in the area looked up the pike to see the road covered with bluecoats. Assuming the Federals were retreating in fear, the Southerners decided to have some fun and stampede the Federals by firing a few shots. The wagons and teams that the terrorized Yankees were sure to abandon would bring additional pleasure. Familiar with the area, the four hid in a thicket next to the road. When the Federals marched by, the men rode out firing their pistols. As they expected, the Yankees reacted immediately, but not as planned. The Yankee officer called out, "Halt! Right wheel! Fire!" To the horror of the Southerners an instant rain of bullets peeled the saplings around them, shot holes through their clothes and saddles, and instigated a burning urge to be elsewhere. Luckily the four managed to get away and the Northerners did not pursue. The Southerners dubbed the encounter the "Battle of Hardup" because of the hard time they had escaping the result of their reckless attack.

Chivalry Lived

At the time of General Hood's defeat before Nashville, Smith's brigade of Cleburne's division was detached and operating with General N. B. Forrest in the vicinity of Murfreesboro. The enemy was on the direct line between Smith's brigade and the main body of the army. The brigade was obliged to make a wide detour by a forced march across the country. The weather was intensely cold and the whole earth covered with sleet and snow. In this march the men suffered terribly, as large numbers of them were barefooted and there were not half a dozen overcoats in the brigade. The head of the column reached Columbia at about nine o'clock at night; "the lame and the halt" were coming up by ones and twos all night.

Early the next morning, the brigade formed to march through the town with the 1st Georgia in the lead. In the first file of fours was a young fellow of about twenty years, who on the march of the day before had been compelled by physical weakness to throw away a part of his burden. He had parted with his blanket and held on to his musket. Now, as they marched, with indomitable pluck he was at the head of the regiment though his trousers were worn to a fringe from the knees down. His bare feet, cracked and bleeding, left their marks upon the frozen road.

At this moment a private of cavalry came riding by, turned and looked at the poor lad, then reined in his horse. Throwing his leg over the pommel of the saddle, he took off first one shoe and then the other. Giving the pair of them to the unshod fellow with these words: "Friend, you need them more than I do," he galloped away. Surely no knight of old ever bore himself more like a true gentleman than he.

Use the Proper Term

The troops fought one particular enemy throughout the war. It was not uncommon to see many men simultaneously engaged in battling this foe. An old man passing by a soldier who had removed his shirt in his skirmishing asked the soldier "Are they fleas?" In a stentorian voice the soldier indignantly replied, "What do you take me to be, a damned dog? No, I'm a soldier, and they're lice."

Watch that Hyperbole!

In the autumn of 1864, General Humphrey Marshall returned to visit the Kentucky brigade he had led before being elected to the Confederate Congress. Arriving in camp, he was surrounded and welcomed by the troops who demanded a speech. Marshall obliged and gave a rousing talk. At one point he enthusiastically stated that the war must be fought to a triumphant conclusion, even though it became necessary to wade waist-deep in blood. Captain Barney Giltner interrupted at that point, saying, "General, that's too deep for me. I only contracted to go in knee-deep!"

Complete

J. Harvey Dorman came upon the body of a dead Federal after a fight at Wytheville. Examining the effects of the man, Dorman found the soldier's diary. He had been killed before making an entry for that day. Wishing to keep the record complete, Dorman made an entry, "May 10, 1864. I was killed today." He then returned the diary so it could be returned with other effects.

Thank You, I Think

General Nathan Bedford Forrest ordered Captain John Kennedy's company of young Mississippi men and twenty-five from another company to hold a vital bridge that spanned the Big Black River. Forrest told him that many Federals were on their way and he must hold the bridge until sundown. The Southerners took their positions and made ready for an attack. Shortly an attack came. Then another, and another. Kennedy and his men were steadily under fire for hours. Federals lay dead all around various approaches to the bridge. Finally the time came when the Southerners could retire. After they reached Forrest, Kennedy asked the general how his men came to be selected for the arduous task. Forrest, well pleased with the performance of Kennedy and his men, replied, "Because I thought you were damned fool enough to stay there."

Alternate Detection Method

One night Southern forces under Generals Nathan Bedford Forrest and Abraham Buford were pursuing Federal General Sturgis after Bryce's Cross Roads. In the dark two Yankee stragglers mistook the Southerners for their own men and rode the length of the first column before meeting General Buford at the head of a second. One asked whose command it was. When Buford replied, "My command, A. Buford," the Yanks said, "Good Lord!" and spurred away, escaping in the dark. When Buford learned the Yanks had ridden the length of the leading column, he cursed and asked how that had been possible. Told that it had been too dark to see their colors, Buford yelled, "See, Hell, smell 'um."

Poor Selection

One cold dark night, two hungry Confederate couriers approached the home of a Kentucky man. One went up and asked for food. He came back to report the man had refused. The other asked the name of the man who had refused to help and was told, "Sample." "Well, I think he's a damned poor sample!"

Blue Not a Preferred Color

In 1863, a wounded Confederate was taken in and cared for by a Missouri family named Hook. Shortly thereafter Federals approached the home, causing the young invalid to fear his presence would lead to the home being burned. Mrs. Hook quickly dressed him in a woman's nightcap and gown and told him to act too weak to talk. As the Federals were about to enter the house, a black woman ran around the corner of the house and yelled that Southern troops were coming. Panicked, the Federals fled without disturbing the Hooks or the begowned soldier. Sixty years later the Hooks' daughter, now Mrs. W. H. Gregg, said that although she no longer bore malice toward the Yankees, the sight of Yankee uniforms still took her back to the 1860s and the emotions of the time. She could forgive, but she couldn't forget.

A Masterly Retreat

While scouting alone, Major Henry T. Stanton was the target for a bushwhacker's rifle. Stanton said that he quickly left the area, proud of the fact that he had not lost a man.

Got the Answer

On May 6, 1864, the second day of fighting in the Wilderness at Spotsylvania, Jeb Stuart needed to know if a line of Federal earthworks had been abandoned. Private Jim O'Mera was selected to get the information. He rode to within seventy yards of the earthworks and then turned to race parallel with them. The earthworks were immediately lit by a fusillade as the Federals fired at him. When a bullet hit his horse, O'Mera stopped, dismounted, unslung his carbine, and coolly fired on the enemy. He then remounted and sped the remaining length of the earthworks. Hurrying to the general, O'Mera saluted and reported, "They're thar yit, Gin'ral."

The Confederate Soldier

He did not serve for pay, for he received a mere pittance for his service. He did not fight for glory, for history does not take care of him. He did not fight for promotion, for he seldom rose above the ranks. He often left a starving family at home—he committed them to God and the charity of his friends. He suffered cruelly from hunger and cold; with his faithful friend, his musket, he was always ready to forget the one and to overcome the other in the heat of battle.

When's Dinner?

Hardtack was a quarter-inch thick cracker made of unleavened flour. A staple of soldiers' diets, it was unpopular and unpalatable in addition to being almost impossible to chew. One Southerner described the accepted method of taking a bite: Put a corner between your teeth and put your chin on a stump. Then have a friend hit the top of your head with a heavy mallet.

Bowie Knives

Thousands of knives of various patterns were made for Southern recruits. Although the hero of the Alamo would have recognized few of them, all were called "Bowie knives" and were considered an important part of the equipment of Southern volunteers of 1861. Company C, 1st Georgia Infantry, was known as the "Bowie Knife Boys." Orators and editors urged soldiers to arm themselves with the knives, saying the Yankees would fear "cold steel." Later the fearsome knives were discarded as useless and unnecessary encumbrances. Returning home without the huge piece of cutlery he had flourished when leaving, one Southern soldier was asked what had become of it. He answered, "I threw it away. The Yanks never let me get close enough to use it."

Irish Green and Black

One of America's favorite forms of entertainment for nearly two hundred years came to this country from Ireland by way of the Caribbean. In the 1650s, after conquering Ireland in a series of massacres, Oliver Cromwell left his brother Henry as the governor of Ireland. Over the next ten years, Henry sold and deported thousands of Irish men, women, and children into slavery to work the tobacco and sugar cane plantations in the Caribbean. There they worked and lived alongside African slaves. Over the course of the next century a hybrid culture of music and dance evolved from the close existence of the two races. Around 1750 a company of itinerant actors and musicians was shipped from the Caribbean to Kentucky to entertain the elite of that state. Called "The Ethiopian Delineators," they were not Ethiopian or even African. In fact, they were Irish, desperate to make a living. They did so by blackening their faces, strumming banjos, and dancing a dance that derived from an African foot stomp and an Irish jig. (The banjo originated in Moslem Africa as a lutelike stringed instrument called a "banjer," which came to the West Indies with West African slaves.) Thus was born one of the most vibrant and fascinating American art forms, the black-faced American minstrels. From then until the twentieth century Irish dominated this form of entertainment.

A "Can Do" Regiment

At the Battle of Gaines' Mill, Virginia, the Confederate advance was held up by a battalion of fourteen Union cannons. Colonel John Bell Hood of the 4th Texas met Brigadier General W. W. Whiting observing the battle. When Whiting commented to Hood that the cannons ought to be taken, Hood asked why they had not been taken. Whiting replied that the position was too strong, saying that his brigade was composed of veteran troops but they could do nothing with it. Hood replied, "I have a regiment that can take it." He galloped off to his regiment while Whiting stood watching after him. The 4th Texas took all of the cannons.

How Touching!

Major Henry T. Stanton came upon a young lady sitting on a log in the forest, singing softly and mournfully to herself. Thinking she had sought the spot for the sake of solitude, he started to quietly withdraw. As he did so, he realized the words she was singing:

> Beauty is skin deep,
> Ugly is to the bone;
> Beauty fades away,
> But ugly holds its own.

Lent Authority

John Hunt Morgan often went after U.S. mail trains in order to get information from Washington, D.C. Once he opened some mailbags containing U.S. Official Correspondence and found a letter from the War Department to a lieutenant in U. S. Grant's army. It contained a captain's commission for the lieutenant. Right under Abraham Lincoln's signature, Morgan wrote "Approved John Morgan" and sent the commission on to the lieutenant.

A Shame He Couldn't Be There

One of Nathan Bedford Forrest's favorite stories concerned an event when Bragg's forces were retreating after Chickamauga. Among the last of the rearguard was Forrest. As he passed an old lady's house, she ran out and urged him to turn back and fight. When Forrest rode on without stopping, the lady shook her fist at him and shouted with rage, "Oh you great big cowardly rascal. I only wish old Forrest was here; he'd make you fight!"

Church Attendance Inspired

After Appomattox, former CSA Brigadier General William Nelson Pendleton returned to rebuild and head an Episcopalian church in Lexington, Virginia, where Robert E. Lee was president of Washington College. At that time the chaplain at the college, a Dr. Pratt, had a very attractive daughter named Grace. Given to long-windedness, Pendleton once told Lee that many students from Lee's school and from VMI had switched from attending his church to the chapel at the college and said he supposed it was Dr. Pratt's sermons. Lee responded, "I rather think it is not so much Dr. Pratt's speeches as it is his Grace."

A Fan of the Rangers

As colonel of the 32nd Indiana Infantry, August Willich went up against Terry's Texas Rangers at Woodsonville, Kentucky. As brigadier general, Willich again met them at Murfreesboro. Both times he lost. In fact he was captured at Murfreesboro. Thus qualified as a judge of the Texans' military prowess, Willich commented when he found he was a prisoner of Terry's Texas Rangers, "*Mein Gott*, I had rather be a private in that regiment than to be a brigadier general in the Federal army."

Wrong Souvenir

Just before the Second Battle of Manassas, Stonewall Jackson and his staff were met on the old Warrenton Road by Jeb Stuart and his men. Stuart had made a raid around Pope's army and captured Pope's headquarters. Stuart called out to Jackson, "Hello, Jackson, I've got Pope's coat. If you don't believe it, there's his name," holding out a magnificent new major general's coat for Jackson's examination. Stuart's staff expected a loud laugh but Jackson's response was, "General Stuart, I would much rather you had brought General Pope than his coat."

Wanted to Be a Good Soldier

In 1863 mines were planted along the Charleston harbor. To prevent any of the garrison from treading upon them, a sentinel was placed to warn them. One of these sentinels was Private Donnolly, of Company G, 1st Georgia, a native of the Emerald Isle. Of any knowledge of ordinary military maneuvers he was calmly innocent. On one occasion a lieutenant of the company asked him, impatiently, "Donnolly, why *don't* you keep step? All the men are complaining about you." And received the reply: "Faith, it's divil a one of 'em can kape shtep wid me!"

General Roswell S. Ripley was riding past Donnolly straight for the dangerous ground when he was suddenly brought to a halt by a loud "Stop!" uttered in the most emphatic tone. The emphasis received additional point from Donnolly's stance, squinting along the barrel of his fully cocked musket, taking dead aim at the general. For a moment there was strong probability of a vacancy among the brigadiers of the Confederate army, but an officer rushed forward, struck up the gun, and explained to General Ripley the reason for his being halted. Subsequently, our sentinel was asked: "Donnolly, what were you going to do?" "I was going to shot him." "And why?" "To kape him from being blown up with the saltpaters, to be sure."

Donnolly's comrades, in view of his little infirmities of drill, had always insisted upon his having a place in the rear rank, but on this day he was heard to say, with much satisfaction: "There's moighty little trouble getting in the front rank now."

Duty Prevailed

A colonel leading his men at Gettysburg shouted encouragement to them in a rich and hearty voice. Reaching the body of a young officer killed a few minutes earlier in a skirmish, the colonel looked at the upturned face. He froze for a moment, then turned, raised his sword again, shouted, "Come on, come on," and plunged ahead. His men, close behind, soon reached the body. One exclaimed, "Good God! It's the lieutenant! His son!" In front the colonel still ran, calling, "Come on!"

A Mighty Poor Farmer

During an artillery duel, Company G of the 17th Mississippi Infantry was pinned down in a cornfield. Every man was as low as he could get among the rows of corn. Lee Hill was reported to have called out, "Damn a man who won't plow a furrow deeper than this!"

Orders to Be Obeyed

Confederate troops entering Maryland were given orders that private property of whatever description was to remain untouched. When some of Kershaw's command took some fence rails to build a fire, their company commanders were sternly lectured, then instructed to surrender their swords and march in the rear of the regiment until further notice. That evening, after a brush with the enemy, the officers were returned to command of their companies. Lieutenant Dan Maffett had not taken his treatment lightly. He told his company, "If you ever touch another rail during the whole continuance of the war, G—— D——n you, I'll have you shot at the stake." "How are we to get over a fence?" inquired one man. "Jump it, creep under it, or go around it, but death is your portion if you ever touch a rail again."

Fighting Blacks

One sentence stands out among the items reported under "Incidents of the Battle" in the *New York Herald* of July 24, 1863:

Washington, July 10, 1863
    Among the rebel prisoners who marched through Gettysburg there
    were observed seven Negroes in uniform and fully accoutred as soldiers.

Wished to Give Company

A startled rabbit hastily fled as General Lafayette McLaws' troops advanced against the 118th Pennsylvania. One Confederate yelled after it, "Go it, old fellow, and I would be glad to go with you if I hadn't a reputation to sustain."

Ever Compassionate

A Yankee soldier, Gamaliel Bradford, Jr., lay wounded as Robert E. Lee and some of his staff passed by. Though faint from loss of blood, Bradford recognized Lee, raised himself, and shouted, "Hurrah for the Union!" Lee heard him, stopped and dismounted, then approached Bradford. Bradford feared Lee was coming to punish him. However, Lee looked down with a sad expression, extended his hand to shake that of Bradford, and told him, "My son, I hope you will soon be well." Bradford said that if he lived to be a thousand he would never forget the expression on Lee's face. When Lee left, Bradford cried himself to sleep on the bloody ground.

Doing Unto Others

When John B. Gordon's Confederates entered the small town of Wrightsville, Pennsylvania, the fleeing Union troops set fire to the long covered bridge over the Susquehanna River. The fire threatened the whole community and Gordon's men helped extinguish the flames. Remaining overnight, the Southerners billeted themselves in houses vacated by the citizens. One of these homes belonged to the Samuel Smith family. Silas Smith, the son of the family, had joined the Union army and gone off to fight. Wounded, he had died in a Southern hospital. The family had given Silas a pocket testament inscribed with his name and address. After the Southerners left, the Smiths returned to their home and found Silas' testament on a table. No message had been left and nothing in the house had been stolen or disturbed. Who left the Bible was never known. Incidentally, the Yankee newspapers published a report of the fire with the explanation that the Confederates set it in an effort to destroy the town.

All the Amenities

An ambulance driver was bent over a log washing his hands in a small creek just in the rear of the line of battle. A spent shell came through the trees and buried itself just under the edge of the log. Irritated, the driver turned and used the heel of his boot to kick the shell into the water. Only a second or so later the shell burst, blowing off the end of the log and deluging the driver with water. The driver surveyed himself coolly, then exclaimed, "Well, I came here to wash my hands, but hang me if I expected a showerbath in such an out of the way place as this."

Supplied by the North

Reuben Conway Macon, Adjutant of the 13th Virginia Infantry, told of meeting a New Orleans "Tiger" at Fredericksburg. These Irishmen, principally from the wharves, were brave fighters, equally noted for their love of plunder. Pointing toward the Yankees, one of Macon's companions said, "Pat, look over yonder. The whole face of the earth is covered with Yankees." The confident Pat replied, "Faith, if they come this way, I will have an overcoat before night."

Took It Right to Him

Dr. Matt Butler, of the 37th Virginia, received a bad wound in his foot and was limping along a road in company with a wounded companion and Jim, a black hospital helper. Jim told the two men that he was going to find them a safe place because the Yankees were close. Walking as fast as they could, they soon reached a house where a woman was baking cornbread by an open fire. The bread smelled awfully good to the men and they asked the woman for some food. She said she had none except for what she was baking and that was for a Yankee colonel, whom she named. After the travelers left, the black found them a good place to hide and then said he was going to get some food. He returned shortly with a gallon of buttermilk and cornbread dripping with butter. The doctor asked, "How in the world did you get it, Jim?" Jim replied that he just told the woman the colonel was waiting for his cornbread.

Heroicly Selfish

Wounded in the leg during a retreat at Gettysburg, Captain John Bassler of the 149th Pennsylvania Infantry was rescued by Lieutenant Batdorf, who placed Bassler over his shoulder and carried him to safety. Confederate bullets zipped by, encouraging Batdorf's progress. Later, Batdorf jokingly told Bassler not to give him too much credit, because his object in carrying him was to shield himself from the bullets.

Gotta Have Some of Those Cows

A wounded officer was urged by his doctor to drink a little whiskey to stimulate his waning strength. A devout teetotaler, the officer refused the offer. Without his knowledge, the doctor prepared a milk punch with some of the whiskey. This the officer drank. Shortly thereafter he was heard extolling the milk given by the local cows.

Says Who?

The 14th North Carolina's Colonel Bennett had been severely wounded and left on the field when his regiment withdrew. Taking a lantern, Chaplain George Patterson went and found the young officer. The chaplain regretfully told the colonel that his regiment had been ordered away and they would have to leave him. The colonel asked the chaplain to read the funeral service over him, saying, "For I know I am as good as dead." The chaplain did so, reading the solemn service by lantern light. He then left the dying man. However, the man did not die. He recovered and lived many more years. In 1886 in a western town the colonel recognized the chaplain, walked up to him, and greeted him. The chaplain did not recognize him and peered at him, then said, "I don't know you, sir. Who are you?" When he said, "I am Colonel Bennett of the 14th North Carolina Regiment," Patterson promptly replied, "Now I know you are lying, for I buried him at Gettysburg!"

Due Respect

A lofty heroism and nobility of soul may exist where an ordinary observer would never expect to find them. In the ranks of Company K, of the 1st Georgia, was a man from Bulloch County. Before his enlistment a charcoal burner, he was of mean exterior, sickly frame and complaining disposition. He had long been a butt for the rough witticisms of his comrades. What troubled him most was that the men told him he had been "dug up," an implication upon the manner of his entry into the world that he resented bitterly.

During the bombardment of this day he had, in the performance of customary guard duty, been posted at the rampart, near the flag staff, to watch for any movements of the enemy that might indicate the formation of an assaulting column. At the end of his tour, Lieutenant Cyrus Carter started from the guard quarters to relieve him. As Carter crossed the parade, he did so with the profound conviction that he would be struck down before reaching the other side, so appalling was the storm of projectiles that tore up the ground around him. What was his surprise, therefore, to find the sentinel, not sheltered behind the parapet as it was intended he should be, but quietly walking back and forth upon its very crest, for the expressed reason that he "couldn't see good down thar." The flagstaff had been shattered at his side, and with a strip torn from his shirt, he had tied the colors to the stump and continued his walk. As may be well supposed our charcoal burner escaped criticism after that.

An English Confederate

When asked why he was fighting for the South, a young Englishman named Dalgetty replied, "I happened over here."

In those days field glasses pretentiously decorated the lowest order of officers as well as the highest. Dalgetty saw this and got three joints of cane, which he adjusted to imitate a spyglass. Fastening it with a profusion of tarred spring he mounted a lofty lookout and leveled his mock glass at the enemy's batteries. Soon after he slid with a thump to the ground, and threw away his spying tube. When asked what ailed him he replied, "I brought the Yanks too close up." Field glasses were seen only with field officers after that.

After an order had gone out, "furloughs only when death is in the family." Dalgetty applied for leave, writing, "I've lost my grandmother." It was approved, and Dalgetty was passing Colonel ———, a splendid officer, "I am sorry to hear of your affliction, when did your grandmother die?" "She was very old, Colonel, and could not have lasted longer." Dalgetty moved on. "But when did the old lady die?" returned the ex-West Pointer. "It is quite an affliction, sir, and we'll miss her," said Dalgetty, still on the move. "Perhaps you are hard of hearing — when did she die?" asked the colonel with a voice sufficient for a brigade front. "She's been dead forty years, sir; I can't lie about it, but I ought to get a furlough on it." The colonel had to break out in a laugh as he saw Dalgetty going doggedly back to camp.

Disguised

Noting that Stonewall Jackson's uniform and cap had become quite dingy, Jeb Stuart presented him with a fine new uniform, including cap and overcoat. The first time that Jackson appeared in his new clothes, his men did not immediately recognize him. There was silence until someone shouted, "Come out of them, Jackson, you can't fool us."

Bagmen

After Second Manassas, Union General John Pope believed the Confederates were retreating and telegraphed Washington that he had "whipped Jackson and had him in a bag." When that news was received, some Congressional dignitaries and their ladies took a carriage ride to Manassas to see the captured Stonewall and his Confederates. This excursion was surprised when Jeb Stuart paid his compliments and informed them they were his prisoners. Stuart sent the ladies home but obliged the men to walk to Richmond as his prisoners.

An Incident at Walthall Junction

Colonel Carlos Tracy, an aide of General Johnson Hagood at the time of the battle of "Walthall Junction," while following Hagood into the field, became separated from him by some intervening obstacle. He noticed a wounded man, bearing the colors of one of the regiments, walking with the flag of the regiment trailing on the ground.

The Confederate left was clearly turned, and as far as he could see, or know, there was not a soldier to be thrown in the way. Seizing the colors borne by the man, Colonel Tracy (then Captain Tracy), rushed forward some distance on his large cream-colored mare, a conspicuous mark for the shot of the enemy, and endeavored by every possible exertion to rally the men. After fifteen or twenty minutes, having succeeded in getting some of the regiments to form in a line with him, an officer of the regiment, bravely and gallantly claimed the flag, and Tracy bowed and yielded it. It was for this gallant conduct Captain Tracy was promoted to the rank of colonel of cavalry, and assigned to the court of General Ewell's corps, as one of the three judge advocates.

This act of Colonel Tracy's was one that few survive, the like of which one finds scattered here and there in the histories of the past—the relation generally ending with the account of the death of the actor therein. This time, though, the hero was providentially saved and his efforts probably turned the fate of the day in favor of the South.

An Unknown Agent of Justice

While on a raid into northeast Missouri, troops under Captain Thomas Stacy captured Unionist William Aylward. Two of Stacy's men had recently been taken prisoner in a skirmish and then executed. Aylward had bragged about bayoneting them. Stacy was instructed to select an appropriate guard for Aylward for the night. The two men he selected just happened to be a brother and cousin of the men Aylward bragged about killing. The following morning, the prisoner was reported to have "escaped in the darkness of the night." That afternoon Aylward's body was found where someone had hanged him.

Refuted

A prisoner, a Yankee officer from New York, complained to a Confederate chaplain, "I came to fight for the Union, to put down this rebellion, and I will fight till I die for the flag of my country!" The chaplain responded that there was no "Union" to fight for, nor was there a rebellion because the people of the South were merely defending their national and constitutional rights. Finally, the chaplain added, no one could believe what he said about fighting to the death because he had surrendered.

Good Reason

At a dinner during the war, Nathan Bedford Forrest was asked why his hair had turned gray while his beard remained dark. The mentally quick Forrest replied that it was possibly because he tended to work his brain more than his jaw.

Religious Services in Wartime

From an article by Reverend Howard Henderson, in the *Western Christian Advocate*, May 25, 1892:

"During the great revival in Gordon's Georgia brigade, baptism by immersion was administered in the Rapidan in open view and easy range of the Federal army. General Gordon was always present, offering a splendid target to the Union pickets on the bank, but to the honor of 'the boys in blue' they refrained from firing, and stood reverentially looking on the sacred scene. No danger was apprehended while the ordinance was being administered. On several occasions the Federal pickets joined in the hymns."

As Lincoln Saw Things

Abraham Lincoln stated many times that the war was to preserve the Union, not to free the slaves. Freeing the slaves only became an issue when Lincoln decided to use it as a war measure. In 1862, several Republican senators urged Lincoln to take action to free the slaves. His response was:

"Gentlemen, I can't do it. But I'll tell you what I can do. I can resign in favor of Mr. Hamlin. Perhaps Mr. Hamlin could do it."

The Union Army as Saviors

On December 9, 1864, Union General Jeff C. Davis marched his troops across pontoon bridges over the rain-swollen Ebenezer Creek near Savannah. After his troops had crossed, he had the bridges removed, stranding many hundreds of frightened fugitive slaves on the shore behind him. Knowing that Confederate cavalry was closely following the Federals, and fearful of what the Confederates might do, hundreds of the slaves plunged into the water hoping to swim across, and many died.

A Different Reason

General Richard Ewell noticed a friend of his, a chaplain, wrapped in a robe and asked him, "Father, were you in the battle yesterday?" "Why do you ask?" "I see you have a Yankee blanket and I thought you captured it." Ewell roared in surprise when the response came: "I was at the battle, General, but I captured nothing. Some of your good boys stole my overcoat, so I have to wear my blanket."

Made Jackasses of the Yanks

On August 28, 1862, while attacking Stonewall Jackson near Groveton, Virginia, the Federals placed a mountain howitzer opposite the 15th Louisiana. The continuing howitzer barrage really enraged the Southerners. After repelling an attack by New York infantry, they charged the howitzer and captured it along with a large squad of Yankees. In the assault the horses of the battery were killed. Wanting to keep the artillery but having no horses to haul them briefly presented a problem to the Southerners. They quickly resolved it. They harnessed the Yankees and compelled them to haul the artillery into the Southern lines.

Whirlwind

One summer day in 1845, twenty-four-year-old Nathan Bedford Forrest rode up to where two women and their driver were stranded at a creek ford. While the driver struggled to free the carriage from a mud hole, two acquaintances of the women sat on horseback watching the driver's efforts. Forrest alit from his horse and waded out to the carriage. With the ladies' permission he carried them one by one to dry ground. Then he reentered the water and helped the driver free the carriage. Before helping the ladies into the carriage he turned to the two spectators, upbraided them for their uselessness, and threatened them if they didn't leave at once.

The ladies were a widow, Elizabeth Montgomery, and her eighteen-year-old daughter, Mary Ann, who had never before met Forrest. Introducing himself, Forrest asked permission to call on Mary Ann. A few days later he did call on her. Arriving at the Montgomery residence, Forrest found the two men who had been watching at the creek. The two left after Forrest threatened them again. When Mary Ann invited him in, he proposed to her, telling her that his business could support her comfortably and securely. Mary Ann hesitated. Although he had impressed her, she had only seen him once before. He told her he was determined to marry her and would bring a marriage license on his next visit. On that third visit, Mary Ann accepted his proposal and the two were married in September.

Recalling His Lineage

After a fatiguing inspection tour of the Rio Grande frontier, General Philip Sheridan was approached by a stranger who asked what the general thought of Texas. Slapping the trail dust off his uniform, Sheridan replied, "If I owned hell and Texas, I would rent Texas out and live in hell!" The remark spread quickly throughout Texas and inspired the praise of one Texas newspaper for Sheridan for sticking up for his place of origin.

Gettysburg

Robert E. Lee never attempted to put any blame for Gettysburg on anyone else when he felt it was rightly his. He told James Longstreet, "It's all my fault. I thought my men were invincible."

Hood and His Brigade

John B. Hood made no effort to curb the footloose behavior of his Texans. He was demanding in battle but turned his back on what the men did in camp. On one occasion, while passing through Richmond, virtually the entire brigade decided to go AWOL. When one of the officers tried to stop them, Hood called to him, "Let 'em go. Let 'em go. They deserve a little indulgence and you'll get them back in time for battle."

On the final day at Manassas John B. Hood's men captured several Union ambulances and put them into action for the Texas Brigade. General N. G. Evans, who was senior to Hood, ordered Hood to turn the ambulances over to him. When Hood refused, Evans placed him under arrest for insubordination. Longstreet then ordered Hood to remain in Virginia. Hood explained his refusal, "I would cheerfully have obeyed directions to deliver them to General Lee's Quartermaster for use of the army, [but] I did not consider it just that I should be required to yield them to another brigade of the division, which was in no manner entitled to them." The power of arrest was sacrosanct to Robert E. Lee and he would not intercede nor override Evans. However he recognized Hood's value and ordered Hood to bring up the rear of his division and accompany it into Maryland. When Hood's men saw General Lee, they began to shout, "Give us Hood!" Lee sent for Hood and told him, "General, here I am just upon the eve of entering battle with one of my best officers under arrest." He then told Hood that if he would apologize about the ambulances he would release him. Hood again refused, repeating the justice of his stand. Lee shook his head, told Hood his arrest was suspended, and then went out to where Hood's Brigade was waiting. Courteously waving his hand, Lee told the troops, "You shall have him, gentlemen." To the accompaniment of wild cheering, Hood moved to the front of the division.

Critical Standards

Robert E. Lee believed there could be discipline without regimentation. As president of Washington College he told the faculty, "Make no needless rules." He wanted responsibilities simple enough to be understood and obeyed by all. When asked by a student for a copy of the school's rules, Lee replied, "We have only one rule here—to act like a gentleman at all times."

Dallas County and the War

Dallas County was one of the very few Texas counties that gained population during the war. It was recognized as one of the leading food-producing counties of Texas. The county was so successful in the production of wheat, corn, forage, meat, and other necessary food supplies that the Confederate government established and maintained a general quartermasters/commissary headquarters at Dallas for the collection of food and supplies for the Army of the Trans-Mississippi Department. A transportation and recruiting department was established in Dallas, while at Lancaster a manufacturing department was established where arms were repaired and pistols manufactured. As the general headquarters for all these departments, Dallas was the home for the officers and men, and often their families. During the five years after the war, the population of the county increased by over 50 percent, primarily from former Confederates attracted by Dallas' prosperity.

A Northern Scavenger

Josiah H. Law, Private, Company B, 4th Georgia Infantry, was killed on July 1, 1863. He was buried on the David Blocher farm, just north of Gettysburg. After the war, Law's body was recovered and expressed to his family in Savannah, Georgia.

There the family found that a gold dental plate had been removed from the skull. Mr. Blocher admitted taking it and refused to give up the plate. Blocher finally agreed to sell the gold teeth to the Law family and sent them after receiving his money.

Conscientious

One of the most respected field officers in Lee's artillery corps was Joseph McGraw, a teamster of Irish blood, aged twenty, who rose to the rank of lieutenant colonel. This remarkable officer was "discovered" by Colonel William J. Pegram, in whose battery ("The Purcell") he enlisted and rapidly advanced through the lower grades. He was a young man of powerful frame and exceptional ability to command men. His courage was proverbial. While he was sitting on his horse at Spotsylvania, a solid shot tore away his left arm, leaving only a stump in the shoulder socket. For an instant his subordinates paused in their work to proffer him assistance, but perceiving their intention, he cried out in unshaken tones—"Don't mind me, men, I'm all right—give 'em hell!" and then fell forward from his saddle without a flinch or a cry of pain. Upon regaining consciousness, Major McGraw refused to receive the usual anesthetic. He exercised his authority as senior officer to the surgeon in attendance upon him to command the latter to remove the shattered stump of his arm. This was done without eliciting a groan from the patient, or a blink from his marvelous blue eyes, while he quietly puffed away at his pipe. One of his officers undertook to commiserate with him over his wound. "Pretty bad; reckon I'll be off duty thirty days," was the laconic reply. When General Lee heard of the wounding of McGraw, he said: "I very much fear the Artillery will lose one of its best officers." Not long after this, Colonel Pegram, sitting in his tent at Petersburg, heard a mounted man approaching, contrary to his orders against such reckless exposure in the trenches. McGraw rode up to the tent, calmly saluted with his right hand, and reported: "Sir, Major Joseph McGraw returns to duty." Just before the withdrawal of the army from Petersburg, he was again promoted and placed in command of twenty-four guns.

Extreme Capabilities

A member of the famed Kentucky "Orphan Brigade" wrote home that rations and clothing were scarce, and the men of the brigade had learned how to get along on next to nothing. "Why, shoot," he bragged, "I can sleep on a fence rail and use a shoestring for my cover!"

Responsibility

From the private journal of a Confederate officer high in command, both at Andersonville and other Southern prisons:

"At one time an order came to Camp Lawton to prepare 2000 men for ex-change. The order from Richmond was to select first the wounded, next the oldest prisoners and sickly, filling up with healthy men according to date. This party went first to Savannah, as arranged, but by some mistake the ships were at Charleston, and the poor wretches had to be taken there; and every one who knew the Southern railroads in those days, and the difficulty or rather impossibility to procure food for such a crowd along the road, will know what those poor fellows suffered. At Charleston they were refused, the commissioner declaring that he was not going to exchange able-bodied men for such specimens of humanity. (The term used was more brutal.) Finding him obdurate, Colonel Ord requested him to take them without exchange. This he refused with a sneering laugh, and the crowd was ordered back. Never did the writer of this witness such woe-begone countenances, in which misery and hopelessness were more strongly painted, than shown by these poor fellows on their return. And the curses leveled against the rulers who thus treated the defenders of their country were fearful, although certainly well deserved. As the stockade gate closed upon them the surgeon in charge said to the writer: 'Poor fellows! the world has closed upon more than half of them; their disappointment will be their death-knell.' His words proved true. Who murdered these men? Let history answer the question."

Not What He Wanted to Hear

The young recruit walking back to camp decided to save a few steps and cut through a farm. About halfway across he noticed a mean-looking bull in the field. Seeing the farmer working in the next field, the young man excitedly yelled, "Hey! Is this bull over here safe?" "Well," came the reply, "he's a darned sight safer than you are."

No Symbol of Slavery to This Man

In a letter home to Texas after the Battle of Corinth, Mississippi, a cavalry officer wrote about his regimental flag:

"I must not forget our old flag—though torn and tattered and faded. In the three days of fighting, although about 18 inches was torn off the end and lost—there is fifteen bullet holes through the flag and three through the staff—and besides this a large rent made by a piece of a bomb. Three color bearers were shot down and the fourth now carries it. If I should live through the war I would want no brighter monument than this faded flag to decorate my parlor walls (provided I ever have a parlor)."

The Supreme Court and Treason

Salmon P. Chase, chief justice of the United States Supreme Court, was responsible for the dismissal of any charge of treason against Jefferson Davis. In conversation with other members of the court he put this query to them: "A man can not be tried for treason unless he is a citizen of the country, can he?" "Certainly not," was the answer of every judge. "Then Mr. Davis can not be tried for treason unless he is a citizen of the United States?" "Assuredly not," was again the answer. "Can you show me under authority of the Constitution or any law of Congress where any man is a citizen of these United States? The people of this country are citizens of the respective States in which they reside and not citizens of the United States." This position was assented to by the other members of the court and Mr. Davis was never brought to trial. This led to the fourteenth amendment to the Constitution, making the people of the country citizens of the United States.

Generous

Marching through Pennsylvania, a member of the 5th Texas Infantry was hailed by a lady who asked where he got his knapsack, which bore in large letters the name, regiment, and company of its former owner. The Texan told her he took it from a dead Yankee at Chancellorsville. When the lady told him, "That was my son," the Texan stopped, removed his possessions, and handed the knapsack to the lady.

Faithful

In the battle of Malvern Hill, Joe Kendall, a cannoneer in Stribling's "Fauquier Battery," lost one of his arms. In the excitement of the conflict he was permitted, upon his insistent request, to hold, with his one hand a number of loose horses, which had been left under cover. "At least I can do that much," he urged. Soon after, his lifeless body was found lying at the feet of the horses, the bridle reins of which were gripped in his stiffened hand. Kendall had bled to death, but remained faithful to his charge even after death!

Knew His General

Following his defeat at Lookout Mountain and Missionary Ridge, Braxton Bragg retreated, falling back to Dalton, Georgia. This was a habit of which his disgruntled troops heartily disapproved. In camp for the winter at Dalton, some men of Cleburne's Division discussed Bragg's many failed campaigns. In an ill-advised attempt to bolster support for Bragg, one soldier stated that at least Bragg was a member of the Church. "What the hell's the use in that!?" shouted a grizzled old veteran. "If Bragg were now in Heaven, he would fall back in less than three days for a better position!"

Relative Values

When Abraham Lincoln heard that Confederates had captured General Edwin Stoughton and fifty horses, he remarked that while he could make a new brigadier general with the sweep of a pen, he really regretted losing those horses.

On-the-Job Recruiting

On February 20, 1864, a two hundred-man detachment of Maryland and New York cavalrymen was searching for partisans near Upperville, Virginia. To their great regret they found some. John Mosby and about fifty of his Rangers attacked them and drove them away after heavy fighting. When the local school released its students for a break just as the Rangers attacked, one student, Cab Maddux, became so excited that he mounted his pony and joined in the chase, brandishing his textbook over his head. That was his last school day until the end of the war, as he promptly joined the Rangers.

Sometimes Decisions Are Easy

On January 1, 1863, Companies D, E, and G of the 42nd Massachusetts were guarding the railroad bridge connecting Galveston with the mainland. During the battle for Galveston that morning, General William R. Scurry demanded the surrender of the regiment. Colonel Burrell, the regiment's commander, asked Scurry for three hours to consider the surrender. Scurry replied, "If you can stand the fire of my battery that length of time, you can have it, but not otherwise." Burrell surrendered the regiment at once unconditionally.

Flame-Out for a Meteor

Three years after graduating from West Point, E. H. Stoughton of Vermont was a U.S. brigadier general. In March of 1863, beguiled by a young Southern lady, the twenty-four-year-old general lay asleep in his bed in Fairfax Court House, Virginia, sleeping off an evening of champagne drinking. The same young lady gave guidance to Colonel John S. Mosby, allowing Mosby and twenty-nine other Confederates to make their way through the Union troops guarding the young general's headquarters. After obtaining entry by saying he had a dispatch for Stoughton, Mosby approached the sleeping general, lifted his shirt and delivered a slap on the man's bare back. The startled and indignant officer awoke to find himself a prisoner. Mosby and his men spent an hour in town before riding out with thirty-nine men and fifty-eight horses. Stoughton gained his release two months later, but the army career that had seemed so bright was over. Receiving no further assignment, he left the army shortly thereafter.

Devastating

One of Union General George McClellan's staff officers reported that in the fight at Gaines' Mill an entire regiment of Union soldiers, with the exception of one man, was killed or severely wounded by one volley of bullets from the 5th South Carolina Infantry. Commanded by Colonel Micah Jenkins, the South Carolinians had marched against a Union regiment that was on its knees with rifles raised, ready to receive them. Jenkins had instructed the men not to fire, but to march with their rifles ready to do so at his command. As they neared the Union troops, Jenkins heard the start of the enemy's command to shoot. When he heard "Ready," Jenkins gave the sharp order, "Fire!" The command was so well received that not an answering shot came back.

Colonel William Johnson Pegram

After the death of Pelham, Colonel William Johnson Pegram, who fell at Five Forks, age twenty-two, was perhaps the best-known figure among the younger field officers of artillery in Lee's army. In four years he had advanced from the grade of private to the rank of colonel by the sheer force of his skill and dauntless character. Without previous military training of any kind, he might have commanded an infantry brigade before he fell. Three separate times he was recommended to be a brigadier. On every great battlefield in Virginia he was conspicuous for both skill and courage, and at all times for his modesty. Very near-sighted, Pegram frequently made personal reconnaissances almost up to the enemy's position, a custom that often elicited complaint from those who were called upon to accompany him. So well known had he become among all arms before the war had progressed very far, that the men in the trenches or on the march were often heard to exclaim: "There's going to be a fight, for here comes that damn little man with the 'specs'!"

Confederate Candle

A "Confederate candle" was a famous Christmas gift, for it lasted nearly all winter and was indeed a labor of love. It was made of yards and yards of cotton wick, which was passed slowly through melted bee's wax until it became thick and firm; then it was coiled and twisted into many fanciful patterns around a smooth upright stick fastened firmly into a wooden block or pedestal.

Unstoppable

Battery A, Cutts' "Sumter (Georgia) Battalion" was in the very back of the rear guard when Lee's army commenced the movement from Spotsylvania to the North Anna. Cut off from the main body by a large force of the enemy's infantry, Lieutenant Rees, in command, ordered the gallop and dashed past the hostile troops with his guns. He then went into action in the enemy's rear, retiring his battery piece by piece. Moving by a long circuit to the west and south, they passed around the enemy's right at Little River. After two days and nights of ceaseless marching, during most of which time they were separated from their own army by the enemy, Rees reported with all his men and guns to his battalion commander. Cut off by the enemy, the battery had circled the rear of a hostile army and managed to rejoin its own command.

Glad to See Homefolks

During the winter of 1863–64 while inspecting picket lines, General Robert Rodes came upon a young soldier lounging on the ground with his rifle leaning on a nearby tree. Rodes asked the boy if he knew he could be court-martialed for his action. Without rising, the boy replied that he didn't know that. "When did you enlist?" snapped Rodes. "Last week." "When were you assigned to picket duty?" "This morning." "Do you know who I am?" "No, sir." "I am General Rodes." Leaping to his feet, the boy ran over to Rodes, stuck out his hand, and said, "Glad to meet you, General Rodes. I'm Dick Maness. How's your folks?" The general gave up and tactfully retired.

Gunning for the Yanks

Pennsylvania-born Confederate General Josiah Gorgas, chief of ordnance, displayed organizational genius at his task. In addition to Richmond, Virginia, and Fayetteville, North Carolina, he established ordnance works in Texas, Arkansas, Louisiana, Mississippi, Alabama, and Georgia. The plant at Selma employed over three thousand employees. These plants made the Confederacy self-sufficient in gunpowder, and almost self-sufficient in ammunition and arms.

Out Of Place!

In the fury of fighting at the Battle of Holly Springs, a disoriented Yankee thought he was surrounded by fellow Yankees when actually all around him were Confederates. Seeing soldiers fleeing, the Yank called out, "Fall in boys and we will whip the darn Rebels yet!" A sudden realization of who his companions were, prompted the quick comment, "By Gee, I'm in the wrong pew!"

In the Land of Lincoln

In the mid-1800s both Indiana and Illinois passed state laws prohibiting Negroes and mulattoes from settling within their borders.

Close Shave

At Gaines' Mill on June 27, 1862, a rifle ball cut off half the mustache of Private A. N. Vaughn.

No Bull

Major Moses B. George, quartermaster for Hood's Brigade, brought a Durham cow with him when he enlisted in 1861. He managed to keep the cow with him through four years of war, with the cow usually following his wagon train. At the end of the war, the cow provided milk for the hungry men going home to Texas.

Duty First

Robert E. Lee always placed duty first. One day Lee summoned his adjutant to ask if there were any matters of army routine upon which his judgment and action were desired. The mail was presented to him; he reviewed the military papers and gave his orders in regard to them. The adjutant then left. When for some cause he returned in a few moments and entered Lee's tent, he was startled to see Lee overcome with grief, an open letter in his hands. That letter contained the sad intelligence of his daughter's death. And he had not so much as opened it until he had disposed of the duties the needs of his country imposed.

Salt

Easily available before war came, salt quickly disappeared from the scene in the South. Without salt, no one could preserve meat. From Texas, the Ledbetter Salt Works in Shackleford County, and the salt works at Grand Saline and Palestine sent large quantities of salt to the armies. The wells at Saltville, Virginia, produced at full capacity, as did the mines at Avery Island, Louisiana, until their capture in 1863. Prices for salt skyrocketed, going from eighty cents a bushel in 1861 to as high as $100 in 1865.

Pretty Neat and Neatly Pretty

Marching through the Pennsylvania countryside prior to Gettysburg, Texans in Hood's Brigade were extremely impressed by the houses and barns they saw. In a letter home on June 29, 1863, John West of Waco wrote that he had not seen a barn in the past three days that wasn't more substantially and carefully fitted out than any house in Texas. He deemed the barns more tastily built than two-thirds the houses in Waco.

An Inspiring Message

Confederate cavalrymen attacked and captured a Federal wagon train at Newtown, Virginia, on May 29, 1864, killing and wounding ten Federals. David Hunter, commander of Federal forces in the Shenandoah Valley, was determined to punish local residents who he believed had helped the Confederates. He sent Major Joseph Stearn and the 1st New York Cavalry to burn the village. According to the regimental histories of the New Yorkers, the crying women and children begging for their homes to be spared aroused such sympathy and concern that Stearn decided to disobey Hunter's order and just return to camp. That is a possible reason. However another possibility came to light when a message was found in Stearn's effects when he died in 1866. It was addressed to Stearn and read: "Sir: I write this note to inform you that if you attempt to execute the barbarous threat of retaliation on citizens for my acts, I will hang every Yankee that falls into my hands. I hold several of your men captured this morning as hostages for your good behavior. Your obt. servt., John S. Mosby, Lt.Col., CSA."

No Brass Hats

The term "brass buttons," often used to refer to an officer, came about because an officer would be more likely to have them than an enlisted man. Although Confederate uniform buttons were planned to be made from brass, due to the lack of manufacturing industry, the most common buttons among enlisted men were made of wood or bone.

Medals

Medals had no tradition in the American military at the time of the War Between the States. Congress had occasionally awarded presentation swords or gold medals to high-ranking officers, but there were no medals or badges for enlisted men. The Confederate Congress established a "Roll of Honor," with the intention of later awarding medals but none were ever struck. Medallions were struck in France during the war for members of the Stonewall Brigade but did not reach North America until after the war. The Southern Cross of Honor was issued by the UDC after the war to veterans or their families. The only medals known to have been awarded during the war were the Davis Guard medals and the Texas Gold Star medals. The Davis Guard medals, made from Mexican silver dollars, were presented by President Davis to all members of the Davis Guard for their 1863 defense of the fort at Sabine Pass. The Texas Gold Star medals were nine gold stars sent to the Texas Brigade by an unidentified Texas lady. In January of 1865, these stars were presented by Colonel Frederick Bass, acting upon the orders of General Robert E. Lee, to nine men chosen by their fellow soldiers as the bravest in the brigade.

The Merryman Case

Serious and resourceful students of U.S. history may find an occasional reference to Lincoln's suspension of writs of habeas corpus, with such suspension responsible for imprisonment of thousands of citizens. However, it is extremely rare for there to be any mention of the Merryman case. Chief Justice R. B. Taney of the United States Supreme Court was outraged by Lincoln's action but was not able to prevail over the military might of the dictator. In regard to writs of habeas corpus, Chief Justice Taney upon the case of John Merryman of Baltimore County, Maryland: Mr. Merryman was seized by military forces while in his home on the morning of May 25, 1861, and imprisoned in Fort McHenry, with no warrant from any legal authority and no attempt to obtain one. General George Cadwalader detained Mr. Merryman on the order of a General Keim and refused to honor a writ of habeas corpus on grounds that the president authorized the action. The military would not give any name of any witness to any crime nor specify any act of which the prisoner was accused. Chief Justice Taney cited specific areas of the Constitution to prove that Lincoln had no authority for his action and that such powers were reserved for the Legislative Department, to be exercised only under explicit circumstances. He went on to cite earlier English law as further proof that Lincoln was acting illegally. While Taney had the law on his side, Lincoln had the power. The illegal imprisonments continued even after Taney sent a sealed copy of his ruling to Lincoln with a request for the president, in fulfillment of his constitutional obligation, to take care that the laws be faithfully executed and that the civil process of the United States be respected and enforced.

Learned Early

Robert E. Lee is revered all across the South, but nowhere more than in Virginia. According to a story from there, a little boy came home from Sunday school and told his mother, "Mama, I'm confused. Was General Lee in the Old Testament or the New?"

Had a Leak?

German-born troops under Federal General Franz Sigel marched toward the Battle of Cross Keys singing, *"Shackson [Jackson] in a shug [jug], boys, Shackson in a shug!"* When they came back worse the wear after meeting Jackson, young Virginia ladies cried out, "Hey, thought Jackson was in a jug!" prompting the response, "Ach, der stopper flew out!"

Cloth

During 1861 and 1862, a plant at the Huntsville, Texas, prison supplied the Confederate armies with almost a million and a half yards of cotton goods and nearly 300,000 yards of woolen goods.

His Birth Inspired His Name

Captain Decimus Et Ultimus Barziza, Company C, 4th Texas Infantry, had many siblings. Translated from the Latin his given names mean "Tenth and Last."

Military Order Number 38

Alabama had seceded from the United States and joined the Confederate States of America. With the war going against the South, the Federal army had occupied most of Alabama. The constitution was in effect annulled. The population was held under duress. Because of the situation, Richard Hooker Wilmer, Episcopal Bishop of Alabama, ordered the prayer for the president of the United States and those in civil authority omitted from the morning and evening prayer services. When he refused to reinstate such prayer, the Federal army issued General Order 38, closing the churches in his diocese. Soldiers were stationed at church doors to prevent entrance. This order stayed in effect until the war was over and civil authority again in control. Bishop Wilmer explained his action: "I could not find it in my heart to send up a prayer for a blessing on what had no existence. I could not ask the Almighty to give health, prosperity and long life to the Commander-in-Chief of this body of men who had devastated our entire country and especially when the officers with swords at their sides came to demand it."

What a Candidate!

The Republican National Committee voted to hold the 1860 convention in Chicago only after receiving a pledge that Illinois would not field a favorite son as a candidate for president. With the Democratic Party divided into three warring factions, the Republican presidential nominee was considered a "shoo-in" for election. William H. Seward of New York, famed as "Mr. Republican," was believed certain to be nominated on the first ballot. Ignoring their promises, the Illinois Republicans made Abraham Lincoln their candidate for president. Lincoln's campaign manager, David Davis, presided over early sessions of the national convention and managed to delay printing of ballots so that it was impossible to take a vote on the first evening. On the following morning bogus admission tickets were distributed to Lincoln supporters in order to pack the convention. When Seward supporters arrived at the convention site, only a few could find seats. Davis went to work, promising contenders for the nomination that support for Lincoln would bring them cabinet posts. On the third ballot, Lincoln was nominated, virtually guaranteeing his election.

Reaping What He Sowed

Colonel Ulric Dahlgren led a picked force of five hundred Union soldiers on a raid toward Richmond, with the intent of murdering Jefferson Davis and his cabinet. Uncertain about where he might ford the swollen James River, Dahlgren accepted the offer of guidance from an adolescent black, Martin Robinson. Led to a place of crossing, Dahlgren looked briefly at the river and decided against attempting a crossing. Instead he decided that young Robinson had betrayed him and had the boy shot on the spot. The next day Dahlgren and his men rode into a hail of bullets from Virginia troops. In a moment of poetic justice Dahlgren was shot and died almost instantly.

Under Fire

From an article by Major General George B. Pickett, Jr.:

"Confederate General George Edward Pickett retained his sense of humor in the midst of battle. When his aide-de-camp, Robert A. Bright, had one of his spurs shot off by grapeshot, the general chided him, 'Captain, you are here to win your spurs and not lose them.' "

Should Have Armed Them

Late in the war, General Richard Taylor visited the camps of the slaves who were working on the fortifications of Mobile. During a conversation with a slave leader, Taylor commented to the man that the men had worked very well. The slave then stated, "If you will give us guns we will fight for these works too. We would rather fight for our own white folks than for strangers."

Fired with Enthusiasm

Federal sharpshooters hidden in bulrushes across the Nansemond River from Fort Huger in Virginia practically neutralized the garrison. The sharpshooters had hit several of the gunners in the fort and killed Captain Ike Turner of the 5th Texas. The Federals were out of sight and impossible to dislodge as they moved from place to place through the tall grass. A private (name unrecorded) in the 4th Texas solved the problem. Amid a shower of bullets, the private swam the river with a block of matches tied on the top of his head. After setting the grass aflame and driving out the sharpshooters, he returned safely to the fort.

What a Surprise

"The North, it seems, have no more objections to slavery than the South have..."—John Stuart Mill, 1861

Served Him Right

In 1861 Commodore William D. "Dirty Bill" Porter of the U.S. Navy proved his fidelity to the Union by divorcing his Southern-born wife. He was therefore without her support and care when he died of heart disease in May 1864.

Honor the Flag

Thirteen Texans died at Antietam defending the flag of the 1st Texas Infantry Regiment. When Union soldiers seized the flag as a trophy they first had to roll a dead officer off of it.

Archibald Gracie, Jr.

Gracie Mansion, the official residence of the mayor of New York City, was the family home of Confederate Brigadier General Archibald Gracie, Jr. Gracie had resigned from the U.S. Army in 1856 to enter his family's business. His father later said that the worst mistake he ever made was sending his son to Mobile to manage the branch there. Gracie fell in love with the South and defied his family to accept a commission in the 3rd Alabama. He soon earned appointment to brigadier general and was killed by a Federal shell while fighting in the trenches near Petersburg.

Confederate Treasure

When Richmond was evacuated at the end of the war, the Confederate Treasury consisting of $300,000 to $350,000 in coins and bullion was sent out of Richmond. Six wagonloads are believed to have reached Washington, Georgia, where they vanished from recorded history. Since then many treasure hunters have sought it in vain.

From the Man Racists Call Racist

Confederate General N. B. Forrest

Memphis, Tennessee—July 1875

"I feel that you are free men, I am a free man, and we can do as we please. I came here as a friend and whenever I can serve any of you I will do so...therefore, let us stand together. Although we differ in color, we should not differ in sentiment."

Robert E. Lee, On Slavery

December 27, 1856

"There are few, I believe, in this enlightened age, who will not acknowledge that slavery as an institution is a moral and political evil."

A Relative Report

Interesting relations of participants in Battle of Galveston:

The Confederate navy commander at the battle was Leon Smith, whose brother was Calvin Smith, Abraham Lincoln's secretary of state.

Major A. M. Lea, with Confederate forces storming the Union gunboat *Harriet Lane*, found his son, Union Lieutenant Edward Lea, dying on the ship's deck.

Another Confederate boarding the *Harriet Lane* grabbed a man by the throat and demanded his surrender. When the man told him, "Look your prisoner in the face," the Southerner realized the Yankee sailor was his brother.

Evidently He Hadn't Watched CNN

On April 9, 1865, the day the Civil War ended, Benjamin Madison Crownober Clark, stationed with the 16th Texas at Galveston, wrote to his family: "I have nothing of importance to write today."

And Justice for All

At Hilton Head, South Carolina, volunteers for pioneer black regiments were recruited with promises they would be treated and paid as white soldiers. Sergeant William Walker, 3rd South Carolina, discovered that he and his comrades actually would receive only $7 per month while whites received $13. When Walker protested the inequities in pay, he was accused of using threatening language while addressing an officer. He was reduced in rank to private, sent to Jacksonville, Florida, and executed by musketry, all for the offense of crusading for equal pay among men fighting for the Union.

Official U.S. Policy

Preamble to the H.R. 97, passed by both Houses of the U.S. Congress:

"Rebel prisoners in our hands are to be subjected to a treatment finding its parallels only in the conduct of savage tribes and resulting in the death of multitudes by the slow but designed process of starvation and by mortal diseases occasioned by insufficient and unhealthy food and wanton exposure of their persons to the inclemency of the weather."

A Man of Principle

At the Johnson's Island prison for Confederate officers, their black servants were with several of the men. The blacks were not prisoners but had no rights and were under constant pressure to leave the officers. George, servant of Colonel I. G. W. Steadman of Alabama was repeatedly interviewed and offered freedom, clothes, good pay, and a good place to live. George's reply to these offers was, "Sir, what you want me to do is desert, and I ain't no deserter. Down South, deserters disgrace their families and I am never going to do that."

Demonstrated Leadership Early

The leadership of General George E. Pickett has often been obscured by myths and errors. Actually his leadership was demonstrated many times. An early example took place at Chapultepec on July 13, 1847. Charging up the hill, Lieutenant James Longstreet fell wounded. Lieutenant Pickett promptly took his place leading the men of the 8th U.S. Infantry. When the sixth color bearer in five days was shot down, Pickett seized the flag and carried it as he charged up the heights. While the battle still raged, Pickett took down the Mexican flag and raised that of the 8th. For his action he was brevetted captain and became famous as "the first man over the wall of Chapultepec."

A Wartime Account

By Dock Owen, Company F, Holcombe Legion, CSA:

"General Longstreet owned a fine iron-grey horse he called 'Selim.' He thought a great deal about that horse and never failed to graze Selim when we were in camp. One day some of the boys happened along by the pasture and on arriving in camp told the General old Selim was dead. He had an Irishman named Mike Logan who looked after the stock for the general. General Longstreet sent after Mike and told him to go down to the pasture, skin old Selim, and bring him the hide; he was going to send it home, have it stuffed and keep it in his library. Mike got his tools and went to the pasture and was absent about six hours, when he returned with the hide on his shoulders. The general asked him what the devil he had been doing. Mike replied, 'General, I had to run that old horse four hours before I could kill him.' "

Double Duty

Three Confederate navy officers also held a commissioned rank in the Confederate army: Commander John Taylor Woods, colonel; Commander Richard L. Page, brigadier general; Captain Rafael Semmes, brigadier general.

No Matter How Well Washed

On each of the many times that Winchester, Virginia, was occupied by Federal troops the family of Dr. William Augustus Davis saved their silver and other valuables by burying them in the family manure pile. For generations thereafter eating with the family silverware always gave rise to momentary curiosity as to the sterility of the eating utensils.

Recognition Before Medals

During the fighting at Murfreesboro on December 31, 1862, the Confederates needed to determine whether a certain battery was Confederate or Federal. Sergeant Oakley of the 4th Tennessee carried the colors of his regiment two hundred yards in front of the line and waved it conspicuously, which action would surely draw the fire of enemies. After showing the colors and assuring the identity of the battery, Oakley returned to his lines. In June of the next year General Leonidas Polk arrived to inspect the 4th Tennessee. The general had learned of Oakley's action and called for the sergeant. After offering his ungloved hand to Oakley with the comment, "I must shake hands with you," Polk raised his hat and continued with great feeling, "I am proud to uncover in the presence of so great a man." The assembled troops gave a great shout of approval for the general and the sergeant.

Always Considerate

According to Colonel Walter H. Taylor, one of Robert E. Lee's staff became offended at a gentle rebuke by Lee for some error he had made and went off in dudgeon. Soon thereafter, General Lee sent an invitation to the officer in question to come and drink buttermilk with him—the strongest refreshment he ever took.

The officer went, but still remained in bad temper. Lee was as polite and considerate as possible and did not despair when the officer left his presence, sulking as before. Before long, as they were on the roadside in the rain, the officer dropped back and fell asleep. When he awoke, he found that about him was the poncho of the general—placed by the general so quietly and unostentatiously that none of the other members of the staff had observed the act.

Alrighty

"Pat," said the captain, "how would you like to be buried in a Protestant grave yard?" "Faith and I'd die first."

Notes on Hood's Texas Brigade

Lieutenant Mark A. Williams, Company C, 3rd Arkansas Infantry, was promoted to captain on December 1, 1862, eleven days after his death on November 20.

Company B, 1st Texas, originally had 102 members. At Appomattox, on April 12, 1865, there were no survivors.

Privates D. M. Walker and Rhodes B. Stephens of Company E, 1st Texas, were discharged just before Second Manassas, due to being under age. They chose to stay and go into battle with their comrades "one last time." Each was killed in the battle.

In the entire Texas Brigade, there was only one member who was not a volunteer. Private J. S. W. Cooke, Company B, 4th Texas, was conscripted June 6, 1862, at Culpeper Court House, Virginia.

Lieutenant J. M. Alexander, Company K, 5th Texas, was captured at Antietam in 1862, Gettysburg in 1863, and Darbytown Road in 1864. Each time he managed to rejoin his company.

The 602 survivors of the Texas Brigade surrendered only 348 rifles to the Federals at Appomattox. Many smashed their weapons against trees rather than surrender them.

Deaf and Dumb

Foraging for food, Ed McCain approached a farmhouse near Drury's Bluff in Virginia. He wrote on a piece of paper that he was a deaf mute and gave the note to the lady of the house. Sympathetic, the lady brought him food and offered him two dollars. Elated, McCain forgot himself and said, "Thank you." Realizing what he had done, he immediately ran from the house like a deer.

Fair Enough

General Roger A. Pryor was sitting in his saddle at Brandy Station when a shell exploded close to his men. After they dodged backward, Pryor was reprimanding them when another shell exploded close to him. Pryor dodged, prompting one of his men to remark, "General, I seen you dodge." Pryor responded, "All right, boys, all of you dodge, but for God's sake, don't run!"

Reciprocity in Action

Bill Arp was once asked if he had actually ever killed any Yankees. Arp said, "Well, I don't want to boast about myself, but I killed as many of them as they did of me."

Father John B. Bannon

Reverend John B. Bannon was one of the most prominent and respected chaplains to serve the South. Born and reared in Ireland, after his ordination he volunteered to follow many of his countrymen to America where they had fled famine. He became one of the leading clergymen in St. Louis, Missouri, and a leader of the Irish community.

The coming of war found the area deeply divided. Many German immigrants in the St. Louis area were hostile to Irish Catholics due to identifying Catholicism with the Austrian Empire, Germany's main enemy. Targeted for arrest by Federal authorities because of views he expressed from his pulpit, Father Bannon escaped and became chaplain of the 1st Missouri Confederate Brigade. The hostility of the Germans led many of the St. Louis Irish to follow Father Bannon into Confederate service. Although his main service was to Catholics, he was widely respected by soldiers of all faiths. Many chaplains prayed with their men before battle and then remained in the rear to comfort the wounded. Bannon believed a chaplain should share his men's hardships and dangers and quickly became known as "the Catholic priest who always went into battle."

When General Van Dorn ordered him off the battlefield at the battle of Elkhorn Tavern, he refused to leave, explaining he must stay to attend those who could not be removed from the field. General Sterling Price called him "the greatest soldier I ever saw."

Visiting Richmond, Father Bannon was surprised when President Jefferson Davis invited him to his home for a meeting. The growing strength of the Union army was being fueled by an influx of immigrants, many of them Irish. President Davis asked Bannon to undertake a secret mission to Ireland to discourage the Irish from enlisting in the Union army. He accepted and his campaign there was highly effective, resulting in a two-thirds drop in Union recruits. He never returned to America. He joined the Jesuit order and became one of its most distinguished Irish members. He was long thought to have died on July 14, 1913, but Anthony Jones of England recently discovered that he actually lived until 1919. Father Bannon is buried in the 2nd Jesuit plot in the Glasnevin cemetery in Dublin.

Unexpectedly Truthful

The hands of an old veteran were drawn out of shape by chronic rheumatism. When religious missionaries called on him and asked him to tell them what the Lord had done for him, he replied, "He has durn nigh ruint me."

A Good Idea

During the war a Yankee soldier called upon a widow living ten miles south of Petersburg. He asked her permission to bury a Yankee on her land. She was quite amenable to the suggestion, telling him, "Certainly sir, you are welcome to bury the whole Yankee army on my land."

Hilarious Reasoning

President Davis told the story of a Georgia soldier who was bucked and gagged for stealing chickens, but screamed with laughter when they removed his gag. Angered, the officer in charge had him tied up by the thumbs. He continued to laugh. Finally the officer asked him why he was laughing. Continuing to laugh, the man said it was because they were punishing the wrong man.

New Life Meant Death

Most of the Union soldiers killed or wounded during the Battle of Fredericksburg were Irish immigrants from the British penal colony of Tasmania in Australia. These men had been sent to Australia as convicted criminals. After serving sentences of up to ten years, they immigrated to America to start a new life and were drafted into the Union army.

What an Invitation

In the winter of 1861–62, D. H. Hill was in command of Confederate forces at Leesburg, Virginia. He learned that his former messmate and dear friend General Charles P. Stone commanded the Union troops across the Potomac at Poolsville. The hostile batteries kept up a constant fire upon each other. Since the useless losses decided nothing, Hill and Stone finally arranged a cease-fire. In the course of their official communications, Hill sent personal greetings to his old friend, adding, "I should be glad to have you and your staff come over and breakfast with me, but if you prefer, bring your whole army. In either case you will receive a warm welcome."

Death Not Acceptable

President Jefferson Davis commuted the sentence of every Confederate deserter condemned to death.

Reprieved

With a knee shattered by a ball during the action at the battle of the Wilderness on 6 May 1864, E. K. Goree, Company H, 5th Texas, was left for dead in the dense undergrowth. He lay in the rain all day and through the night before being picked up by a burial detail the following day. Finding him alive, the detail placed him behind a soldier on horseback to be taken to a field hospital. Goree was again left for dead when he fainted and fell from the horse. He lay on the wet ground for hours before being found again and taken to the hospital. Surviving the wound and two days in the rain, Goree lived another fifty years.

Bloodiest Battles of the War

Battle	Length in days	Casualties
Gettysburg	3	51,116
Sharpsburg	1	22,726
Seven Days	7	36,463

Not Peculiar to the South

Africans who were sold as slaves by European merchants were first enslaved by other Africans who had done so for the very purpose of selling them. For centuries African empires prospered based on the slave trade, and the slave was Africa's chief export. When Europe banned the slave trade, African economies were staggered. Slavery has never been stamped out in Africa, still existing in the Sudan and Mauritania. Compare the number of slaves imported to the United States, not just to the South, with those brought to other parts of the Americas:

4,000,000 taken to Brazil by the Portuguese
2,500,000 taken to Spanish possessions
2,000,000 taken to the British West Indies
1,600,000 taken to the French West Indies
500,000 taken to the U.S.

Why He Didn't "Take The Oath"

"I have not yet changed, nor do I expect to change, my mind as to the principles which prompted and the circumstances which actuated me to espouse the cause of my State in the War for Southern Independence."—Lieutenant Benjamin Hamilton Cathy, 39th North Carolina Infantry

Orders from Higher Authority

When Irish native Tim Casey enlisted as an infantryman in the Holcomb Legion, the enrolling officer asked him for his last residence. Casey thought a moment and said, "Faith sor, I dunno, but it'll be the cimitery, Oi'm thinking."

Casey later managed a transfer to the cavalry although he was not a horseman. Before he mounted his first horse, the drillmaster gave him instructions that he must not dismount without "orders from head-quarters." Unknown to Casey his mount was a wild mustang. When Casey mounted his horse and stuck the spurs to it, the horse immediately threw him. The drillmaster galloped back and asked Casey if he had orders from headquarters to dismount. Case ruefully responded that his orders had come from hindquarters.

Confederate Casualties

Confederate casualties of the war:

Killed in action	94,000
Died of Disease	64,000
Died as Prisoners of War	31,000
Wounded in Action	194,026
Total Casualties (1861–1865)	**483,026**

On the average each of the 600,000–1,000,000 men who served in the Confederate army fell victim to disease and wounds approximately six times during the war (3,600,000–6,000,000 cases).

Confederate regiments sustaining the greatest losses in one battle were:

Regiment	Killed	Wounded	Battle
26th North Carolina	86	588	Gettysburg
6th Alabama	91	277	Seven Pines
4th North Carolina	77	286	Seven Pines
44th Georgia	71	264	Mechanicsville

Lee's Foreign Legion

The 10th Louisiana Infantry was called "Lee's Foreign Legion" because soldiers from around the world fought in it.

Lawbreakers

Participants in the fighting at Culp's Hill during the battle at Gettysburg were breaking a local law. At the top of the hill was a sign forbidding the discharge of firearms.

Deadly

During the War Between the States, an area of barely twenty square miles in Virginia became America's bloodiest battleground. It included Fredericksburg, Chancellorsville, The Wilderness, Spotsylvania, and Cold Harbor. In this small area more than half a million men fought in deadly combat. Here, more men were killed and wounded than were killed and wounded in the Revolutionary War, the

War of 1812, the War with Mexico and all of the Indian wars combined. Nineteen generals, 10 Union and 9 Confederate, met death here.

A Historic Vessel

The USS *Cairo* (pronounced Kay-ro), became the first ship in history to be sunk by an electrically detonated torpedo. On December 12, 1862, the 175-foot ironclad Union gunboat struck a Confederate torpedo in the Yazoo River, just north of Vicksburg. All 160 men on board escaped because the *Cairo* took twelve minutes to sink. and sank close to the riverbank. A few years ago the *Cairo* was raised from its watery grave and is now on display in the Vicksburg National Military Park.

Relative Damage

When Colonel John Singleton Mosby and his men went ten miles behind Union lines and captured U.S. General Edwin Henry Stoughton, 2 captains, 30 enlisted men, and 59 Union horses at Fairfax Court House, Virginia, March 8, 1863, Abraham Lincoln evaluated his losses by commenting, "I can make brigadier generals, but I can't make horses."

All Indian Battle

Confederate Indians fought Union Indians in an 1863 battle at Chusto-Talasa "Caving Banks," Honey Springs, Oklahoma. The battle ended in a draw with five hundred dead.

Family Dedication

The men of the family of Texan James Selen Stout were nothing if not dedicated to the Confederacy. On October 12, 1861, Hopkins County farmer Stout and his two eldest sons, Frank and John, enlisted in Captain James Leftwich's infantry company. They considered younger brother Francis too young to go, so they left him at home. Francis promptly ran off and joined a different Texas regiment. Henry Stout, James' father, was born in 1799, but he enlisted also, and served as a second lieutenant in the 10th Texas Cavalry until discharged due to age. Fighting at Shiloh in 1862, James and John were wounded. James' wound was so severe that he was discharged. John's wound left him with a permanently dislocated right ankle but he returned to duty anyway.

A Head of His Time

Phrenology: The study of the skull based on a belief that it is indicative of character and mental capacity.

During a lecture in Memphis several years before the War Between the States, Dr, Orson G. Fowler, a noted New York phrenologist, asked for a volunteer to assist him. After examining the head of the local businessman who had stepped forward, the doctor announced his findings: "Here is a man who would have been a Caesar, a Hannibal or Napoleon if he had an opportunity. He has the qualities of a great military genius. If he could not go over the Alps, he would go through them." The subject of that examination was future Confederate General Nathan Bedford Forrest.

No Combat Loss

Noble Leslie Devotie was a founder of Sigma Alpha Epsilon fraternity. A perhaps lesser claim to fame was that he became the first man to die in the Civil War when he fell off a ship and drowned.

Sympathized

U.S. General Grenville Mellen Dodge, ultimately responsible for the hanging of Sam Davis as a Confederate spy, contributed $10 to the building of a monument to Davis in Nashville after the war.

Brothers

When Little Rock, Arkansas, was taken by Federal troops during the war, Union General Thomas H. Benton posted troops to protect Albert Pike's Masonic Library. Benton was Grand Master of the Masonic Lodge in Iowa.

Worst Prison Camp

Andersonville was not the worst prison camp of the Civil War in terms of percentages of death. That distinction belongs to the Union prison camp at Rock Island, Illinois, which had an estimated 72 percent death rate as compared to Andersonville's 27 percent.

A Lot in Common

The following were fought in Virginia on June 30, 1862: White Oak Swamp, Frayser's Farm, Glendale, Charles City Cross Roads, Nelson's Farm, Turkey Bend, New Market Cross Roads. The seven names all refer to the same battle.

A Clear Northern View

"If we of the North were called upon to endure one half as much as the Southern people and soldiers do, we would abandon the cause and let the Southern Confederacy be established. We pronounce their cause unholy, but they consider it sacred enough to suffer and die for. Our forefathers in the Revolutionary struggle could not have endured more than these Rebels. A nation preserved with liberty trampled underfoot is much worse than a nation in fragments but with the spirit of liberty still alive. Southerners persistently claim that their rebellion is for the purpose of preserving this form of government."—Private John H. Haley, 17th Maine Regiment, U.S.A.

What Battle Was That?

Federals named battles after nearby physical features. Confederates named them after nearby towns. *Chickamauga* is one of the few battles given the same name by both the North and the South. The town of Chickamauga and Chickamauga Creek are both near the site of the battle.

A Good Excuse

A Southern brigade commander planned to play a trick on General James Longstreet during an inspection. Knowing that Longstreet's horse was frightened by the sound of a bass drum, he ordered the regimental bass drum player to beat the drum when the general passed. When the appointed time came, he saw that the drummer did not have his drum. He called the drummer aside and asked where the drum was. The drummer whispered that he had stolen sixteen chickens the night before and hidden them in the drum and said that half the chickens were for the brigadier. The general loudly said, "All right, if you are sick, go back to your quarters. You shan't do duty for me when you are sick!"

Additional Stanza for "Dixie"

Because of fears that this stanza might offend the religious-minded, it was never used, though Daniel Emmett sometimes included it in souvenir copies:

> Dis worl' was made in jiss six days,
> An' finished up in various ways;
> Look away! Look away! Look away! Dixie Land!
> Dey den made Dixie trim and nice,
> But Adam called it "paradise,"
> Look away! Look away! Look away! Dixie Land!

Need a Necktie?

In the Old Capitol Museum in Jackson there is an authentic General William T. Sherman necktie. A Sherman necktie is a railroad rail heated over a fire and bent around a tree. This very successful method was used by Sherman to render the rail system in the South useless. The "necktie" in Jackson was found buried in a muddy bank of the Pearl River, just a few hundred yards from the museum. The same museum borders some of the tracks Sherman destroyed during his destructive sweep throughout the South.

A Matter of Size

At Fredericksburg, imminent death was everywhere. When some of the 12th Regiment of South Carolina Volunteers were disposed to duck out of the way of the minié balls flying thick and fast, Colonel Cadwalader Jones ordered the men to stand firm. Immediately thereafter a cannonball whistled close by the colonel. When he dodged, his men laughed. The colonel quickly amended his original order: "You may dodge the big ones."

A General Invitation
by Lieutenant Innes Randolph, CS Engineers
("The wit of the ANV")

Come! Leave the noisy LONGSTREET;
 Fly to the FIELDS with me;
 Trip o'er the HETH with flying feet,
 And skip along the LEE!
 There EWELL find the flowers that BEE
 Along the STONEWALL still;
 And RANSOM buds of flowery pea

 For OULD or YOUNG, no COOKE essays
 The very STEWART's turn;
 The BUTLER, these *al fresco* days
 Just lets the pipe CLEBURNE.
 Across the RHODES the FORREST boughs
 A gloomy ARCHWAY form,
 Where sadly pipes the EARLY bird
 That never caught the worm!

 Come ! Hasten, for the BEE is gone,
 The WHEAT lies on the plains –
 And braid a GARLAND ere the BRANCH
 FALLS IN THE BLASTING RAINS!
 Haste! Dazzling JOHNSTON beyond PRICE
 SHINES BRIGHTLY FROM THE SWARD;
 AND NONE WOULD RAISE HOOD in a trice
 To such a BEAUREGARD!

Protected

When the Battle of Malvern Hill began, a rabbit was in the field between the two armies. A shell burst near the rabbit and the frightened creature began trying to find safety. More shells, troops moving, horses galloping, all made the poor rabbit frantic. It ran into a field where a Confederate regiment lay flat on the ground to avoid flying bullets. It ran up to a soldier and tried to hide under his arms. The soldier, feeling how he himself needed protection, spread the skirt of his coat over the trembling animal. When the regiment was ordered forward, the rabbit tamely stayed close to the soldier and moved with him wherever he went during the rest of that bloody day. When night came and the battle was over, the rabbit finally hopped away, quietly and unmolested.

If You Want One That Bad...

During the fighting around Atlanta in July 1864, after General George Maney exhorted his men to charge and take a Union battery, General Patrick Cleburne and his men were standing next to Maney's troops. Cleburne felt he should encourage his men also, and told them, "You hear what General Maney says, boys. If they don't take it, by the eternal God, you have got to take it!" One of Cleburne's Irish veterans failed to see why all the fuss was raised over possession of one battery. He shouted back, "Faith, gin'ral, we'll take up a collection and buy you a battery, by jiminy!"

Related by Marriage

Sam and Keith Blalock joined the 26th North Carolina, claiming to be distantly related old friends. A few months later, "Sam" was discovered to be Keith's wife, Malinda, who had donned men's clothing and gone with him when he went to fight the Yankees.

Speaking from Experience

In late 1865, General Joseph Johnston was on a Chesapeake Bay steamer where a young man was insisting that the South had been conquered but not subdued. When Johnston asked the bellicose young man in whose or what command he had served in the war, he proved to be one of those "invisible in war, invincible in peace." He told Johnston that unfortunately circumstances had made it impossible for him to be in the Confederate army, prompting Johnston to tell him, "Well, sir, I was. You may not be subdued, but I am!"

A Unit to Be Proud Of

Tennessee furnished many military units to the Confederate army. However, Company G, 15th Tennessee Infantry, was not among them. The men of that unit were actually Southern sympathizers from Illinois.

Family Treasure

It was an extremely hot day in July 1862, when a group of Confederate officers stopped at a house near Richmond. None of the officers were dressed in a fine uniform. When the lady of the house was asked for a drink of water, she eyed the men and unenthusiastically agreed. She went into the house and brought out a stone pitcher of water with no dipper or cup to drink from. She handed it to the first man in line who, unknown to her, was Stonewall Jackson. Noting the deference of the other men, she asked one of them who was drinking from her pitcher. Learning it was Jackson, she gazed at him intently as if to engrave the scene in her memory. When Jackson finished drinking and handed back the pitcher, the lady emptied the contents onto the ground and took the pitcher into the house. She returned with another pitcher and gave it to the staff. Asked why she had taken the other pitcher away, she replied that after it had touched the lips of Jackson no one else would ever drink from it. It would be kept as a family memento of Stonewall's visit to her home.

A Patriotic Young Lady

On July 20, 1864, after a battle near Winchester, Virginia, defeated Confederates were forced to make a rapid retreat and leave their dead and wounded. That evening Tessie Russell and other young ladies of the town came to the battlefield to aid and comfort the wounded. Tessie came upon a young Confederate suffering great agony. She raised his head to give him some ease. He gave a sigh of relief and sank his head back into her arms. His moans gave way to regular breathing as he fell asleep. Time passed and Tessie found herself and the young man alone on that part of the battlefield. Her position was cramped and painful, causing her to try to get comfortable. Each time she did so the soldier moaned and awoke. A passing Federal surgeon came by, looked at the soldier, and told Miss Russell that if he could sleep until morning he might live. On the other hand his fever was at the point that if he woke he might die. Disregarding her own suffering, she resolved to remain still and support his head until his life was assured. After a night of agony for her, the young man awoke and smiled at her. She had saved his life. Made seriously ill by that night, Miss Russell could not raise her hand for several days.

As Abraham Lincoln Saw Things

In a letter to Salmon P. Chase: "The [Emancipation] proclamation has no constitutional or legal justification except as a war measure."

Justifying his suspension of the habeas corpus Lincoln wrote: "The suspension of the habeas corpus was for the purpose that men may be arrested and held in prison who cannot be proved guilty of any defined crime." Commenting further he wrote to an Albany committee of Democrats, "Arrests are not made so much for what has been done as for what might be done."

A Grievous Loss to the South

The U.S. paid for its own arms and equipment as well as those of Southern troops who were often outfitted with arms and equipment seized from the Union army. After Union General Pope and his invading army were sent flying after Second Manassas, Lincoln replaced Pope with McClellan. That prompted this exchange: "Have you heard the news? Lee has resigned!" " Good G——! What for?" "He has resigned because he says he cannot feed and supply his army any longer, now that his commissary, General Pope, has been removed."

Horse Thief Achieved High Office

In his memoirs General U. S. Grant admitted that while near Vicksburg he stole a small horse from Jefferson Davis' Brierfield Plantation. He named the horse "Jeff Davis."

What a March!

In his Shenandoah Valley campaign of 1862, Stonewall Jackson marched his 16,000 men more than six hundred miles in thirty-five days. In that time they fought five major battles and defeated four separate Union armies totaling 63,000 men.

Closely Connected

In the WBTS generals often knew their opposition personally. Before the war, the U.S. Army officer corps was small, with most being West Point graduates. Robert E. Lee was a superintendent of West Point and of his last class (1856) 14 served in the Confederate army and 23 served in the Union. At First Manassas, Confederate P. G. T. Beauregard faced Irwin McDowell, an 1838 classmate. Confederate A. P. Hill and Federal George McClellan were rivals for the same girl. McClellan was an 1846 classmate of Stonewall Jackson.

In addition to West Point there were Mexican War connections. Beauregard and McClellan were both on the staff of Winfield Scott. John Pemberton, later U. S. Grant's foe at Vicksburg, thanked Grant for his role in capturing Mexico City. James Longstreet and Winfield Scott Hancock fought together at Churubusco, against each other at Gettysburg. George H. Thomas and Braxton Bragg were fellow artillery officers at Buena Vista. Albert Sidney Johnston and Joseph Hooker served together at Monterey, as did Joseph E. Johnston and George Meade at Vera Cruz. When Jeb Stuart and his cavalry rode completely around the Union army during the Seven Days, Stuart's father-in-law, Philip St. George Cooke, commanded the cavalry pursuing him.

Solved His Problem

Sergeant William Campbell, 11th Mississippi Cavalry, captured and a prisoner in Nashville, had lost all of his clothing except his undergarments and was sorely troubled with concern that he would be shipped north in that sad state. A young Nashville lady visiting the prison learned of his need and left, but soon returned. After having the prisoners turn their backs, she took off a pair of pants she had smuggled in under her petticoat. She handed the pants to a prisoner to give to the sergeant, telling him to wear them as she did to get them into the prison. The sergeant never forgot her kindness.

Young But Patriotic

At 11, George S. Lamkin, of Winona, Mississippi, joined Stanford's Mississippi Battery. He was severely wounded at Shiloh before he was 12.

E. G. Baxter, of Clark County, Kentucky, was 12 when he enlisted in Company A, 7th Kentucky Cavalry. (A year later he was a second lieutenant.) Also 12 was John Bailey Tyler, of Frederick, Maryland, when he joined D Troop, 1st Maryland Cavalry.

At 13, M. W. Jewett, of Ivanhoe, Virginia, was a private in the 59th Virginia. He served at Charleston, South Carolina, in Florida, and in the siege of Petersburg.

At 14, John T. Mason, of Fairfax County, Virginia, served with the 17th Virginia at First Manassas, before training as a Confederate navy midshipman and serving on the cruiser *Shenandoah*. Matthew J. McDonald was also 14 when he joined Company I, 1st Georgia Cavalry. W. D. Peak, of Oliver Springs, Tennessee, was also 14 when he joined Company A, 26th Tennessee.

At 16, Billings Steele, a grandson of Francis Scott Key, left his home near Annapolis, Maryland, crossed the Potomac, and joined Colonel John Mosby's rangers.

Couldn't Doubt His Generals

A deputation from New England was leaving the office of Abraham Lincoln after a meeting. One of the delegates turned and asked Lincoln the size of the Confederate army. Without hesitation Lincoln replied, "Sir, I have the very best possible reason for knowing the number to be one million of men, for whenever one of our generals engages a rebel army he reports that he has encountered a force twice his strength; now I know we have half a million of soldiers in the field, so I am bound to believe the rebels have twice that number."

That's Walking Fast

Harvey R. Bishop was a young private in Company F of the 29th Virginia Infantry. He was a survivor of the famed Pickett's Charge at Gettysburg where so many men lost their lives. Years later he told his son that he never heard a sweeter sound than the bugle calling retreat. When his son asked him if he had run when the bugle sounded, he said no, but he had passed a whole bunch of guys who *were* running!

Confederate Amazons

LaGrange, Georgia, was so patriotic that every man enlisted in the Confederate army. To protect LaGrange, a women's home guard was formed and named for Nancy Hart, a Revolutionary heroine. When Wilson's Raiders were about to invade the defenseless city, the Nancy Harts marched out to do battle. This so impressed the Union colonel (coincidentally named LaGrange) that he marched on without burning the city.

Slain for Defending His Rights

On May 23, 1861, Virginia seceded from the U.S. Early the next morning Federal troops occupied Alexandria. Colonel Elmer Ellsworth, an arrogant officer of the New York Fire Zouaves, spied a Confederate flag erected over the Marshall House. The proprietor of the hotel, James W. Jackson, had hoisted the flag to symbolize his advocacy of the Southern right to secede from the Union. When Ellsworth took the flag as a trophy, Jackson shot and killed him. A Zouave, Corporal Francis Brownell, then shot and bayoneted Jackson. Today a small bronze plaque on the red brick exterior of the Holiday Inn in Alexandria's Old Town district tells the story. "The Marshall House stood upon this site and within the building on the early morning of May 24, 1861, James W. Jackson was killed by Federal soldiers while defending his property and personal rights."

Captivating

General J. E. B. Stuart was riding with his men in western Virginia and found he had outdistanced them and was by himself. Just as he realized that, he came upon a company of Pennsylvanians. Thinking fast, Stuart mustered as authoritative a tone as he could and ordered the men to tear down the fence. Accustomed to obeying orders, the troops did not question his command and began to tear down the fence. Emboldened by his success, Stuart then roared, "Throw down your arms or you are all dead men!" Even though they outnumbered him 49 to one, they obeyed and discarded their arms. When Stuart's men caught up with him, he was sitting there with his prisoners, almost an entire company.

No Pirates

When the Southern privateer *Savannah* was captured near Charleston by the USS *Perry* on June 3, 1861, the members of the crew were taken in irons to the "Tombs" prison in New York. On October 23, 1861, they went on trial for piracy and faced death sentences if convicted. However, the jurors could not be convinced by the prosecution that sailors should be charged with piracy but soldiers should become prisoners of war. A hung jury led to the Southern sailors being held until exchanged for captured Union officers.

Why Butler Was Called "Spoons"

General Benjamin Franklin "Beast" Butler was placed in command of occupied New Orleans and held that position for eight months. When he left he had a net worth $3,000,000 greater than when he arrived. In the Confederate Memorial Hall Museum in New Orleans is a letter Butler's successor, General Nathaniel Banks, wrote to his wife summing up Butler's actions:

"I never despaired of our country until I came here. Our affairs have been terribly managed here. The strongest government in the world could not bear up under such responsibility and wrong. Everybody connected with the government has been employed in stealing other people's property. Sugar, silver-plate, horses, carriages, everything they could lay hands on. There has been open trade with the enemy. No attention has been given to Military affairs...This State could have been made and ought to now be strongly for the Union and against the Confederate States. Instead of that, they have been robbed of their silver forks and spoons, jewelry, ornaments, plate, pictures, books, carriages, horses, houses, plantations and Negroes, not for the benefit of the Government but for individual plunders. They see women of the town sleeping in their beds and houses, and they are terribly bitter against the Government, that permits such things."

At Home in the Field

Noting the Spartan tastes of General Robert E. Lee, Richard Taylor commented, "General Lee was never so uncomfortable as when he was comfortable."

Not Without Purpose

To his staff, Major General D. H. Hill appeared bent on throwing away his life during one of the battles of the Seven Days near Richmond. With a cigar jutting defiantly between his clenched teeth, he rode the length of his infantry line, completely exposed to the fire of his army. When he returned unscathed, they pleaded with him not to take such chances. He snapped back, "I did it for a purpose. I saw that our men were wavering and I wanted to give them confidence."

Faithful to the End

Thad W. Bullock, first corporal of Company K, 1st Texas, reverted to the rank of private in order to accompany the body of a friend to San Augustine, Texas. Although he returned to his company he never regained his corporal's stripes.

Defiant

Hood's Texas Brigade numbered 602 at Appomattox but turned in only 348 rifles. Many of the men smashed their guns against trees rather than surrender them.

Couldn't Be Soft

Toughness sometimes had to be demonstrated to the untrained officers, as well as to the men in the ranks. Eppa Hunton, a Virginia lawyer-turned-soldier, never forgot General Nathan "Shanks" Evans' response to his appeal for reinforcements at the battle of Ball's Bluff: "Tell Hunton to hold the ground until every damn man falls."

Do What Makes Sense

William "Extra Billy" Smith was a political general and a former governor of Virginia who delighted in ridiculing the regulars, "West P'inters," as he called them. At Seven Pines, his command had been instructed to hold its fire as it advanced. When it came under withering fire from concealed sharpshooters, his Virginians appealed to him for permission to open fire. Smith needed no urging, and burst out, "Of course you can't stand it, boys. It's all this infernal tactics and West Point tomfoolery. Damn it, fire. and flush the game!"

General Forrest and His Slaves

Forty-five of Nathan Bedford Forrest's own slaves served through the war with him. Forrest told a Congressional committee after the war, "I said to forty-five colored fellows on my plantation that I was going into the army; and that if they would go with me, if we got whipped they would be free anyhow, and that if we succeeded and slavery was perpetuated, if they would act faithfully with me to the end of the war, I would set them free. Eighteen months before the war closed I was satisfied that we were going to be defeated, and I gave those forty-five men, or forty-four of them, their free papers, for fear I might get killed."

Memo to Je$$e and Company

"Think about it: We went into slavery pagans; we came out Christians. We went into slavery pieces of property; we came out American Citizens. We went into slavery with chains clanking about our wrists; we came out with American ballots in our hands...When we rid ourselves of prejudice, or racial feeling, and look the facts in the face, we must acknowledge, notwithstanding the cruelty and moral wrong of slavery, we are in a stronger and more hopeful position, materially, intellectually, morally, and religiously, than is true of an equal number of black people in any other portion of the globe." —Booker T. Washington, who, in fact, had been a slave

Not A Master of Persuasion

When Major Frank Paxton was nominated by Stonewall Jackson to become brigadier general in command of the Stonewall Brigade, Colonel Andrew Jackson Grigsby, temporary commander of the brigade, was outraged that he had not been chosen. He rode swiftly to Richmond to plead his case with President Jefferson Davis. The discussion quickly became heated. Offended by Grigsby, President Davis finally said, "Do you know who I am? I am the President of the Confederacy." Grigsby rose and raged, "Do you know who I am? I am Andrew Jackson Grigsby of Rockbridge County, Virginia, late colonel of the Bloody 27th Virginia of the Stonewall Brigade, and as good a man as you or anyone else, by God!" For some reason this didn't win over the president and the colonel was soon out of the army.

Non-Uniform

Firing on friendly troops occurred frequently at First Manassas. Not only did the Confederate flag in use at the battle resemble the U.S. flag, but some Confederate troops wore blue, while some Union wore gray. Highland kilts were worn by a New York City regiment. Both sides had Zouave units wearing the fez and baggy trousers of French colonial troops.

Imagine That

Enthusiastic cavalryman: "Now, if you can just imagine me mounted…"

Unimpressed infantryman: "Nah, I'm having enough problems thinking of you on horseback."

Needed a Good Model

John Bell Hood was a man of imposing presence, as rugged as any of the fierce fighters serving under him. At Gaines Mill, a young Texan was nervous and shaky as he prepared to go into battle for the first time. Looking behind him he saw Hood looking as unconcerned as if he were on dress parade, resting on one foot with one hand raised above his head to grasp the limb of a tree. The young man decided that if the towering general could stand it so could he. He entered battle with his fears resolved.

As Useful As (Use Your Own Simile)

One of the U.S. Navy crewmen on the USS *Monitor* when it moved into action against the CSS *Virginia* was a sail maker.

An Apt Identification

W. M. Vaught of Cushing, Texas, served with the 8th Texas Infantry, a unit under General John Walker's command. After marching with his unit in its many transfers around the Trans-Mississippi, Vaught thought the name Walker's Division was particularly fitting.

Charlie

Charlie served with the Troup Artillery, a Georgia battery in the Army of Northern Virginia. His enthusiasm was apparent and he was popular with everyone in the battery. He even received a snappy salute from Robert E. Lee when the general noted Charlie sitting prominently on the box of an artillery limber as the guns rolled by during an 1863 review. Charlie was killed by an artillery shell near Petersburg a short time before the end of the war and the entire battery turned out for his burial. It was said there was not a dry eye among the soldiers as they laid their canine friend to rest.

No Breaking Parole

A group of young ladies were visiting a plantation near Baton Rouge when the crew of the Confederate gunboat *Arkansas* appeared. The girls told the crewmen that they could not invite them to enter because the plantation owner was on parole by the Federal authorities. However, the owner's daughter told them, if they should choose to order entrance, "women could not resist armed men." They did choose to order and the men and women were soon paired up for a party lasting until the following day. When the sailors left they were given bottles of gin as going-away gifts.

What's That Again?

In some ways ill-prepared for his teaching responsibilities at VMI, Major Stonewall Jackson stayed ahead of his students only by reading and memorizing the textbooks used in the course. His lectures were essentially quotes from the books. He was precise to a fault in small details. He once asked a cadet, "What are the three simple machines?" When the cadet proudly replied, "The inclined plane, the level, and the wheel," Jackson snapped, "No sir, the level, the wheel, and the inclined plane." That was the order they were listed in the textbook and therefore the way they were to be identified.

Jackson a Man of Principle

Stonewall Jackson was beside Richard Taylor as the Louisiana Brigade advanced under heavy artillery fire near Winchester. When some of the troops ducked, Taylor rasped at them, "What the hell are you dodging for?" Jackson stared reproachfully at Taylor, saying there was no excuse for such language, especially on Sunday. He placed his hand on Taylor's shoulder and commented, "I am afraid you are a wicked fellow."

A Testimonial

Camp Morton, in Indianapolis, Indiana, was a Federal prison for captured Confederates. On the site of that prison is a mass grave holding the remains of about 1,200 Confederates. Of that number, 26 were Black, 7 were Hispanic, 7 were Native Americans, and at least one was Jewish. To walk away from that prison as a free man, any of those 26 Black Southerners needed only to raise his hand in an oath to the Union. They chose to stay, even though death was their reward.

The Best Policy

A spirited young Virginian, Miss N——, needed a pass to visit her brother, a Confederate soldier held prisoner by the Yanks. A friend, Francis P. Blair, agreed to get her an audience with Abraham Lincoln to ask for it and warned the rather impulsive girl to be prudent and not express her strong Southern sympathies. Ushered into Lincoln's presence, the two stated the object of their visit. Lincoln leaned forward to look into her face and asked, "You are loyal, of course?" With her eyes flashing she responded with emotion and honesty, "Yes, loyal to the heart's core—to Virginia!" Lincoln gazed at her intently, then wrote briefly on a paper and handed it to her, terminating the visit. Outside, Blair reproached her, saying he had warned her. Miss N—— made no reply but opened the paper. On it was written, "Pass Miss N——; she is an honest girl and can be trusted."

Triskaidekaphobia

Before the WBTS the U.S. Congress considered an amendment to the Constitution to preserve slavery in the South. It would have been the 13th. After the war a 13th amendment was actually enacted. It abolished slavery.

Did He Qualify?

Invited to the home of a lady he had never met, John C. Breckinridge was surprised to receive a request for references when he arrived early and in civilian clothes. He replied, "Former Vice President of the United States, former United States Senator, and Major General, Provisional Army of the Confederate States of America." Embarrassed, his hostess explained that she thought he was an applicant for a job as a footman.

Pretty Good Pay for the Time

The only Confederate troops who received "mustering out" pay were some five hundred troops in San Antonio. Learning the war was over, they confiscated $80,000 in Confederate government silver and divided it among themselves, netting each about $160.

Final General Losses

The last Confederate general to die in the war was Brigadier General James Dearing. He was wounded on April 6, 1865, during the retreat to Appomattox, in an exchange of pistol fire with a Union officer. Dearing died seventeen days later.

The last Union general to be killed in the war was Brigadier General Thomas A. Smyth. He was wounded April 7, 1865, during the Appomattox campaign and died two days later.

Random Bursts

For every three horses required by the cavalry, artillery, or supply columns, an additional two horses were required to transport fodder.

There were 37 different nationalities in the ranks of one Louisiana regiment.

Soldiers on both sides soon learned that the barrel of a musket could hold nearly a pint of whiskey.

During the siege of Vicksburg in 1863, there were 39 Missouri regiments: 22 in blue, 17 in gray.

Reflecting the heavy losses throughout the Confederate Army of Tennessee, at the end of 1864 the 3rd and 18th Tennessee regiments had a total strength of twelve men.

Although "The Confederate States of America" appeared on currency, laws, and military regulations, that term was never officially adopted by the Southern states.

Confederate General Nathan B. Forrest had 29 horses shot out from under him in battle.

Robert E. Lee's hair was black at the start of the war, completely white at the end.

Confederate Brigadier General William R. Cox was wounded eleven times between April of 1861 and Appomattox, or approximately once every four months.

Sea Duty

The Union navy burned or destroyed 355 vessels, worth about $7,000,000. In addition, nearly 1,150 ships were captured and sent to Admiralty courts during the war. These had a total value of approximately $25,000,000, which was divided among the officers and men of the capturing vessels. Such action prompted a young U.S. sailor to drop to his knees as his ship prepared to go into action. When an officer asked a young sailor why he was kneeling, the lad responded that he was praying that the enemy's bullets would be distributed the same way as prize money, principally among the officers.

A Confederate Spy

Thomas Nelson Conrad was a Georgetown headmaster until he was deported after Federals discovered his students raising and lowering window shades to transmit messages. Disguised, he slipped back into Washington and took up quarters near the War Department. He searched out War Department clerks sympathetic to the South and arranged for them to leave documents on their desks when they went to lunch. Conrad then slipped into the building, read the material, and forwarded the information to Richmond.

Major C. Roberdeau Wheat

The hard-drinking founder of Wheat's Tiger Zouaves (the 1st Louisiana Special Battalion) was a match for his rowdy men. He had used his wealth to live the life of a soldier of fortune. In law school when the Mexican War broke out, he left school to serve in the U.S. Army. He later fought with several filibustering expeditions, became an officer in the Mexican army, and was warring in Italy when he returned to Louisiana to fight for the Confederacy. Shortly before being killed at Gaines' Mill, Wheat reportedly had a drink with a fellow officer and told the other man, "Something tells old Bob this is the last drink he'll ever take in this world."

The Gray Ghost

Lawyer-turned-warrior John Singleton Mosby was the officer most praised in Robert E. Lee's wartime papers. Mosby had been a student when his hair-trigger temper led to his shooting a man who threatened him. While in prison for that, he had decided to become an attorney and did so after his release. A Unionist until Virginia's secession, he enlisted as a private in the 1st Virginia Cavalry and became a scout for Jeb Stuart. Mosby began his career as a partisan in January 1863. For the rest of the war, he and his rangers made life miserable for the Northern invaders. Their exploits were so legendary as to lead to a section of northern Virginia becoming known as Mosby's Confederacy. Northern efforts to eliminate Mosby's forces were fruitless, and Mosby ended the war a full colonel in charge of eight hundred men. Rather than surrender his command, he disbanded it. In a somewhat odd development, Mosby later became friends with U. S. Grant, who had once ordered his troops to hang Mosby without a trial. It has been estimated that Mosby's efforts prolonged the life of the Confederacy by as much as six months.

Rapid Promotions

Edmund Kirby made the fastest rise in rank in the Union army. As he lay dying in 1863 from wounds received at Chancellorsville, Abraham Lincoln promoted him from first lieutenant to brigadier general. The fastest rise in the Confederate army was that of Victor J. B. Girardey, promoted by Robert E. Lee from captain to brigadier general in 1864 in recognition of his service during the battle of the Crater. General Girardey died in battle about six weeks later.

Honest Appraisals
(Opinions of U.S. Army officers)

A Lieutenant General on Brigadier General Napoleon Bonaparte Buford: "He could scarcely make a respectable hospital nurse if put in petticoats, and certainly is unfit for any other military position. He has always been a deadweight to carry, becoming more burthensome with his increased rank."

Lieutenant General Winfield Scott on Secretary of War Simon Cameron: "There goes a bad man."

Major General George B. McClellan on Henry Halleck: "...very dull and very incompetent."

Major General John Pope on Major General Franz Sigel: "...the God damndest coward I ever knew."

Brigadier General Luigi di Cesnola on Colonel James H. Van Alen of the 3rd New York Cavalry: "radically incapable of commanding his regiment, much less leading it into battle."

Sharing the Rewards

Urging his troops to do their best in the battle then opening, a Confederate chaplain told them, "Remember, boys, that he who is killed will sup tonight in paradise." One of his flock called back, "Come along and take supper with us."

Gotta Watch Those People

In late 1861, a coach proceeding through an army camp near Washington, D.C., appeared suspicious to pickets of the 3rd New York Artillery. They took the coach's three occupants into custody. The men were not prisoners long. One was the president of the United States, one was the secretary of state, and the third was the commander of the Army of the Potomac.

Needed an Untainted Name

Patriotic Irishmen of Charleston, South Carolina, volunteered for the *Meargh Guards*, named for an Irish national hero, Thomas F. Meargh. Shortly after the fall of Fort Sumter, when the troops learned that Meargh had raised a company for the Federal 69th New York, the unit became the *Emerald Light Infantry*.

Worked on Commission

Two of Robert E. Lee's sons, George Washington Lee and William Henry Fitzhugh Lee, were major generals. His youngest son, Robert E. Lee, Jr., enlisted as a private and worked his way to a captaincy. Lee's brother, Sidney Smith Lee, was a captain in the Confederate navy. Lee's nephew, Fitzhugh Lee, was a lieutenant general. A cousin, James Terrill, was a brigadier general. All Confederate, of course.

Called to Serve

Even older men felt the need to help defend their country. George Taylor at the age of sixty was a private in the 60th Virginia Infantry. Nicknamed "father of the regiment," Taylor was recognized for his gallantry at the battle of Frayser's Farm.

Mournful Occasions

Captain Alexander Todd was a half-brother of Mary Todd Lincoln, Abraham Lincoln's wife. Captain Todd served on the staff of his brother-in-law, Confederate General Benjamin Helm, who was married to Mrs. Lincoln's younger sister, Emilie. Captain Todd shared the unfortunate fate of Stonewall Jackson. He was killed by "friendly fire" near Baton Rouge when Southern infantry fired on returning Confederate cavalry. Mary Lincoln did not grieve for her sibling, saying she saw no reason to mourn one of the Rebels who would hang her husband if possible. Benjamin Helm's death was a different story. The Lincolns had doted on Emilie, looking on her almost as a daughter, and Helm had been a prewar favorite of Lincoln. When Helm died in battle at Chickamauga in 1863, the Lincolns took Emilie into the White House and observed a mourning period by flying the U.S. flag at half-mast, to say the least, unusual for the death of a Confederate officer.

Equally Tactful

Robert E. Lee found his views obscured by Brigadier General Archibald Gracie, Jr., who seemed always in front of him as the two inspected the lines around Petersburg. Tactfully, Lee remarked, "General, you should not expose yourself so much." Gracie, who had been trying to shield Lee, replied, "If I should not, General Lee, why should you?" Lee smiled and moved to a safer location.

Making the Best of a War

After the Confederate victory at Palmetto Ranch on May 12, 1865, Confederate General James E. Slaughter took his forces across the Rio Grande River into Mexico. There he sold his artillery to the Imperial Mexican Major General Tomas Meija for $20,000 in gold. Slaughter lived several years thereafter in Mexico.

Battle of the Crater

From the memoirs of William Henry von Eberstein, Sergeant Major, 61st North Carolina Infantry:

"The Yankees had mined under one of the forts around Petersburg. On the 30th of July [1864], they sprung their mine and blew up our fort. We lost several men and guns by this blow up. After a short while the Yankees made a heavy charge against the break they had made. They charged with their Negroes in front and the white Yankees behind them with their bayonets fixed. It was certain death for a Negro not to advance upon the charge. Our regiment, the 61st under the command of Major Henry Harding, was sent to assist in repelling the charge. When the Yankees attacked and our men found the attackers were Negroes, the cry of 'No Quarter' was given. Men clubbed with their rifles, others drove their bayonets through them. It was a fierce hand to hand fight. The poor Negroes would cry for quarter but no quarter was received. The whole were killed. It was a heavy slaughter. Some two thousand were killed or more. The Yankees themselves reported that owing to delay, the slaughter of their troops had been heavy. They lost their men and did not accomplish what they had expected to have done."

Battlefield Ethics
(or the lack thereof)

The last Jewish Confederate officer to fall in battle was Lieutenant Joshua L. Moses of the Washington Artillery. United States Colored Troops shot him *after* he surrendered at Fort Blakely, Alabama, on April 9, 1865. His last words were "For God's sake, spare my men! They have surrendered!"

A Vital Difference

When the U.S. Navy forces ravaging the land along the Mississippi were characterized as looters, Union Rear Admiral David Dixon Porter defended them by stating, "Armies loot; navies take prizes."

"Jones" Would Have Done Better

Colonel Wladimir Krzyzanowski had an outstanding military record in the Union army but never received a promotion to brigadier general. Purportedly, the reason was that the U.S. senators who would have to confirm his promotion couldn't pronounce his name.

Needed a Better Deal

Meeting a Billy Yank in the Rappahannock to trade tobacco for coffee, a Johnny Reb asked if there was anything else Billy might like to trade. "Well," said Billy, "do you happen to have a lame old horse?" "What in the world would you want with a lame old horse?" "Would you take General Burnside?" asked Billy. "Nope, think I'll keep my lame old horse!"

Northern Supplies Welcomed

Late in August 1862, Stonewall Jackson seized the Federal supply depot at Manassas Junction. His men were soon feasting on delicacies such as ham, lobster, cakes, fruits, etc. Fine cigars circulated freely. Salt, clothing, and wagons were also secured. Jackson wanted his troops to stay ready for battle and tried to ensure they would not partake of the abundant quantities of whiskey and brandy found in the supplies. Stating that he feared the liquor more than Union General Pope's whole army, Jackson ordered some of his most trusted officers to spill the liquor on the ground. Try as they may, those hard-working officers were unable to prevent all of the fast-thinking troops from filling their canteens with the sought after liquids. (Some walked away with canteens filled half with brandy and half with strawberry syrup.) With stomachs and thirsts sated and military accoutrements refitted, the Confederates destroyed what they could not cart away. When resultant fires reached the ammunition trains, it was reported that the explosions rivaled the loudest of battles.

Last General

In 1862 William Flank Perry resigned as president of East Alabama Female College to enlist as a private in the 44th Alabama. A few weeks later he was elected its major. After Sharpsburg, Perry became colonel of the regiment. He led that regiment until Cold Harbor, after which he led Law's Brigade until Appomattox. After being repeatedly recommended for promotion by his superiors, Perry was commissioned a brigadier general to rank from 21 February 1865. He was the last general officer commissioned in the Confederate States Army.

Put That on the Menu

Complaints about hospital food are nothing new. In 1862 an army nurse described her charges' food in unglowing terms: beef that seemed to have been preserved for use in the Revolution, pork that looked like it had just come in from the street, army bread made of sawdust, butter with salt churned by Lot's wife in biblical times, blackberries stewed to look like preserved cockroaches, mild and muddy coffee, tea that seemed to be made from three huckleberry leaves boiled in a quart of water.

With No Writ of Habeas Corpus

In the words of Abraham Lincoln, "The suspension of the habeas corpus was for the purpose that men may be arrested and held in prison who cannot be proved guilty of any defined crime."

In a meeting between U.S. Secretary of State William Seward and British Minister to the U.S. Lord Lyons, Secretary Seward said to Lord Lyons: "My Lord, I can touch a bell at my right and order the arrest of a man in Ohio; I can again touch the bell and order the arrest of a man in New York, and no power on earth save that of the President can release them. Can the Queen of England do as much?"

"No," replied the astonished Englishman. "Were she to attempt such an act her head would roll from her shoulders."

A Little Help, Please!

At the beginning of the war, soldiers were required to use stamps to post their letters, just as everyone else. One soldier resorted to poetry on the exterior of his envelope to invoke the post office's grace:

Soldier's letter, nary red
Hardtack and no soft bread
Postmaster, please put it through,
I've nary a cent, but six months due.

A Common History

Albert Sidney Johnston, George B. Crittenden, Thomas Green, Joseph L. Hogg, Ben McCulloch, and Jerome Bonaparte Robinson were all Confederate generals who had another military connection. All had served in the Army of the Republic of Texas.

Buddy, Have Another Drink!

In many regiments possession of alcohol was officially banned to the enlisted men. With the great ingenuity of men under pressure, troops denied the right to buy hooch created their own by fermenting whatever they could obtain, usually fruits and/or grains, occasionally adding meat for flavoring. Some of the names given the resulting liquors indicate their flavors and effects: "pop-skull," "bust head," "old red eye," "rifle knock knee," "oh, be joyful." Knowing his canteen's contents might be checked, one man carried his hoard of alcohol in the barrel of his rifle. Sometimes the imbibing of homemade liquor was purposeful—to avoid the contaminated water that was often the only water available. In these cases the liquor probably saved some lives because the high alcohol content killed the germs in the local waters used in the fermentation.

Enlisted Commanders

George W. Kipps, 1st Sergeant of Company K, 4th Texas, commanded his company at the Wilderness on May 6, 1864, as no officers were present for duty. At Malvern Hill on July 1, 1862, Companies I and K of the 1st Texas were both commanded by privates due to heavy casualties a few days earlier on June 27, at Gaines' Mill.

A Strong Belief

Stonewall Jackson was so strong in his regard of the sacredness of Sunday as a holy day that he would not send a message if it would be carried on its way on Sunday. He is said to have refused a batch of gunpowder because it had been procured on Sunday.

Not As Popularly Portrayed

In his initial *Life of Lincoln*, William Henry Herndon, intimate friend and junior law partner of Abraham Lincoln, described a man far different from the man portrayed in his book after the negative views had been deleted. Of Lincoln's piety, Herndon stated, "Lincoln was a deep-grounded infidel. He disliked and despised churches. He never entered a church except to scoff and ridicule. Before running for an office he wrote a book against Christianity and the Bible. His friend Hill burned the book."

The War Afloat

For his Tennessee River advance on Shiloh, U. S. Grant assembled what may have been the most immense fleet in history. There were 14 armored riverboats and 153 other vessels. The USS *Tiger* and USS *Lexington* were the first gunboats ever to appear on the Tennessee River.

Did Pretty Well for a Neophyte

After resigning from the U.S. Army, Robert E. Lee was appointed to head the military forces of Virginia. Up to that point, Lee's experience in field command was extremely limited. Once in 1856 for four weeks he had led a scouting expedition with four squadrons of horse soldiers. He had no battlefield experience in command of troops.

Recognized

Continuing rains and the passage of artillery units and wagon trains had turned the Virginia road west of New Kent Court House into a three-foot deep mud pond. Texas infantry units were floundering along, slowly making their way toward Richmond. General William H. C. Whiting exhorted the men to move on, finally losing his patience. He rode up to where they were struggling through the mire and yelled, "Hurry up, men, hurry up! Don't mind a little mud!" One man responded, "Do ye call this a *little mud*? Suppose you git down here and try it, stranger; I'll hold your horse." "Do you know whom you address, sir? I am General Whiting." "General, don't you reckon I know a *general* from a long-tongued courier?" said the fellow, disappearing into the darkness. After such an exchange took place several times, the general gave up on the Texans and rode away.

Understatement

Brigadier General Martin Edward Green was noted for his coolness under fire. In battle near Corinth, a bullet hit his horse in the neck. When he stopped to stem the blood, the horse was hit by another bullet. While the general cared for his horse, a bullet hit the horse in the head, killing it. The bullets continued to fly, clipping twigs and branches and even scraping the general's skin. He turned and quietly commented, "I believe those damned scoundrels are trying to kill me!"

Messed with the Wrong Man

In a raid along the Mississippi River, the men of a Union boat carried off the ten-year-old son of a slave named Jenkins. Jenkins had already resisted all appeals for him to desert his master. Enraged by the kidnapping, Jenkins boarded the boat with knife in hand and declared in fierce tones, "Give me back my boy or I will make the decks of this boat slippery with your blood. You are nothing but a set of vile robbers and plunderers, and I will spill the last drop of my blood but I will have my child. Give him to me or I will plunge my knife into the heart of the first man I reach." The soldiers recognized the danger they were in and released the boy before some of them were killed. Jenkins took the boy and returned to his contented home.

Neither Lady a Fan of Bragg

Conversing about the battle of Chickamauga, one elderly lady commented that since General Bragg was a Christian, she wished he were dead and in heaven, adding that it would be a god-send for the Confederacy. The other replied, "Why, my dear, if the general were near the gates of heaven and invited in, at that moment he would fall back!"

Shared Emotions

When Confederate President Jefferson Davis' small son Joe died, Abraham Lincoln sent Davis a message of condolence. When Union President Lincoln's small son Willie died, Jefferson Davis sent Lincoln a message of condolence. Such solicitude was unusual for the heads of two countries at war.

Reunited

On April 30, 1864, President Davis' five-year-old son, Joe, died in a fall from a railing at the Confederate White House in Richmond. The boy was buried in Hollywood Cemetery. The Davis family left the house in April 1865 as the Union was about to enter. For twenty-eight years numerous persons reported seeing an apparition wandering about the street near the Confederate White House. It was a small boy, about five years of age, and resembling Joe Davis, mumbling, "He's gone! He's gone!" In the spring of 1893, Varina Davis consented to the reburial of her husband in Hollywood Cemetery. At that time little Joe's body was moved next to his father's. The apparition of the little lost boy was never seen again.

Only Logical Choice

At Petersburg, U. S. Grant issued an order for the arrest of anyone found within the Union lines without an official pass. When an elderly black was brought to him, Grant saw that he was no danger but questioned him in a teasing manner. As the black was about to leave, he turned to Grant and asked if he could ask the general a question. Smiling, Grant agreed. The man then asked where Grant was going when he moved the next time. Grant told him, "I'm going one of four places. I'm going to Richmond, to Petersburg, to Heaven, or to Hell!" The old man thought for a moment and then said, "You can't go to Richmond because General Lee is there. You can't go to Petersburg because General Beauregard is there. You sure can't go to Heaven because General Stonewall Jackson is there. So I don't see but one place left for you to go, sir!"

Who Said That?

A Confederate soldier, exhausted by fighting at Petersburg, fell into a deep sleep among the bodies of fallen comrades. Later he was rudely awakened by being dragged across a field by a member of a burial squad. He screamed to the man, "Hold on...you're not going to bury me!" The man dropped him as though he were red-hot and ran away as fast as he could. He evidently wasn't ready for a conversation with a dead man!

Not the Most Prized Appellation

To avoid capture by John Singleton Mosby in Fairfax Court House, Virginia, Union Lieutenant Colonel Robert Johnstone scrambled out into his backyard. Clad in his nightshirt he hid under an outhouse. For the rest of his military career the 5th New York Cavalry officer was dogged with the humiliating nickname "Outhouse" Johnstone.

Favored over Colts

A favorite weapon of Confederate cavalry was the imported .44 caliber Kerr revolver produced by the London Armory Company. It had a five-shot cylinder and could be fired either single- or double-action. The Kerr pistol saw more use than all other Southern handguns combined.

A Different Kind of Pain

On the battlefield there was often non-physical pain. Major John G. Taylor of the 21st Mississippi Infantry wrote home after First Manassas in 1861, describing a pain he felt:

"I saw many affecting sights—a beautiful boy about 12 years old...lay among the dead. I dismounted to examine the boy being struck with his beautiful face and rich flowing hair. His sword was by his side and his hands were pressed upon the wound that killed him. In his jacket pocket I found a little Bible with his name, 'Joseph Simon, presented by his mother' & then followed the scripture 'Remember now thou Creator in the days of thy youth...' It affected me more than anything else I saw that day."

Rush This to the General

After the battle at Elkhorn Tavern, 3rd Texas cavalrymen were guarding the road for retreating infantrymen. A request from Colonel Elkanah Greer for the man with the fastest horse to deliver a message to General Van Dorn aroused apprehension as well as curiosity. Reporting to Greer, Douglas Cater was handed a folded message and sent speeding on his way. With the roads crowded by troops, Cater made a hard ride through the brush to reach the general. Van Dorn's aide, Colonel Dabney Maury, took the message and read it. With a smile lighting his face, Maury refolded the paper, handed it back to Cater, and told him, "Tell him to keep it." Puzzled by an apparently flippant response to an important message, Cater opened the paper and read: "General, I have captured three barrels of whiskey. What shall I do with it?" Angrily Cater shredded the paper, threw it to the ground, and returned to his company without delivering any response.

Battle Flags

Battle flags had practical uses in addition to serving as inspirational symbols. The flags were made large so they could be seen in spite of the smoke and haze of battle. Regiments were usually made up of 500 to 1,000 men. Soldiers were trained to watch their regimental flags so they would know where they were supposed to be. If the flag advanced, the men were to do the same. If the flag withdrew, the men could fall back with honor and in good conscience. The flags told the field commander where his units were on the field. On the battlefield the banners served as rallying points where the men could reform their lines if the battle lines became disorganized. Carrying the flag was a position of great honor. Men competed for the position even though they knew that carrying the flag into battle shortened their life expectancy.

A Silent Army

The fighting was so fierce during the one-day Battle of Sharpsburg that entire regiments ceased existence. Despite that ferocity, one-third of Union General George B. McClellan's 75,000-man Army of the Potomac never fired a shot.

The Cost of War

At the beginning of the war, recruits for the Southern cavalry had to supply their own clothing, weapons, horse, and other needs. The cost made the cavalry impossible for poor men. When Private A. W. Sparks volunteered for the 9th Texas Cavalry his equipment was valued as follows:

Horse*	$100
Saddle	25
Saddlebags	4
2 Blankets	7
Bridle	2
Underclothing, shorts, & drawers	8
Shotgun	25
Coat and pants	16
Boots	6
Canteen, cup, knife, and belt	3
Total	$196

*If a man lost his horse by death or capture, he was afoot until he could obtain another. Purchase was not an option on a private's pay.

Company Designations

Regiments in both Confederate and Union armies contained ten companies, with a letter designation "A" through "I" and "K" to each. The letter "J" was not used due to its similarity to "I" in script. (It has been conjectured that this may also have been due to "J" being considered unlucky because of its use in "jinx" and "Judas.") Each company captain drew lots to determine his company letter designation. The men often resented giving up the unit names they had chosen when they first organized, such as the *Mounted Rifles, Titus Grays,* and *Cypress Rangers.* Company affiliations were important because many times a company was associated with a particular company or area and the members often related, leading to a real camaraderie among the men.

Sharp Shooting

W. G. Langdon of Boston, a veteran watch and clock maker, produced an excellent handmade heavy rifle for snipers. Equipped with a telescopic sight, only twenty of these rifles were made, all for the U.S. War Department at a cost of $150 each. Another favorite sniper's weapon was the Whitworth target rifle with telescopic sight, imported from England. However, at $1,250 each, only wealthy men could buy a Whitworth. When the popular Spencer repeating rifle was introduced, its initial cost was $35. At war's end any Union combat veteran could buy one for $8.

A Most Unusual Engagement

Fort Enge was one of the Texas forts built to keep the Indians away from the pioneer settlements. In October of 1861, Sergeant N. Barrett and seventeen other members of the 2nd Texas Mounted Rifles were ordered to locate a band of reputedly hostile Lipan Apaches who were roaming the country. The cavalrymen were poorly armed. Although all had procured cavalry swords, they had no handguns, only shotguns and old percussion rifles.

The soldiers followed the Indians for three days, through a steady rain. The Indians proved to be a war party, not just Indians on the move. The bad weather sapped the alertness of the soldiers but not that of the Indians. The cold and miserable troopers were longing for a halt and a warm fire where they could dry themselves. Suddenly a large number of Indians sprang up and surrounded and attacked the cavalrymen. The sergeant barked orders for his men to fire at their attackers. He was dismayed to find that wet and useless powder prevented any weapon from firing. Quickly he ordered his men to draw their sabers and cut through the encircling Indians. Fighting desperately, sabers against spears and tomahawks, the cavalrymen finally broke free, although with four men lost. Ten Lipans were slain and a few others wounded. The oddity of this encounter was that it may have been the only Civil War action fought without firearms.

Some Might Take It As a Compliment

Despite their actual ages, privates throughout the Confederacy were commonly called "boys." Some really were boys, such as John Sloan of Company C, 9th Texas Cavalry, who was thirteen. Others were old enough to be grandfathers, such as a sixty-three-year-old "boy" in an East Texas cavalry unit.

Jubal and the South Carolinians

General Jubal Early has been described as half shrewdness and half sarcasm. Strongly opposed to secession, he had bitterly criticized in the Virginia Convention of 1861 the conduct of South Carolina. After the war began, he had in his brigade a South Carolina regiment that he always put in the most ticklish spot in battle. When his brigade was ordered into battle near Richmond, he as usual put the South Carolinians at the front. Riding up to them, he squeaked at the top of his voice, "Yes, I'll send you to the front, and I'll keep you there, too! You got us into this fix and, hang it, you've got to get us out!"

Southern Men

Senator George F. Hoar of Massachusetts was usually biased against the South, but he surely did understand Southern men. Speaking of the South on the floor of the U.S. Senate on the 23rd of February, 1889, Senator Hoar said:

"They have some qualities which I cannot even presume to claim in an equal degree for the people among whom I, myself, dwell. They have an aptness for command that makes the Southern gentleman, wherever he goes, not a peer only, but a prince. They have a love for home; they have, the best of them, and the most of them, inherited from the great race from which they come, the sense of duty, and the instinct of honor as no other people on the face of the earth. They are lovers of home. They have not the mean traits which grow up somewhere in places where money-making is the chief end of life. They have, above all, and giving value to all, that supreme and superb constancy which, without regard to personal ambition and without yielding to the temptation of wealth, without getting tired and without getting diverted, can pursue a great public object, in and out, year after year and generation after generation."

Varied Duty

During a six-month period in 1863, infantrymen of Hood's Texas Brigade fought in the first trench warfare in America, fought against gunboats, and were briefly mounted as a cavalry unit.

Couldn't Stop His Advancement

On December 1, 1862, Lieutenant Mark A. Williams, of the 3rd Arkansas, was promoted to captain. Such a promotion would not have been unusual except for the fact that he had died eleven days before, on November 20, 1862.

A Tragic Loss

Each spring the Battle of Champion Hill is reenacted near the small town of Edwards, Mississippi, on the actual battle site. This battle of the Vicksburg campaign was one of the most decisive battles of the entire war. The Confederate loss of weapons and troops contributed heavily to the loss of Vicksburg and the Mississippi River.

Gallant 26th

In the Battle of Gettysburg the 26th North Carolina Regiment took losses that may have been the highest in numbers and percentages of any regiment on either side in any one battle in the war. Every man in one company of the 26th was wounded. Its orderly sergeant made out his report with a bullet in each leg.

Had to Find the Right Words

When their enlistment period was ending, some Mississippi troops announced they were going home. General Sterling Price changed their minds by telling them, "All of you who wish to reenlist, step forward; all of you who want to be shot, remain still."

Serious About His Religion

Confederate chaplain Isaac Tichenor was conducting services one Sunday morning when he was interrupted by a Yankee sniper. Reverend Tichenor grabbed a musket, sent the sniper to his Maker, and returned to his prayers.

Got His Attention

The Honorable Benjamin H. Hill of Georgia was debating the Honorable William L. Yancey of Alabama in the Confederate Senate when he felt compelled to prove the strength of his argument. He did so—by smashing Yancey in the face with an inkwell.

What Did They See?

In June 1862, Jeb Stuart led his cavalrymen on a scouting raid completely around George McClellan's invaders. The only man lost was Captain William Latane, who died leading a charge against a Yankee picket post.

On June 13, 1962, Bill Latane, great-great-grand-nephew of Captain Latane, together with another man and two ladies, picnicked at a spot near where Captain Latane died. The couples soon found themselves watching a "reenactment" with Confederates charging Union cavalrymen. Bill Latane saw and picked up what appeared to be a very old handkerchief with embroidered initials "W.L." As they watched, the captain leading the Confederates struck a Federal officer with his sword, then died, just as had happened with Captain Latane. Bill Latane realized that the handkerchief he held seemed to be wet with blood. Just then a convoy of modern military vehicles distracted the couples. When they looked back, the "reenactors" had vanished.

Later a museum curator authenticated the handkerchief as a genuine Civil War relic. When the authorities were consulted about the "reenactment," it was learned that one had been planned for that location but had been cancelled at the last moment due to a military convoy moving through the area.

Hardly Paid To Win

Dueling was not uncommon in the Old South, but it did have its opponents. Thomas Jefferson once tried to introduce legislation in Virginia as strict as that in colonial Massachusetts. There the survivor of a fatal duel was to be executed, have a stake driven through his heart, and be buried without a casket.

No Laughing Matter

In 1862, Mrs. Eugenia Philips of New Orleans was banished to Ship Island, off the coast of Mississippi, by order of Union General Benjamin F. Butler. She had been seen laughing as a Union officer's funeral train passed her home. Butler ordered her exiled as punishment for "unpatriotic levity."

An Advancement?

Coffee was on the "must have" list for both Union and Confederate soldiers. Although Confederates often had to "make do" with substitutes for coffee, stockpiles of coffee beans were plentiful in the North. However, due to the bulk of the beans, commanders often prohibited carrying them. Ever mindful of demand, Northern merchants devised a solution to the problem. A thick paste was devised of powdered coffee beans mixed with sugar and milk. Combined with hot water this produced a cup of coffee a thirsty soldier would eagerly drink, the predecessor to today's instant coffee.

Confederate Money Well Spent

The most famous English purchase by Confederate agent James Bulloch was a teak-plated clipper equipped with both sails and a 250-horsepower engine. Originally the *Sea King*, the ship was renamed in honor of a Virginia valley and became a Confederate raider. As the *Shenandoah* the raider captured thirty-eight prizes before being surrendered at Liverpool in 1865. Purchased and renamed by the Sultan of Zanzibar, the former *Shenandoah* sank in the Indian Ocean in 1879.

Last

Major Aaron P. Brown of the Georgia State Militia was the surgeon in charge of a field hospital at Upson, Georgia. After Appomattox, sick and wounded men continued to arrive at the hospital and Brown continued to perform surgery and treat the men. On 23 August 1865 Federal cavalry entered the village and surrounded the tiny hospital. With weapons leveled, the Federals demanded the hospital's surrender. Regarding resistance as futile, the still-uniformed surgeon capitulated. This was the last surrender of Confederate troops.

Made Naval History

On January 30, 1863, a four-gun Confederate battery on the bank of the Stono River near Charleston, South Carolina, opened fire on the heavily armed USS *Isaac P. Smith* patrolling the river. As the Federal ship sped away, its boilers were hit three times by carefully directed fire. The disabled *Isaac P. Smith* became the only warship to surrender to a field battery. It was quickly repaired and joined the Confederate defense of Charleston.

Changed Gray for Black

Lieutenant Edward D. White, a Louisiana cavalry officer, was taken prisoner at Port Hudson during the Vicksburg campaign. Thirty years after the end of the war, White became the only former prisoner of war to become an associate justice on the U.S. Supreme Court. He remained there until his death in 1921.

Upwardly Mobile

Victor Jean Baptiste Girardey, born in France and raised as an orphan in Georgia and Louisiana, enlisted when Jefferson Davis called for volunteers. A lieutenant by

October 1861, he was promoted to captain in January 1862. He fought without special distinction during the Seven Days battles and at Chancellorsville and Gettysburg. However, at Petersburg he acted outstandingly. Without orders he led two brigades against Federals in the Battle of the Crater. When his performance at Petersburg was brought to the attention of Robert E. Lee, Lee saw to it that Girardey received appropriate recognition. He became the only Confederate to jump from captain to brigadier general.

Sent the Yanks to Their Reward

During hand-to-hand combat near Fredericksburg, some of Brigadier General Carnot Posey's brigade wavered. Reverend T. L. Duke, chaplain of the 19th Mississippi, seized a musket, raced to the front of his regiment, and directed the movements of skirmishers. For this he became the only Confederate chaplain to be officially cited for gallantry in battle.

A Willing Bargain

Following the collapse of Federal lines at Brice's Crossroads, the battered Union forces fled toward safety at Memphis. Nathan Bedford Forrest and his troops maintained such pressure on the retreating command of Brigadier General Samuel D. Sturgis that Sturgis remarked to a subordinate, "For God's sake, if Mr. Forrest will let me alone, I will let him alone!"

An Unusual Success

Born into a very poor family, Nathan Bedford Forrest grew up with no formal education. Becoming a livestock dealer at sixteen, Forrest managed to educate himself to conduct his business. He supported his family by his livestock dealing until he accumulated enough capital to enter the slave trade. He purchased enough land to become an important cotton planter and was worth over a million dollars when the war erupted. Enlisting in the 7th Tennessee Cavalry, he may have been the only millionaire private in the Confederate army. After raising a cavalry battalion on his own he was promoted to lieutenant colonel. Feared and respected by the North, Forrest did not surrender until he learned of Lee's surrender at Appomattox. A member of the original Ku Klux Klan, he left it when he found its methods too harsh. No other man in either the Confederate or the Union army started as a private and ended as a lieutenant general.

Battlefield No Place for Formality

Major J. C. Rogers was leading the 5th Texas across Plum Run at Gettysburg, fighting for a hold on the slope of Little Round Top. In the middle of the wild fight, Rogers was astounded by the formality of a message when an aide of General Evander

Law told him, "General Law presents his compliments and says hold this place at all hazard." Rogers bellowed, "Compliments, hell! Who wants compliments in such a damned place as this? Go back and ask General Law if he expects me to hold the whole world with the 5th Texas Regiment!"

Friendly Enemies

Many stories have been told of the men in the field swapping goods, such as tobacco for coffee, but rarely have quarters been mentioned. During the winter of 1863–1864, the Southern and Union armies along the Rapidan River had outposts that were often near to each other. In some cases the lines overlapped, due to the differing ways the two armies posted their pickets. The Confederates posted their pickets a little further during the day than they did at night. The Federals did the opposite. At one point there was a picket post with a log cabin and a fireplace. The pickets worked out a deal. During the day the Confederates would use the post, and the Federals would use it at night. Each party left firewood for the other's use and left the area before the other was due to arrive. This arrangement lasted several months.

One Way or the Other

As the battle at Fredericksburg was about to begin, Generals James Longstreet and Stonewall Jackson eyed the long lines of advancing Federals. In an attempt to remove the grim look from Jackson's face, Longstreet joshingly asked Jackson if all those Yankee troops didn't scare him. Never noted for his jocularity, Jackson somberly replied that he guessed everyone would soon find out; either they would scare him or he would scare them!

Had His Orders

Stonewall Jackson issued orders that each soldier should "know nothing" when questioned by anyone but his lawful superiors. One day Jackson came upon a Texan who had left his ranks to pick some cherries. The following exchange took place:

Jackson: Where are you going?

Texan: I don't know.

Jackson: What is your regiment?

Texan: I don't know.

Jackson: Well, what do you know?

Texan: I don't know nothin'.

Jackson: Well, why do you always answer, "I don't know"?

Texan: Because them's ol' Stonewall's orders an' I'm agoin to obey 'em or bust.

Jackson: Is that all you know?

Texan: No, I know I want some of them cherries.

Jackson: Go on and get them.

Not Open to Debate

Sergeant William Walker, Company A, 3rd South Carolina Infantry (African Descent), was angry and complained when his unit went unpaid long after the quarterly payday came and went. After he protested to an officer he was charged with using threatening language. Court-martialed, he was reduced in rank to private and sentenced to be shot. On February 29, 1864, Walker was executed for the crime of asking the Federal government to pay a just debt.

Better Things to Do

Assigned to color bearing duty during the Battle of Chickamauga, a Confederate Irishman in the 10th Tennessee refused, saying, "By the Holy Saint Patrick, Colonel, there's so much good shooting here, I haven't a minute's time to waste fooling with that flag!"

Power to Spare

Father James Mullin was pastor of St. Patrick's in New Orleans. Union General "Beast" Butler once questioned him about a report that he had refused to bury a Union soldier. Father Mullin denied the statement, saying he would cheerfully bury the whole Union army. Irate, General Butler asked Father Mullin, "Do you know, sir, that I can send you to Fort St. Phillip and keep you there?" Without a pause, Father Mullin replied, "And do you know, General Butler, that I can send your soul to hell and keep it there?" With many Irish Catholics in his army and fearful to offend them, Butler immediately released the gallant priest.

His "War Suit"

Confederate troops of Major General Sterling Price could always tell when he was getting ready to fight: He would don a favorite multicolored plaid hunting shirt.

Imposing

As the Confederate army marched on the road to Gettysburg, Robert E. Lee rode by the home of a patriotic Chambersburg matron waving a Union flag. Staring at him, she stopped waving the Stars and Stripes to cry out, "Oh I wish he was ours!"

Some Would Say an Apt Location

Surrounded by Confederates when Union troops retreated on the first day at Gettysburg, Union Brigadier General Alexander Schimmelfennig hid for three days in a pig sty.

Probably Got a Bang Out Of It

Pierre G. T. Beauregard was once arrested for participating in a duel—with shotguns!

Recognition

At Wilson's Creek on 10 August 1861, troops of the 1st Iowa held their fire in recognition of the gallantry of a brave Texan who rode out to retrieve a flag that had fallen between the lines.

A Discovery of Great Magnitude

Early in the war, knowledge of an important discovery quickly became widespread throughout the troops on both sides: The barrel of a musket could hold about a pint of whiskey!

Sectionalism Not Just American

Hearing his native language coming from the Union lines, a German volunteer on picket duty in the Confederate army called out that he too was German. In reply he heard, "From what part do you come, countryman?" When he answered, "Bavaria," a rifle ball was sent his way.

Quite a Critique

Union Brigadier General Irvin McDowell expressed surprise when William T. Sherman told him he had only requested a colonel's rank when rejoining the army. "Why didn't you ask for a brigadier general's rank? You're just as fit as I am." Sherman was frank, answering, "I know it!"

Effective Antifreeze

Stonewall Jackson was strict in his avoidance of hard liquor. However, once in January 1862, in order to warm himself on a cold winter day, he drank a glass of whiskey in the belief it was wine. He soon opened his coat, commenting on the heat, and became more talkative than any other time during the war.

Proper Reasoning

A Georgia colonel, reprimanded for an unauthorized (although successful) charge, explained his reasoning. His ammunition was getting low and he was afraid he would run out!

Muddling On

On February 12, 1862, W. C. Simmons began a letter home by combining a couple of popular opening clichés. He stated that it "is with pleasure this morning that I take my Seat and pen in hand to drop you a few lines."

Advanced Technology

The USS *Monitor* was the first warship to have flush toilets.

Southern Math

Johnston's Elementary Arithmetic was used to teach children in Raleigh, North Carolina. It utilized the following patriotic problems:

* A Confederate soldier captured 8 Yankees a day for 9 days; how many did he capture in all?
* If one Confederate soldier kills 90 Yankees, how many Yankees can 10 Confederate soldiers kill?
* If one Confederate soldier can whip 7 Yankees, how many soldiers can whip 49 Yankees?

Stood Up for Each Other

Brothers Jack and Jasper Walker both served with the 13th North Carolina. Wounded at Gettysburg on July 1, Jasper lost a leg as a result of the wound. Shortly thereafter, Jack also had his leg amputated as the result of a wound. After the war, the two were often seen walking around town together on their wooden legs. On his wedding day, Jasper fell and broke his wooden leg. He borrowed his brother's wooden leg and the wedding took place as planned. Later the brothers were fond of saying that Jasper was the only man to get married standing on someone else's leg.

Unwelcome Rations

A staple issue of both Confederate and Union armies was a flour and water biscuit of steely consistency, commonly known as "hardtack." Among its other names were hard bread, sheet iron crackers, and hard crackers. Soldiers claimed hardtack over the heart could stop a bullet. To make it edible, they ground hardtack into a powder, soaked it in coffee, fried it, toasted it, and boiled it. There were even tales of beating it with musket butts to soften it.

Unusual Status

Julia Grant, wife of General U. S. Grant, owned three slaves. She always kept one, also named Julia, with her. Following the fall of Richmond, Mrs. Grant toured the ravaged city, bringing with her the slave Julia. If Lincoln's Emancipation Proclamation had actually freed the slaves in Confederate Richmond, Mrs. Grant's servant was perhaps the only slave in the city!

A Real Beauty

Hetty Cary and two of her cousins were deemed "the prettiest women in Virginia." When Federal troops marched by her home she defiantly waved a Confederate flag. Declining to arrest her, a Federal colonel commented, "She is beautiful enough to do as she damned pleases."

Gallantry in Action

Colonel W. H. Martin of the 1st Arkansas saw that a small wood had caught fire and that it sheltered some Union wounded. Jumping on a parapet, he waved a white flag and shouted, "We won't fire until you get them away." His men then held their fire until the Union wounded were removed. At the end of that truce a Yankee major presented Martin with a pair of pistols in gratitude for his action.

In the Dark, All Cats Look Alike

Leonidas Polk was approached by an officer bringing his troops into action at Perryville as night fell in October 1862. The man told him, "I have come to your assistance with my brigade, sir," and identified himself and his unit. The Confederate lieutenant general responded to the surprised Union officer, "There is some mistake about this. You are my prisoner." That same night, Polk rode up to an officer and angrily demanded the man stop his troops from firing on friendly troops. It was only as he left that he discovered he had ordered a Yankee regiment to cease fire!

Nothing Elaborate Required

When Fort Donelson was surrendered there was so much confusion that Confederate General Bushrod Johnson escaped by merely casually walking through the Union lines.

Unusual Imprisonment

Confederate Brigadier General William N. R. Beall was captured in July 1863. He was released under parole to work in New York City supervising the procurement of supplies for prisoner-of-war Confederates. His work was funded by the sale of cotton passed through the lines for that purpose.

Tying Up the Enemy

Confederate cavalry and guerrillas were so effective in the last two years of the war with their raids on Union lines of communication and supply that approximately 30 percent of the Union army was utilized to guard against them.

Never AWOL

At the start of the war, Pierre G. T. Beauregard served briefly as a private in the Orleans Guard. Thereafter his name was always included in roll calls. When his name was called, the color sergeant would respond, "Absent on duty!"

Some Changes Lasted

Among the long-lasting changes that the war brought about was that for the first time homemakers could buy flour in five-pound bags rather than having to buy it by the barrel.

Caffeine Addicts

Except for those troops able to trade tobacco for coffee, Southerners during the war were forced to try all sorts of substitutes for coffee, which became almost totally unavailable due to the blockade. Peas, acorns, rice, beans, okra seeds, cotton-seeds, rye, wheat, and even sweet potatoes went into coffeepots. In Louisiana, chicory was used to stretch the supply of coffee. Jeb Stuart particularly liked a "coffee" made from roasted and ground corn.

Fly Now!

John Pope, commander of the Federal army of Virginia in 1862, invented the buttoned fly for trousers. Prior to that trousers featured a flap such as that worn by sailors until recently.

Respected by All

In the aftermath of the "Trent Affair," negative feelings against Britain ran high in the U.S. However, despite the threat of war between the two nations, when Queen Victoria's husband, Prince Albert, died in December 1861, flags in New York and several other cities were lowered to half-staff in recognition of his efforts for peace.

A Matter of Trust

When officers on duty at western posts in 1861 resigned from the U.S. Army to "Go South," they sometimes left their families behind, trusting in the chivalry of their comrades to see them safely home. In no case was the trust betrayed.

Master Tailors

The Richmond depot of the Confederacy's Quartermaster Department employed sixty men to cut cloth and about 2,000 women sewing, mostly by hand. During 1862 the depot produced an average of 2,500 uniforms per day.

Careful What You Ask For

Thaddeus Stevens, Radical Republican Senator from Pennsylvania, was hardnosed about nearly everything, particularly about corruption. He held Simon Cameron, secretary of war, in very low esteem due to Cameron's reputation for dishonesty. When the subject of Cameron's honesty arose during a conversation between Stevens and Abraham Lincoln, Lincoln asked Stevens, "You don't mean to say you think Cameron would steal?" Stevens' quick reply was, "No, I don't think he'd steal a red-hot stove!" Amused by the remark, Lincoln repeated it to Cameron who demanded that Stevens publicly retract the statement. Stevens scolded Lincoln for repeating a private conversation and refused any retraction. Pressed by Lincoln to withdraw the remark to preserve peace in the government, Stevens finally assented, saying, "I believe I told you he would not steal a red-hot stove. I will now take that back."

Secretaries of the Treasury

Four men held the position of secretary of the treasury of the Confederate States of America:

> C. G. Memminger
> George Trenholm
> John Regan, who held the post temporarily while also Postmaster
> Micajah Clark

Main Sources of Revenue for CSA

1. An export tariff on cotton and tobacco
2. Produce loans (cotton used as collateral for loans)
3. Bond issues
4. Treasury notes

Flying the Flag

The first ship to fly the Confederate Flag was the CSS *Huntress*, which survived the war only to sink off Japan in 1869.

Civil War Flags

There were three types of flags flown during the WBTS: a color, a standard, and an ensign.

A color was carried by dismounted troops.

A standard was carried by mounted units.

An ensign was flown from a ship.

Liked How He Was Guarded

Taken prisoner in 1863, the bold and dashing John Hunt Morgan and his officers were treated as criminals and sent to the Ohio State Prison rather than a prisoner of war camp. They immediately began planning an escape. Several months later they were successful. Morgan decided to "hide in plain sight" and go first to Cincinnati rather than head directly for the South. After boarding a train Morgan boldly took a seat next to a Federal officer. The two began a friendly conversation during which Morgan enjoyed a drink from the officer's brandy flask. As the train passed the state prison, the Federal commented, "That's where they've got old John Morgan." Morgan replied, "Yes, and I hope they always guard him as well as they do now!" (After several close calls Morgan made his way back to the Confederacy, but sadly lost his life during a surprise Federal attack the following year.)

Patricide Not Acceptable Behavior

During the Battle of Shiloh, a Union Kentuckian was captured by his Confederate brother. The Union soldier warned his brother not to shoot at a particular Union officer because "that's father!"

Foraging Not Approved Activity

Confederate Major General Benjamin Cheatham caught a young Confederate up in a tree stealing fruit. The fright of the young man quickly dissipated when he heard the general say, "Young man, drop me down a few of those fine apples."

Worked on Commission

Edward C. Stockton may have had the most unusual military career of anyone in the War Between the States. Shortly after graduating from Annapolis in 1850, he was expelled from the U.S. Navy. He engaged in various civilian activities until war broke out. He became a lieutenant in the South Carolina State Navy in early 1861, a second lieutenant in the Confederate States Marines from May through September of 1861, a captain in the 21st South Carolina Infantry from January through April of 1862, and finished the war as a lieutenant in the Confederate States Navy.

Learning the Nomenclature

Prince Camille de Polignac spoke English fluently but American slang baffled him. Approached by a young Confederate who identified himself as a member of "Colonel Senser's layout," the puzzled de Polignac asked "Colonel Senser's what?" The young man responded "Colonel Senser's layout. You know. It belongs to your shebang!" Groaned de Polignac, "I have been militaire all my life. I was educated for ze army. I have heard of ze compagnie, ze battalion, ze regiment, ze brigade, ze division, and ze army corps, but—my soul to ze ——— ef evair I hear of ze layout or ze shebang before!"

A Different Way to Hunt

Wade Hampton loomed large in person as well as in the history of South Carolina and the South. A tall and powerfully built man, he loved hunting and was a crack shot. However, once he had cornered a bear, he relished a "mano a mano" combat, going up against the bear with nothing but his hunting knife. He had both witnesses and scars to prove that he killed as many as eighty bears in "hand to claws" combat!

No Beau Brummell

Confederate General William E. (Grumble) Jones was known as the worst dressed general in the war. He normally wore jeans, hickory shirt and homespun coat.

A Striking Victory

In consideration of resources the war's most striking victory was the Confederate victory at Sabine Pass, Texas. Richard W. Dowling, defending with forty-three men and six cannon, drove off a Federal force of 15,000 men. Dowling never lost a man!

No Term of Endearment

Union General Hugh Judson "Kill Cavalry" Kilpatrick did not earn his nickname by his ability to kill cavalry troops. It was given to Kilpatrick by his own men because he was so reckless in the field and they suffered needless casualties.

No Success Story

Benjamin F. Butler and his Union army lost every battle, every campaign, and every engagement his units fought.

Surprise, Surprise!

Alfred Ely of New York was the first sitting congressman to be captured during a battle. He was one of those who rode out to witness an expected Federal victory at Manassas.

No Worry!

When General Jackson was being transferred to Guiney's Station following his surgery and amputation, his doctor worried about Jackson being captured by Union forces. Regarding his possible capture, Jackson told the doctor, "If the enemy does come, I am not afraid of them; I have always been kind to their wounded and I am sure they will be kind to me."

Knew the Territory

When J. E. B. Stuart completed his famous trip around the Union army, he was guided by John Singleton Mosby, later of Mosby's Rangers fame.

An Unusual Pet

Confederate soldiers of Company B of the 43rd Mississippi regiment had a really unusual "pet." It was a camel, used to transport supplies. In a forced march toward Iuka, Mississippi, just prior to the battle of Corinth, the camel blundered into the line of march and spooked horses so badly that there was a terrible stampede. The camel was accidentally killed during the siege of Vicksburg.

In Case He Had a Chance to Hunt

Confederate General Turner Ashby rode with a brass spyglass hanging on one side of his saddle and a fox hunting horn on the other side.

Big Bangs

A canister was a shell containing about ninety-six iron balls. A case shot was a shell with timed fuses that would burst over the attacking troops' heads, sending pieces of the projectile into them. Round shot was aimed in front of the attacking troops so that it would skip along the ground causing great havoc.

Sickening Thoughts

"Green apple quickstep" was the soldier's name for diarrhea. The Southern field cure for it was tea made from the bark of either slippery elm, sweet gum, or dogwood. The most common malady affecting Southerners was measles.

Advocated Hanging Lee

Henry Adams said, "I think that Lee should have been hanged. It was all the worse that he was a good man and a fine character and acted conscientiously. It's always the good men who do the most harm in the world."

Simon Cameron

Simon Cameron was Abraham Lincoln's first secretary of war. He was famous as a political machine boss and political opportunist. He once defined an honest politician as someone who "once bought, stays bought." He's also known as one who never forgot a friend or forgave an enemy. Cameron served less than a year, resigning after stories of his unscrupulous dealings in contracting for war materiel came to light. His actions in procuring inferior army uniforms and blankets that would shred and fall apart gave rise to the word "shoddy" for any poorly manufactured product.

Forrest's Wounds

Confederate General Nathan Bedford Forrest was physically wounded in battle just three times. At Shiloh, he was shot through the left hip and the bullet lodged in his spinal column. He was wounded again just prior to the Battle of Chickamauga; and he was shot in the right foot at the Battle of Tupelo. However, his Civil War medical history is more colorful if we add the contusions he suffered each of the six times he was "unhorsed" in battle, with only one instance in which the horse was shot out from under him. The most unusual shooting occurred when one of his officers tried to kill him. Including all these instances, the total number of times Forrest was wounded during the Civil War is ten.

Was Not Highly Valued

In 1861 U. S. Grant was threatened with being relieved of his command. After Shiloh, Governor David Todd of Ohio wanted him court-martialed. Grant was described to Abraham Lincoln as "a drunken wooden-headed tanner."

An Unusual Reaction

Stonewall Jackson refused to use pepper on his food, saying it gave him pains in his left leg.

DESSERTS

The First Thanksgiving

Over a year before the arrival of the more celebrated Pilgrim Fathers in New England, thirty-eight adventurers from Gloucestershire, England, landed in Virginia on December 4, 1619. They named their landing site "Berkely Plantation" to honor their leader, Richard Berkeley. Thankful for a safe landing, the men observed in prayer the first Thanksgiving in America. At Berkeley that occasion is still commemorated on December 4 annually. During the War Between the States, Union President Abraham Lincoln proclaimed Thanksgiving as a national day, choosing to venerate an event in Massachusetts rather than one in a seceded state.

Wearing of the Gray

Thirty years after the War, an old soldier from Georgia was readying himself to attend a Confederate reunion in Richmond. Discussing his plans with a good friend, the veteran mentioned that he would be wearing his old gray uniform even though it was badly worn. The friend, who was in good financial shape, offered to give him a new black broadcloth suit to wear in lieu of the uniform. The veteran replied, "No, I might get killed and if I reached heaven Bob Lee wouldn't know me, and if I went to hell, ol' Jubal Early would kick me out!"

A Documented Travesty

Dr. James I. Robertson, Jr., respected historian, succinctly analyzed the PBS "Civil War" series: "The less you know about the Civil War, the more you'll enjoy the program." Dr. Robertson said that as a historian the main problem he had with the series was not the terrible imbalance of the series, but the number of factual errors it contained. Factual errors are those whereby data is presented materially different from actual facts, not such inconsequential items as showing the body of the same man after several different battles. Dr. Robertson counted seventeen factual errors in a one half-hour segment; on a prorate basis that adds up to hundreds of errors in a series which truly could have been a "classic."

211

War of Cultures

The War Between the States has been the subject of continuous efforts to justify social, sectional, and racial goals and actions by rewriting the prologue and diary of the period. In the view of responsible scholars such as Charles A. Beard, slavery was incidental to the real causes of the war: an agricultural economy in the South versus industrialization in the North. Slavery, a labor system of plantation agriculture, was not a crucial or even major issue. Beard wrote, "Merely by the accidents of climate, soil, and geography, was it a sectional struggle."

The war ended seventy years of Southern leadership in the national government and transferred to the North full control of the nation's economy and even its polity and policies. Wartime legislation enacted by the Union Congress fostered consolidation of power in the North through centralization of finances, increased tariffs, and Federal subsidies. Northern wealth and capital increased by 50 percent in the 1860s; Southern wealth was reduced by 60 percent. Southern industrial capacities, including thousands of miles of railroads, were intentionally destroyed by the Yankee invaders during the war. The South lost more than half of its farm machinery, 40 percent of its livestock, and a fourth of its white males of military age. Emphasis has been placed on emancipation as *the* major result of the war; the wholesale long-term assault on the South's economic resources has received scant notice.

No Quitters

A Confederate steamer, the *William H. Webb*, was at Shreveport, Louisiana, on the Red River, in 1865 when it heard Confederate armies were surrendering. The crew did not care for that option. Camouflaged as a cargo vessel, the *Webb* flew the Union flag at half-mast as though in mourning for Lincoln, and started for the open seas, three hundred miles away. No Union ship in the Red River challenged the steamer, not even a whole flotilla it passed. Entering the Mississippi River, the crew went ashore and cut the telegraph lines to New Orleans. Lights shielded, safety valve tied down, they headed for the Gulf of Mexico, safely passing one Union warship after another. When the *Webb* was finally identified as a Confederate vessel, the Yankees on the river "flipped their lids," spreading tales that Jefferson Davis was on the *Webb*, John Wilkes Booth was the ship's pilot, and Confederate gold filled her hold. With the need for secrecy gone, the *Webb* raised a Southern battle flag and began to try to fight its way to the open seas, actually getting past New Orleans before the brave crew was forced to scuttle her and take to the woods.

The Cause

From a speech of Colonel Robert Aldrich at an annual reunion of Hart's Battery, as reported in the *Confederate Veteran* of October 1894:

"It was then called the War for Southern rights, and it was right then and is right now, and as long as I can say anything, I will always say that my countrymen fought and bled and died for their rights. There was nothing wrong about it except the result."

Mexia Reunion Grounds

In Mexia, Texas, the Joseph F. Johnston Reunion Grounds are still dedicated to the memory of Confederate veterans. When Texas still looked to Confederate veterans for state leadership, numerous parks were established on riverbanks and pleasant sites for popular annual encampments. In 1892, United Confederate Veterans Camp 94 purchased a seventy-acre tract at Mexia and established the Reunion Grounds. Lots were sold to shareholders. Streets were named for Confederate heroes. During the week of the full moon each August, members and families came to encampments. Special trains ran from Dallas, Fort Worth, and Houston. In peak years five thousand people would attend. Setting up housekeeping in tents, shacks, or brush arbors, they feasted on fried chicken, barbecue, sweet potato pie, stew, and watermelons, while enjoying speeches by statesmen, orations by old soldiers, reviews, concerts, and memorial programs. Until 1940 dawn and dusk salutes fired by Old Valverde, WBTS cannon, were heard far into neighboring counties.

To Those Who Say There Were No Black Confederates

Morehouse College is a traditional black college located at the highest point in Atlanta, Georgia. The battle of Atlanta was fought here. The oldest building on the Morehouse campus is Graves Hall, constructed in 1889. According to the Morehouse web page, black Confederate soldiers are buried underneath the hall.

Picture This!

Throughout the years the Confederate Research Center in Hillsboro, Texas, has been offered many items for its museum. Therefore there was nothing unusual about an offer when a Dallas resident offered to give the center a 12x18 oil painting of the Battle of Antietam. There were mixed feelings when the painting arrived; the center was thinking inches, the donor meant feet!

What Civil War?

It is not by accident that Northern apologists have encouraged the use of the term "Civil War" to designate the era 1861–65. Otherwise they would have to admit the unwarranted aggression of the Union forces after the Southern states seceded. A civil war is defined as one taking place within the bounds of a single country between two or more parties fighting for control of that country. Even the Yankees recognized (after the war) the secession of the South by requiring Southern states to qualify for re-admission.

Southern troops fought to protect their homes and hearths, never attempting the subjugation of the nation from which their states had withdrawn. One Southerner always made it a point when he heard the term "Civil War" to politely ask to which one the speaker was referring, English or Spanish?

New Evidence against Sherman

The long-lasting hatred of many Atlanta Georgians for Federal General William T. Sherman was well justified, as evidenced anew recently. Over 7,500 nineteenth-century artifacts were recovered when the site for a new Atlanta Federal Center was cleared. Some of the items will be displayed in the new center. One of the items was a Hotchkiss artillery shell, one of hundreds fired into the area by Sherman's troops. The Hotchkiss shell contained fifteen marble-sized lead balls designed to rip through human flesh. At the time of that attack the area was entirely residential. There was no structure, fort, or any other military target. The Federals had fired on unprotected civilians.

So True!

Originally published in the August 1868 issue of General D. H. Hill's newspaper, *The Land We Love:*

"Shortly after the surrender of the Confederate armies a body of Yankee troops were stationed at Talladega, Alabama. Amongst the officers of this command was a coarse, burly, and arrogant Dutchman who availed himself of every opportunity to outrage the feelings of Confederate officers. Upon one occasion this Dutchman was going to Selma with a gallant officer of the late 10th Alabama when the following conversation took place between them:

Yank: 'You all fought for pay. We fought for honor.'

Confederate: 'Well, that's very natural and proper, we fought for that which we had the least and you did the same.'

Exit Yank."

Confederate Monument in Arlington Cemetery

The Confederate Monument in Arlington Cemetery was erected by the United Daughters of the Confederacy. The sculptor was Moses Ezekial, one of the great sculptors of his day and a Confederate veteran. Ezekial contributed his services. Peace is the central theme of the 32 1/2 foot high monument. It is surmounted by a heroic-sized figure of a woman crowned with olive leaves, her face turned toward the South. In her outstretched left hand is a laurel wreath. In the right hand is a plow stock and a pruning hook. Around the memorial is a verse from Isaiah: *They shall beat their swords into plowshares, and their spears into pruning hooks.* A circular frieze of thirty-two life-sized figures shows Southern soldiers going off to war. Their sad homecoming dominates the middle part of the monument. Over it are carved the seals of the Southern states. The south side of the monument bears the dedication: *To our dead heroes, by the United Daughters of the Confederacy. "Victrix causa diis placuit sed victa Catoni." (The victorious cause was pleasing to the gods, but the lost cause to Cato.)* On the north side is an inscription written by Dr. Randolph Harrison McKim, another Confederate veteran: *Not for fame or reward, not for place or for rank, not lured by ambition or goaded by necessity, but in simple obedience to duty as they understood it, these men suffered all, sacrificed all, dared all, and died.* The monument was dedicated on June 14, 1914, with President Woodrow Wilson making the principal address to an audience that included several thousand Confederate and Union veterans. This is the site of an annual memorial service hosted by the Confederate Memorial Committee, the United Daughters of the Confederacy and the Sons of Confederate Veterans. These services always are well attended, with representatives and legislators from all Southern states.

Decoration Day

In 1868, on the first Decoration Day to be celebrated in Arlington Cemetery, Southern ladies requested permission to place flowers on the graves of Confederate dead. Not only were they refused permission to do so, they were curtly denied entry. By day's end flowers were piled high on the graves of the Yankee dead, while graves of the Southerners lay bare. That night a blustery wind arose. When dawn came, the Southern graves were covered with the flowers formerly on Northern graves.

Honors to the Blacks in Gray

Canton, Mississippi, is the location for what may be the most unusual Confederate monument in the nation. The handsome granite obelisk was erected sometime before 1900 and honors the "loyalty and service" of the blacks who served in Harvey's Scouts, a crack cavalry unit that distinguished itself while opposing Sherman in Mississippi and Georgia.

A Good Reason

From *Reminiscence of the Civil War*, by General John B. Gordon:

"The only explanation of the unparalleled spontaneity that pervaded all classes of the Southern people was the impulse of self-defense."

A Very Good Reason

Asked why Confederate troops continued to fight after they knew defeat was certain, Senator John Sharp Williams said that they were simply afraid to go home, face the Southern women, and admit they had quit.

Southerners All

In the frieze of figures circling the Confederate monument at Arlington National Cemetery are three black representatives of Southern patriotism: a soldier, a mother, and a small child. Their features are easily noticeable and there can be no doubt about their racial identity. The sculptor, a Confederate veteran, placed the blacks amid the other fighters and families of the Confederacy because he wished the memorial to be a truthful representation of the Southern war experience.

A Better Basis for Judgment

After riding on a train shortly after Appomattox, U. S. Grant reported hearing a conversation between two other passengers, one a civilian, the other a newly paroled Confederate soldier. "You shouldn't have surrendered," said the civilian. "You should have taken to the mountains and fought guerilla warfare." The ex-soldier indulgently listened to many such comments before losing his patience. He finally faced his critic and raised his voice to state, "Look! I've been in thirty-five battles since this war began and I'm plumb satisfied."

Lee in Defeat

After the surrender at Appomattox, with the armies still occupying the positions of the prior day, several Southern officers assembled at the tent of Robert E. Lee. Sorrow dominated the conversation until John B. Gordon asked General Lee what their subsequent course should be. Resolve replaced grief on General Lee's face as he responded: "I can only say to you gentlemen what I said to Mrs. Lee this morning: 'We must cultivate and strengthen our virtue. Human virtue ought at least to be equal to human calamity.' "

Experiences of Our Men

In the early years of the twentieth century, Mamie Yeary of the Pearl Witt Chapter of the UDC worked to preserve the personal histories of all Confederate veterans in Texas. Her goal was to reach all such veterans living in Texas at that time, not just those who had enlisted from Texas. The result was a lengthy volume, *Reminiscences of the Boys in Gray*, published in 1912. While many of the tales suffered slightly from "memory lapses," this is a remarkable biographical compilation of the experiences of our men. It has been of real benefit for many researchers.

The Truth Has Been Known

The following was taken from a textbook called *A Youth's History of the Civil War*, by R. G. Horton, published by Van Evrie, Horton & Company, New York, New York:

"Mr. Lincoln, finding a geographical party in the process of formation (Republican), assumed the leadership of a dictator. He overthrew the government as it was formed by issuing a military edict or decree which changed the fundamental law of the land, and declared that he would maintain this by all the military and naval power of the United States."

Since even Southern children do not read such material in their schoolbooks today, it is surprising that this was found in a Northern textbook published in 1867.

None of His Buddies Ever Told

In 1911, Albert J. Cashier, a pensioned Union Civil War veteran of the 95th Illinois Volunteer Infantry, was involved in an automobile accident. It was then discovered that "Albert" was a woman, Jenny Hodges!

And the Victors Wrote Our History

William Tecumseh Smith said cynically that "the truth is not always palatable and should not always be told." Union General George Meade declared, "I have great contempt for History." U.S. Senator Benjamin Wade of Ohio, member of the Committee on the Conduct of the War, admitted, "If I tell the whole truth, I shall blast too many reputations." Don Platt, Union soldier, diplomat, and author, observed that "the historian shapes his ware…to suit the customer."

The Grayclad Warriors

(Confederate Monument Inscription)
The knightliest of the knightly race
who, since the days of old,
Have kept the lamp of chivalry
alight in hearts of gold.

Hang In There!

If we ever feel discouraged about having to fight an up-hill battle with our efforts to preserve and present our Southern heritage and protect the good name of our Confederate ancestors, we should keep in mind a statement by Calvin Coolidge, the comparatively unknown and rarely quoted U.S. president:

"Nothing in this world can take the place of persistence. Talent will not; nothing is more common than unsuccessful men with talent. Genius will not; unrewarded genius is almost a proverb. Education will not; the world is full of educated derelicts. Persistence and determination alone are omnipotent. The slogan 'Press on' has solved and always will solve the problems of the human race."

To Honor Stonewall

In July 1891, when the impressive statue of Stonewall Jackson was dedicated over his grave, 30,000 people gathered in Lexington, Virginia. On the day before the dedication, survivors of the Stonewall Brigade, dressed in faded and tattered gray uniforms, were the center of attention in the town.

That night when citizens of the town wanted to ensure the old soldiers comfortable lodging, a diligent search of homes and hotels yielded not one of the men. Near midnight the brigade was found, huddled in blankets around Jackson's statue in the cemetery. Urged to leave the damp ground and partake of the town's hospitality, none of the men stirred. Finally one said, "Thank you sirs, but we've slept around him many a night on the battlefield, and we want to bivouac once more with Old Jack." And they did.

The next day, July 21, was the thirtieth anniversary of the memorable battle where Thomas Jonathan Jackson became forever "Stonewall." The day began with a procession featuring a brand-new Confederate battle flag made especially for the occasion. When the graveside ceremonies ended, the Stonewall Brigade fell into ranks and marched slowly to the cemetery gate. There one of the veterans paused and gazed around at the land he had defended with the general. When his eyes reached Jackson's grave, he removed his hat and shouted in a choking voice, "Goodbye, old man, goodbye! We've done all we can for you!"

South Carolina Confederate Honored

On December 11, 1993, the General States Rights Gist Camp of the SCV held ceremonies to dedicate a headstone for the West Springs, South Carolina, grave of Private John Alex Sarter, Company B, 18th South Carolina Infantry. South Carolina Division Commander Bob Brown was the keynote speaker. Private Sarter was a slave in Union County, South Carolina, when the war began. After entering Confederate service along with his master, Alex Sarter remained at the front in Virginia following his master's death. He was issued a gun and equipment and assigned to picket duty. Captured by Yankees at Petersburg, he was forced to dig in the tunnel used by his captors for the Battle of the Crater. After that battle he escaped and returned to Union County where he lived till his death in 1933.

Private Sarter drew a pension for his Confederate service. His son said that the pension started out at $19.98 in his first year and increased $1 each year thereafter.

A Question of Priority

Although attacks on the Southern states during the war were justified on the grounds that they had never left the Union and were simply in rebellion, those states had to petition to rejoin the Union. Before Louisiana was accepted "back" in the Union, it had to change its motto from "Justice, Union, and Confidence" to "Union, Justice, and Confidence," placing the Union ahead of Justice. Seems like that was the Yankee concept during the war, too!

Lazarus

Major W. M. F. Bayliss of Virginia recalled the story of Lazarus in the Bible and a general conference of bishops in Washington, D.C., shortly after the end of the war. The Yankee bishops were in a jubilant mood, while the Virginia bishop remained rather sad. After he sat through an oratorical ennobling of the Northern cause and glorification of its victory, the Virginian was asked for a few words. Smiling, he complied and remarked gently, "The South, gentlemen, suggests Lazarus to me." "How so?" asked a Northern bishop. The Virginian sighed and answered, "Licked by dogs, licked by dogs."

Wrong Terminology?

A carpetbagger was a Yankee who moved South after 1865 and took advantage of Reconstruction politics for power and profit. A scalawag was a homegrown opportunist who was already in the South and did the same thing. The most important executive offices in the Texas state government were governor, lieutenant governor, comptroller, attorney general, treasurer, and land commissioner. Of the eleven men who held those offices between July of 1867 and January of 1874, (a) six were native Southerners, (b) three were Northerners who had moved to Texas before the war, (c) one was foreign-born but already a Texas resident in 1860, (d) only one could be classified a carpetbagger (George W. Honey, who became treasurer in 1869). During that same six and one-half year period, only 10 percent of Texas Supreme Court judges were carpetbaggers, only 13 percent of district judges, only 6 percent of the 1868–69 Convention delegates, only 8 percent of the 12th Legislature, and only 5 percent of local officials. Although reference is often made to "carpetbagger rule" in Texas, it probably should be called "scalawag rule."

The General's Lady

Mrs. Helen Dortch Longstreet was a very unusual lady. She married General James Longstreet in 1895 when he was 76 and she was 34. He died in 1904. In 1942 Mrs. Longstreet became the only wife of a Confederate general to serve as a World War II "Rosie the Riveter." She worked at the Bell Bomber Plant in Georgia, helping to assemble bombers.

Up with the Confederacy!

Author's editorial in *Rebel Rouser*

Southern state governors, officials, employees, or legislators, and U.S. senators or representatives from Southern states who do not honor and defend Confederate emblems and history disgrace their positions and should resign. Such people are turning their backs on men who risked (and sometimes lost) lives, limbs, and everything they held dear in defense of the Confederacy. Whether the men went voluntarily or were conscripts, they were there in the service of the states that sent them forth to do battle, the same states these scalawag politicians supposedly represent. Now we are asked (required?) to accept slurs on the honor of these men and let their true history die away in the name of political correctness and social harmony. Well, anyone who really wants harmony better include a few bars of "Dixie"! We are told that those Confederates of yesteryear were misguided and/or shameful and should be written out of our lives and heritage. Further, we are told that the war was over one hundred thirty years ago, so we should forget it. Well, Christ died two thousand years ago and we better not forget him. Not even biased historians, columnists, and anchor people can change facts, even if they can change perceptions. I'm still learning why I need to remember. Meantime, you glorious Stars and Bars, as the grizzled old Johnny Reb said, "Fergit, Hell!"

Concisely Stated

On the Confederate monument on the state capitol grounds in Austin, Texas:

DIED FOR STATE RIGHTS GUARANTEED

UNDER THE CONSTITUTION

Never Changing

Some years after the war, while he was visiting Baltimore, General Robert E. Lee was urged to go as far north as New York where he was assured of a cordial welcome. When he hesitated, his reluctance was interpreted to mean that he dreaded the prominence into which such a trip would thrust him. The suggestion was made that he might travel by night in the stateroom of a sleeping car and thus avoid meeting people. With his eyes flashing, he answered, "I could not sneak into New York City. If I ever go, I will go by daylight and go like a man!"

Jawohl, Sir

From the *World Almanac*, 1900, page 87:

"Of the Union Army, the 'patriots who saved the Union,' over one million were not born in those 'free states.' It was not unusual for a Union regiment to contain not one enlisted man who could speak English."

A Matter of Opinion

While in her eighties, a daughter of an officer on Stonewall Jackson's staff enrolled in a university summer course on the history of the South. When the instructor commented that it was best that the North had won the war, the lady smoldered. When he said it again, she rose and asked, "How do you know? We didn't even get a chance to try it our way."

The Last Battle

When and where did the last battle of the War Between the States take place? Well, probably not when and where you think!

In 1903, two Confederate veterans, residents of an island off the mouth of Mobile Bay, visited the mainland to pick up a load of supplies. On their itinerary was a local saloon where they took on quite a load of another type. Alternately rowing and sampling a jug, they were bemoaning the intolerable end of the War Between the States when they saw a U.S. battleship entering the bay. As the ship drew abreast of them, the sight of the U.S. flag aroused anger in the men who for the moment were emotionally forty years in the past. Grabbing a fowling piece, the two took turns firing a shot "across the bow" of the ship. After a load of shot hit the bridge, a gig was lowered and the two old men were taken on board the ship. There they demanded to see the captain. Brought to his cabin, they demanded the surrender of the ship. The captain possessed good manners and a sense of humor in addition to a quick understanding of the situation. Inviting the men to be seated, he offered them cigars, then politely and gravely begged for a discussion of terms. These were presented during a conversation over several bottles of champagne. Finally a formal truce was drawn. This peace treaty between the United States and "the Confederacy" was signed and sealed in duplicate. Under the terms the ship was allowed to proceed, but not to sail near the men's island, and the captain was allowed to keep his sword. Afterward the captain escorted the "Confederates" on deck where they were piped over the side with full naval formality. A launch waited there to tow them to their island. As the dory was towed away, one of the old men rose in the boat, raised the returned fowling piece, and fired a salute. The battleship fired a salute in return. Thus ended the last battle of the War Between the States.

Afterward

As stated by General Stephen D. Lee, when president of Mississippi Agricultural and Mechanical College: "Great as was the courage shown by the Southern people in four years of war, they showed even greater courage in the eleven long years of Reconstruction."

A Man of His Word

With the war over, U. S. Grant and his armies were encamped around Washington, D.C. Grant was engaged in a game of billiards when an officer hurried in and whispered to Grant. Grant immediately went outside, took the horse of a mounted sentinel and rode rapidly to the War Department. Striding into the office of Secretary Stanton, Grant told him that he had learned that Stanton had issued orders for the arrest of Robert E. Lee. Stanton replied that officers would be dispatched for them shortly to arrest all prominent Rebels. Grant quickly said that when General Lee surrendered he had been given Grant's word that neither he nor his followers would be disturbed so long as they honored their parole. He then suggested that Stanton cancel the orders. Stanton angrily told Grant, "General Grant, are you aware whom you are talking to? I am Secretary of War." Grant snapped back, "And I am General Grant. Issue those orders at your peril," then turned and walked out. Stanton decided it would not be a good idea to arrest the Confederates.

Giving Due Credit

A veteran of the Army of Northern Virginia, Douglas Southall Freeman's father once advised him, "Never depreciate the enemy. What honor was there for a Confederate if he was supposed to be fighting a coward? They were not cowards, those men of the North. Indeed, there never was a greater army in the world than the Army of the Potomac save one," and he drew himself up with pride, "which modesty forbids me to mention."

Unpardonable Pride

Informed after the war that former Confederates could obtain pardons by asking for them, one Confederate said, "Pardon for what? We haven't pardoned you Yankees yet!"

Whose Was the Fault?

On October 7, 1869, Robert E. Lee posed for a portrait by Swiss painter Frank Buchser. While talking with Buchser, Lee said that the charge of murder against Henry Wirz was the most unjust calumny in the world and that his execution was judicial murder. He stated that the Confederates had made every effort to further the exchange of prisoners, but the North refused to cooperate. He criticized Grant on a personal basis, asserting that the Confederates had even offered to give the prisoners freedom if the Union would only supply transportation, but Grant refused the offer. The Confederates had already informed the North that the South did not have doctors and medicines for the prisoners and offered to allow the Union to provide doctors, medicines, and care, guaranteeing no diversion to Confederate use. Even this was refused. The South did everything it could to relieve the prisoners' problems. The North used the presence of the prisoners to cause additional strain on Southern resources. On whose shoulders rests the responsibility for prisoner deaths?

The War

A Georgia veteran asserted, "If this was a civil war, I hope to never fight in an uncivil one!"

What a Deal

In 1954 the U.S. government contacted the Grosvenor Estate regarding purchasing land for an embassy in London. They received a letter from the Duke of Westminster that while the estate did not usually sell the freehold of any property, such a sale would be considered if the U.S. would simply return to the duke's family land confiscated after the American Civil War. The U.S. immediately looked into the matter, but the deal fell through when it was determined that the purchase would cost 12,000 acres in Florida, including a substantial part of Miami.

Where's "Dixie"?

Dixie State College—St. George, Utah

Dixie National Forest—HQ in Cedar City, Utah

Dixie Chili—HQ in Newport, Kentucky

Dixie, a life-size Brachiosaurus—Benicia, California

Dixieland jazz—website in Kouvola, Finland:
    http://cat.teho.net/software/dixie/e-site

Heartfelt

In January of 1903 General James Longstreet was buried. Following the funeral, friends gathered at the grave to bid him farewell. As the casket, draped with Confederate and American flags, was being lowered, an old Confederate stepped forward and threw his old uniform and enlistment papers into the grave, saying, "I've served my time. And the general, he's served his time, too. I reckon I won't need my uniform and papers again, but I'd like to leave them with him for always."

Southern Soldiers

An 1896 *Boston Evening Gazette* editorial reprinted in the March 1896 *Confederate Veteran:*

"A few members of the Grand Army of the Republic in Woburn are complaining that the textbooks used in teaching history to the public school children of that town are robbing them of some of their hard-earned laurels. They seem to advocate a return to the style of book in vogue twenty-five years ago when pupils were taught that Jefferson Davis was a little bit worse than old Satan himself, and that Southern chivalry meant cowardly brutality. How can it detract from the glory of brave men to tell their posterity that the foes they conquered were among the finest soldiers that the world has ever seen? What generous Northern veteran would strive to rob the South of that which belongs to her as the mother of those intrepid heroes who followed Pickett to annihilation at Gettysburg? Our united country is proud of them. The fame of their unsurpassed valor is part of our national heritage. Every truly patriotic American hopes that when the call comes for the men of Virginia, of South Carolina and of Alabama to stand under the old flag, shoulder to shoulder with the men of Massachusetts, of Pennsylvania and of Illinois, there shall arise another Lee, another Jackson and another Johnston. What stainless knight of mediaeval romance can claim precedence over these? To cast one false slur upon their fame is to insult the memory of Grant, of Sherman and of Sheridan." *(Editor's note: Can you imagine such an editorial in today's newspapers, North OR South?)*

Hallowed Ground for Jewish Confederates

On Shockoe Hill in Richmond, Virginia, is the only Jewish military cemetery in the world outside the state of Israel. On a plaque are these words: TO THE GLORY OF GOD AND MEMORY OF THE HEBREW CONFEDERATE SOLDIERS RESTING IN THIS HALLOWED SPOT. ERECTED BY THE HEBREW LADIES MEMORIAL ASSOCIATION, RICHMOND, VIRGINIA, ORGANIZED 1866.

As Seen in the East

China's Premier Zhu visited Washington recently. European news sources report that in reference to China's preparations to use force if necessary to reclaim Taiwan, Zhu said such action would be nothing more than Lincoln's attack on Southern states that seceded in 1861.

Abilities Recognized

When war in Cuba was threatening the U.S. in 1869, William Tecumseh Sherman, commander of the United States Army, must have been a very surprised man when he received a letter from Nathan Bedford Forrest. At one time Sherman had vowed to use every resource he had to kill Forrest. In his letter Forrest offered his services in the event of war. Sherman wrote Forrest that any war in Cuba would probably be a naval matter. He then forwarded the letter to the War Department with a note saying if it "were up to me in the event of a war requiring cavalry, I would unhesitatingly accept his services and give him a prominent place. I believe now he would fight against our national enemies as vehemently as he did against us, and that is saying enough."

Confederates Recognized

In 1917 the U.S. government officially paid a tribute to the military genius of Confederate generals. To prepare draftees and National Guardsmen for service in the First World War, four training camps were named for Confederate generals. Robert E. Lee was honored by Camp Lee at Petersburg, Virginia. John B. Gordon was honored by Camp Gordon at Atlanta, Georgia. Camp Wheeler, the National Guard Camp at Macon, Georgia, honored Joseph Wheeler. The National Guard Camp at Alexandria, Virginia, was named Camp Beauregard to honor P. G. T. Beauregard.

If You Can't Lick 'Em

In 1923, the Honorable Charles M. Stedman of Greensboro, North Carolina, was the sole and last Confederate veteran serving in the U.S. House of Representatives.

From the Surrender Scene

No artists or photographers were present when Lee and Grant met in Wilmer McLean's parlor to negotiate the surrender of the Army of Northern Virginia. Later in the year, Henry Orr did a sketch of the event, based on a verbal description by McLean. Thereafter artists used their own concepts of the scene. Union officers bought much of the room's furnishings. A small oval table upon which Colonel Eli Parker wrote the terms agreed upon by Lee and Grant was purchased by General Philip Sheridan, given to General George Custer, and wound up in the Smithsonian. A marble top table first used by General Lee, and then by his aide to draft Lee's response to Grant, was bought by General Edward Ord, whose widow sold it to a wealthy Chicagoan who gave it to the Chicago Historical Society. The chair used by Grant was bought by Colonel Capehart, and that of Lee by Colonel Whittaker. Candlesticks were bought by a Captain Sharpe. The paper manifold and stylus used by Parker, along with copies one and three of Grant's terms, are at Princeton University. Copy two of the terms was kept by Parker and is now in the New York Historical Society. The original of Lee's letter of acceptance went to the U.S. War Department and was lost. A copy of Lee's letter was obtained by his aide, Charles Marshall, and is now at Stratford Hall, Lee's birthplace in Virginia.

Confederate Army Life

As remembered in 1908 by J. T. Respess, Cottonwood, Texas:

"We 'fit, bled and died' when occasion demanded but when not engaged in 'fitten and bleeding and dying' we had as good a time as occasion and circumstances would permit, and woe it was to the potato patch, goober patch (we were Georgians), hog lot, chicken roost, or bee gum that became contiguous to our camps."

Statement of Captain J. K. P. Blackburn, Terry's Texas Rangers

"I believed then, and I still believe now, if the terms of peace had been left to the men who faced each other in battle day after day, they would have stopped the war at once on terms acceptable to both sides (except the civil rulers) and honorable to all alike. These men that always bore the brunt of battle never had and never will have any bad feelings toward each other."

U.S. Navy Honored Buchanan

In 1862, Franklin Buchanan was the first captain of the CSS *Virginia*. On January 19, 1919, Buchanan was honored by the launching of a U.S. destroyer named after him.

Showed His Southern Ancestry

"I do not want a government that will take care of me. I want a government that will make other men take their hands off me so I can take care of myself."— Woodrow Wilson, President, U.S.A.

An Aggressive Prayer

During the 1999 Battle of Chickamauga (re-enactment), a Tennessee chaplain gave an inspiring prayer for his troops:

"Lord, as we prepare to close with the enemy on the field of battle, give us the strength, the courage, and the will to kill every last one of the sorry sons of bitches."

An English View of the Confederacy and Its Cause

By Col. G. F. R. Henderson, CB, 1886:

"Let none be deceived by the statements of those from whom unreasoning prejudice still hides the truth. It was not to preserve slavery, not in open rebellion against the Federal Constitution, that the Confederates stood in arms, but in the defence of their rights as citizens of sovereign and independent States bound to the Union by a voluntary compact, which they were free to maintain or cancel as they would. Such was the faith of the Southern people. That it was inexpedient may be admitted; that it was illegitimate has not yet been proved."

Recognized Guilt

After the war, a lady from Virginia was seated with her husband in Trinity Church in New York. She was surprised to see that the Yankee lady seated in front of her was wearing a fine shawl that had been stolen from her Virginia home by Yankee pillagers. The shawl was identified by a tiny darn. The lady leaned forward and whispered, "That is my shawl you have on. We are stopping at the St. Nicholas." The wearer turned crimson and said nothing. The shawl was delivered to the hotel early the next day.

What the South Wanted

"All that the South has ever desired was that the Union as established by our forefathers should be preserved and that the government as originally organized should be administered in purity and truth." — Robert E. Lee

An Odd Twist

Scurry County, Texas, is the only county in the U.S. that is named for a Confederate general and has a county seat named for a Union private. The county was named for Confederate General William R. Scurry. The county seat, Snyder, was named for Union Private William Henry Snyder.

A Principled Man

"The principle for which we contend is bound to reassert itself, though it may be at another time and in another form."—President Jefferson Davis

Richard Henry Lee Comments

The following quotation was taken from a speech given by Colonel Richard Henry Lee, of Virginia, at the dedication of the Confederate monument at Old Chapel in Clarke County, Virginia, in 1893:

"Twenty eight years have passed since the close of our civil war. Time, I trust has healed the wounds of war, but with the revolving years the causes and events of that terrible struggle seem to be forgotten, or if not forgotten, considered as unimportant events of history. And even the history of those events, and the causes that led to that struggle, are not set forth fairly and truthfully. It is stated in books and papers that Southern children read and study that all the blood-shedding and destruction of property of that conflict was because the South rebelled without cause against the best government the world ever saw; that although Southern soldiers were heroes in the field, skillfully massed and led, they and their leaders were rebels and traitors who fought to overthrow the Union, and to preserve human slavery, and that their defeat was necessary for free government and the welfare of the human family.

As a Confederate soldier and as a citizen of Virginia, I deny the charge, and denounce it as a calumny. We were not rebels; we did not fight to perpetuate human slavery, but for our rights and privileges under a government established over us by our fathers and in defense of our homes.

My friends, as I look upon the graves around me, and yon monument, the most comforting thought to me is this: 'The Lord God Omnipotent reigneth.' God is in history—in all history; was in our history during our war, and although the final result was not according to our desires and hopes, sure am I that the time will come when we will acknowledge that he in mercy and not in wrath afflicted us. I do not know when or how this will appear. Who knows but that the devotion of the South to the true principles of the constitution may not in the future cause the fructification of those principles and their growth throughout the land? Who knows but that the example of courage and devotion to duty of our leaders and soldiers, our mothers, wives, and sisters, may not hereafter influence the leaders of our whole people to put duty and honor before power and place, and to do and think only of the things that are true, honest and of good report?"

Unusual

In 1883 when the mother of Union General Ulysses S. Grant died, the minister presiding over her funeral was H. A. M. Henderson, once the Confederate officer in charge of the Confederate prison camp at Cahaba, Alabama.

Unrelenting

When Abraham Lincoln visited Richmond following its fall in 1865, he toured Jefferson Davis' home, the White House of the Confederacy. News of Lincoln's visit to the mansion brought this reaction from one Richmond lady, "Our President's house! Ah, it is a bitter pill! I would that the dear old house, with all its associations so sacred to Southerners, so sweet to us as a family, had shared in the general conflagration…Oh, how gladly I would have seen it burn! "

Carpetbaggers and Scalawags

"Carpetbaggers" were Northerners who came south after the war, with the name being derived from their supposed habit of bringing their worldly possessions crammed into cheap carpetbags. Their counter egos, Southerners who sided with the Yankees, were "scalawags." That name can be traced to the Shetland Islands town of Scalloway that was known for its scrubby cattle.

What Happened, Folks?

From an 1892 *History of Dallas County*:

"To record in history the brave and valiant deeds of those who from a consciousness of duty fought for their country's interest, either on the battlefield or otherwise, is the duty of every historian who undertakes to write that people's career. And in no spirit of sectionalism does the compiler write of the Confederates, but with the sentiment, 'All honor to whom honor is due,' would say that the brave deeds of the noble and gallant Confederate soldiers of the South will ever be honored and revered by their descendants, and will be kept fresh and green in their memories for time immemorial."

Showing the Colors

During the battle for Okinawa in WWII, the heart of the Japanese main line of resistance was General Ushijima's central command post in the tunnels under the ancient Shuri Castle. Captain Julian Dusenbury's Company A of the First Battalion, Fifth Marine Regiment, First Marine Division, was ordered to make an assault on that building on May 29, 1945. They quickly and effectively captured Ushijima's headquarters. To signal the enemy and demoralize him it is important to raise your own banner upon achieving a major objective. This also gives your own side a boost in morale. Captain Dusenbury did not have a U.S. flag but "just happened to have" in his helmet liner a Confederate flag from his native South Carolina. He raised that flag for all to see, making it the first American flag to fly over a conquered Okinawa.

Biblical

Zebulon Vance, wartime governor of North Carolina, was imprisoned by the Union army after the war. Vance, a personable man, often engaged in banter with his guards, who appreciated his wit. Feeling under the weather one day, Vance sought solitude by giving the guards a riddle to ponder so they would discuss it and not badger him: "How were Lazarus and the late CSA alike?" After much debate among the guards, they guessed incorrectly. Vance, having gained his desired respite, informed them that the only correct answer was that both had been licked by a pack of dogs!

A View of Lincoln

"It must be admitted, truth compels me to admit...Abraham Lincoln was not, in the fullest sense of the word, either our man or our model. In his interests, in his associations, in his habits of thought, and in his prejudices, he was a white man. He was preeminently the white man's president, entirely devoted to the welfare of white men. He was ready and willing at any time during the last years of his administration to deny, postpone, and sacrifice the rights of humanity in the colored people, to promote the welfare of the white people of his country."—Frederick Douglass, noted African-American leader

Accurately Looked Ahead

"Surrender means that the history of this heroic struggle will be written by the enemy, that our youth will be trained by Northern school teachers, learn from Northern school books THEIR version of the war, and taught to regard our gallant dead as traitors and our maimed veterans as fit subjects of derision."—General Patrick Cleburne, CSA

Fortunes of War

A sword in the Smithsonian Institution bears three inscriptions that together show the uncertainties of war. The first inscription: *Presented by Co. L, 1st N.Y. Vet. Cav. as a mark of Esteem to C.W. Brandt.* The second: *Captured March 10th 1864 and Presented to Lt. Col. John Singleton Mosby.* The final: *Recaptured Sept. 1864, by the 13th N.Y. Cavalry, Colonel H.S. Gansevoort.*

Belatedly Recognized a Disaster

After five years under the yoke of Reconstruction and its military dictatorship, Robert E. Lee was asked by a Union general to make a statement indicating how happy he was to be back in the Union and under the Stars and Stripes. Lee refused. He told Fletcher Stockdale, Confederate governor of Texas, "Governor, if I had foreseen the use those people [the Yankees] designed to make of their victory, there would have been no surrender at Appomattox Courthouse; no sir, not by me. Had I foreseen these results of subjugation, I would have preferred to die at Appomattox, with my brave men, with my sword in my hand."

Blacks in Gray

Many people today wish to ignore black Confederates because those soldiers fail to fit their explanation of the war. Unfortunately many of those are blacks who almost completely deny this chapter in their history. Officially, for most of the war regular Confederate military service for blacks was not encouraged. Most blacks who served as soldiers did so as members of local militia and home guard units. In April of 1861, a black militia company in Nashville, Tennessee, offered its services to the Confederate government. The next month a recruiting office for free blacks opened in Memphis. On June 28, 1861, the Tennessee legislature passed the first law enacted by a government, North or South, that conferred military privileges and duties on blacks. On November 23, 1861, a grand review in New Orleans included a regiment of 1,400 "free colored men." In November 1863, Major General D. H. Maury officially authorized enlistment of the first blacks in a regular Confederate army, the members of the Creole Guard of Mobile, Alabama. In 1907 Captain John Dinkins wrote and delivered a glowing tribute to blacks of the South during the war. He said he did not believe any people at any time proved themselves more loyal; that for months many families were wholly dependent upon the loyalty of blacks for survival, and that throughout the war no incendiary language or insurrectionary movement was heard of or hinted at. Dinkins was not running for political office when he delivered that talk. He was addressing the United Confederate Veterans reunion in Shreveport, Louisiana.

Timing Was Everything

Many years after the war, Henry W. Graber of Terry's Texas Rangers was joined by Major J. J. Weiler of the 17th Indiana Mounted Infantry in petitioning the state of Indiana to return to Texas a unit flag lost by the Rangers during a hurried retreat from Rome, Georgia, in 1864. The Indiana legislature passed an act to do so. In 1899, Governor James A. Mount and a large number of Union veterans traveled to Texas to make the presentation. Though the Rangers insisted the flag had not been captured but merely found on the road, furled in its case, they admitted they had been in a rapid retreat when they lost it. "Graber," said Governor Mount, "I thought you Rangers never ran." Replied Graber, "Governor, if they hadn't run a thousand times, there would not have been one left to tell the tale. We always knew when to quit and didn't require a bugle to bring us out."

Charitable Indeed

When the great fire of Chicago caused such a great loss in October of 1871, the mayor appealed to all Southern states for relief. General Wade Hampton was a resident of Columbia, a city burned by the Yankees. The general generously sent a bale of fodder for the cow that kicked over the lamp that started the Chicago fire.

Dedication Remarks

Washington Gardner, commander of the Grand Army of the Republic, the Union veterans group, spoke at the dedication of the Confederate Memorial in Arlington National Cemetery on June 4, 1914. He said, "The heroic devotion and lofty self-sacrifice of these honored dead is held in grateful and affectionate memory…Neither side will ever have to apologize for the sincerity or the devotion of its adherents."

In those same ceremonies Bennett Young, commander of the United Confederate Veterans, was uncompromising in his view of the war. "We still glory in the records of our beloved and immortal dead. Their surviving comrades and their children still believe that for which they suffered and laid down their lives was just; that their premises in the civil war were according to our Constitution. The men of the Confederacy submit, but they have no words to recall, nor history to change. The South gave 200,000 lives, the best and most precious offering it had, as an assurance of honesty of conviction, unfaltering faith and integrity of purpose. The sword said the South was wrong, but the sword is not necessarily guided by conscience and reason. The power of numbers and the longest guns cannot destroy principle nor obliterate truth. Right lives forever."

Federal Agents

A U.S. secretary of the treasury commented on Federal agents who plundered the South during Reconstruction: "I am sure that I sent some honest agents to the South, but it seems very doubtful that any of them remained honest very long."

The Principal Southern Principle

After the war, Robert E. Lee was called before the U.S. Congress to testify. There a questioner attempted to make out a case of treason against him for taking up arms against the Northern invaders. General Lee responded by referring to the Act of Secession of Virginia:

"In withdrawing herself from the United States, she carried me along as a citizen of Virginia, and that her laws and her acts were binding upon me."

Integrity Recognized

In Dayton, Virginia, four miles south of Harrisonburg on Highway 42, the only monument in the South erected by Southerners to the memory of a Union officer is located. During the destruction of the Valley by Sheridan in '64, a three-man Union patrol came upon a three-man Confederate scouting party inside their lines. In the ensuing exchange of fire, a member of Sheridan's staff was killed. Sheridan, thinking that the attackers were bushwhackers, ordered that Dayton and all the houses within five miles be burned to avoid further secret attacks. The monument reads:

In Memory of Lt. Col. Thomas F. Wildes
116th Ohio Regiment
Who when ordered by General Sheridan to burn the Town of Dayton, Virginia, in retaliation for the death of a Union officer, refused to obey that order risking court-martial and disgrace. His refusal and plea to General Sheridan resulted in a countermand to the order and saved this town from total destruction.

A Proud First

In 1871, Liberty, Mississippi, became the first town in the U.S. to erect a Confederate monument.

Where Flowers Healed a Nation

Although other locales claim or are given credit, Friendship Cemetery in Columbus, Mississippi, is where Memorial Day actually began on April 25, 1866. The war had been over for a year when the ladies of the town decorated the graves of both Confederate and Union soldiers in the cemetery with beautiful bouquets and garlands of flowers. Touched by this act, the local commanding Union general gave orders calling for the same observance throughout his command annually thereafter. As a direct result, Americans now celebrate Memorial Day, an annual recognition of our war dead."

Travelling Men

The only continent that does not have a Confederate grave is Antarctica.

Unwavering

John F. Talbert, a South Carolina veteran, was firm in his beliefs about the cause for which he fought. The following was excerpted from a letter he wrote to his cousin Hillary on October 10, 1889:

Our old Confederate flag has been furled forever. While our armies bore it, nothing was done to dishonor it. We carried on the War according to the rules of civilized warfare and when our cause failed, we laid it aside without a stain or blemish on its folds. It was followed by men who fought for the most holy and sacred of causes, and we are today proud of that cause and the record they made in the struggle for States Rights. We have nothing to apologize for...We fought for what we thought was right...In speaking of the late unpleasantness you may say, "Well, John, forgive and forget." I am like the woman who when told she must "forgive and forget" said, "Yes, I'll forgive and forget, but I will *always remember.*"

Our Responsibility
J. Taylor Ellyson

"Let us be certain that our children know that the War Between the States was not a contest for the preservation of slavery, as some would have them to believe, but that it was a great struggle for the maintenance of Constitutional rights, and that men who fought were warriors tried and true, who bore the flags of a Nation's trust, and fell in a cause, though lost, still just, and died for me and you."

Unknown Soldier

A Confederate soldier was the first person buried in the Morris Cemetery, five miles south of Gilmer, Texas. On the way home at the end of the war, he became very ill and stopped at the William Morris home. There he died without ever revealing his name.

Gettysburg Address Appraised

Noted author H. L. Mencken "cut to the chase" in considering Lincoln's Gettysburg Address. He correctly evaluated it as "poetry, not logic; beauty, not sense." He analyzed Lincoln's statement that the Union soldiers sacrificed their lives to the cause of self-determination so that "government of the people, by the people, for the people should not perish from the Earth." His conclusion? "It is difficult to imagine anything more untrue. The Union soldiers in the battle actually fought against self-determination; it was the Confederates who fought for the right of people to govern themselves."

We Outlasted 'Em

Albert Woolson, the last Union veteran, died in 1958. Walter Williams, the last Confederate veteran, died in 1959.

Recognize These Battlefields?

During the war, skirmishes and battles were fought at more than 10,000 locations. Though seemingly memorable, names of many these engagements have been forgotten, such as Wet Glaze, Missouri; Convalescent Corral, Mississippi; Gum Swamp, North Carolina; Droop Mountain, Virginia; and Bear Wallow, Kentucky.

Wish He Hadn't Felt That Way

"I'll never write my memoirs. I would be trading on the blood of my men."— General Robert E. Lee

His Words Were Lost

"The war is over—the rebels are our countrymen again."—U. S. Grant, Appomattox, April 9, 1865

Inscription from Confederate Monument

(SPARTANBURG, SOUTH CAROLINA)

(erected 1910)

LET THIS MONUMENT TEACH OUR CHILDREN AND OUR CHILDREN'S CHILDREN TO HONOR THE MEMORY AND THE HEROIC DEEDS OF THE SOUTHERN SOLDIER, WHO FOUGHT FOR RIGHTS GUARANTEED HIM UNDER THE CONSTITUTION. FOUR YEARS OUR ARMIES CONTENDED AGAINST GREAT ODDS, ENDURING INCREDIBLE HARDSHIPS, AND CEASING TO STRUGGLE ONLY WHEN THE SOUTH WAS EXHAUSTED, AND COULD NO LONGER FURNISH RECRUITS OR SUPPLIES.

Florida Well Represented

A statue of Confederate general Edmund Kirby Smith represents Florida in the U.S. Capitol.

Our Duty

"Duty is ours; consequences are God's."—Stonewall Jackson

Deadly Target

American forces operating in the Ia Drang valley in South Vietnam on a search-and-destroy mission in 1966 were hit by overwhelming forces of VC and NVA. When things looked hopeless, soldiers from Alabama, Mississippi, and Louisiana unfurled Confederate battle flags and tied them to trees. They were determined to stand and defend to the last man. Given those flags by their families, the men had been told, "Don't disappoint your ancestors." On Hill 187, that sector was the only area that held, allowing dust-offs and reinforcements to be brought in. Later, captured prisoners who were interrogated wanted to know what country that flag represented. When they were told the Confederate States of America, they replied, "It is suicide to attack their position." After that, Confederate battle flags were carried by some forward units occupying fixed positions.

Lee on Gettysburg

Although Robert E. Lee never went public with his frustrations, he did hold strong opinions about the roles played by some of his Confederate subordinates. During his postwar days as president of Washington College, he privately discussed the war with one of his professors, Colonel William Allen, formerly Stonewall Jackson's ordnance chief. On 15 April 1868, in discussing Gettysburg, Lee told Allen he did not know the Federal army was at Gettysburg and could not believe it, as he specifically had ordered Stuart to keep him informed of the position of the enemy, and Stuart had sent no word. In Lee's opinion, Stuart's failure to carry out his instructions forced the battle of Gettysburg, and the imperfect, halting way in which his corps commanders fought the battle gave victory finally to the foe. Lee believed that Gettysburg could have been won if he could have gotten one decided simultaneous attack on the whole line, but his subordinates would not act in concert. On 19 February 1870, Lee returned to the subject of Gettysburg to comment that before he went to Gettysburg in 1863, he had secured President Davis' promise to move Beauregard and his troops to Manassas to threaten Washington while Lee went into Pennsylvania. Failure to so position Beauregard weakened Lee's strategy.

Some Have Long Memories

After his wife accidentally knocked down a historical marker commemorating the Civil War battle of Blue's Gap, a West Virginian called the state police to report the damage. When the trooper who answered asked, "Who won that battle?" the caller replied, "The Union." The trooper told the caller, "Well, don't worry about it," and hung up.

Justified

Robert Brown had been a slave of the Jefferson Davis family and was devoted to his former master. Prior to the president's release from prison, Mrs. Davis sent the older children to Canada where they could be shielded. Robert Brown went along to protect and care for the children. On board the ship to Canada, Brown came upon a white Northerner who had cornered Little Jeff and was making insulting remarks about the boy's father. Brown interrupted the man to ask, "Do you consider me your equal?" "Certainly," was the reply. "Then take this from your equal," said Brown, and he knocked the man down. The ship's captain considered the blow justified and refused to accept any charges from the Northerner.

North and South

In a graveyard in Wilmington, North Carolina, stands a somewhat odd statue erected to honor Confederate soldiers. It is a soldier casually resting on his musket, with his wrist draped over the muzzle. An exact copy of the statue stands in the town square of Chambersburg, Pennsylvania, honoring Union soldiers. Both statues were bought from a manufacturer who carefully avoided anything that could identify the soldier as Northern or Southern. The oddity of the statues may be seen in their muskets. The hammer is at full cock and the soldier is about to shoot his hand off.

Unforgiving

Victors often fail to understand the depths of the emotions of wartime victims. On April 17, 1865, Eliza Frances Andrews, a young refugee from Washington, Georgia, noted in her diary, "I used to have some Christian feeling towards Yankees, but now that they have invaded our country and killed so many of our men and desecrated so many homes, I can't believe that when Christ said 'Love your enemies' he meant Yankees."

Not As Planned

Several years ago at a reenactment in Virginia, a practical joke was planned. One of the men was covered with leaves while prone on a grave in a small cemetery. The idea was that when someone walked by, the covered man would rise from under the leaves and scare the passerby. Before the "buried man" could play his trick, however, he started screaming, leaped up, and ran. Obviously terrified, he said that while he was under the leaves, something cold had reached from beneath him to touch his face.

Their Blood Showed in World War II

General George S. Patton, commander of the 3rd, 7th, and 15th Armies, was the grandson of Colonel George S. Patton, 22nd Virginia Infantry. General Patton died late in 1945 as the result of an auto accident.

Brigadier General Nathan Bedford Forrest III was the great-grandson of Confederate General Nathan Bedford Forrest. Chief of staff of the 2nd Air Force, he died during a bombing raid on Kiel, Germany.

Lieutenant General Simon Bolivar Buckner, Jr., son of Confederate Lieutenant General Simon Bolivar Buckner, commanded the 10th U.S. Army. He was killed during the invasion of Okinawa.

Elmira, New York

Woodlawn National Cemetery in Elmira, New York, may be the only cemetery where a mass grave holds both Confederate and Federal bodies. The worst train wreck in U.S. history took place on July 15, 1864. One of the trains was a prison train. That head-on collision took the lives of all but one man on the prison train. Forty-nine Confederate prisoners, seventeen Federal guards, the train's engineer, two firemen, and a brakeman were killed in the accident. The dead Union troops were all guards from the Federal 11th Veteran Reserve Corps. The Confederates belonged to eight units from North Carolina, six from Virginia, and six from South Carolina.

Uneven Numbers

In Mississippi seventeen years after the war, John Allen was running for Congress against former Confederate General William Tucker. Tucker closed a speech by pointing to a nearby clump of trees and saying that after a hard-fought battle he had slept under those very trees. He asked that all those who remembered those trying days to remember him when they voted. Allen spoke then. He said that Tucker had indeed slept under those trees and he knew that to be true because he had guarded Tucker while he slept. He then told the audience that all those who had been generals should vote for Tucker, but all those who guarded the generals while they slept should vote for him. Needless to say, Allen won!

What a Shame!

An entrepreneur obtained 100,000 Civil-War era glass photographic plates shortly before World War I. To the despair of historians he destroyed the plates to recover their silver and glass content.

The Heritage We Honor
Jefferson Davis, 1871

"There is little left for us to do, who still live, but that little is of worth. It is to preserve the traditions of our fathers and to keep in honorable remembrance the deeds of our brothers, happiest of whom we must reckon those who fell before the night of despotism closed upon this country."

What Would He Think *Today?*

"If I had foreseen the use those people designed to make of their victory, there would have been no surrender at Appomattox Courthouse; no sir, not by me. Had I foreseen the results of subjugation, I would have preferred to die at Appomattox with my brave men, my sword in this right hand."—General Robert E. Lee

A Perpetual Truth
Confederate Monument. Decatur, Mississippi
The men who wore the gray were right, and right can never die.

Regarding a Pardon
Jefferson Davis, speaking to the Mississippi legislature in 1884
"It has been said that I should apply to the United States for a pardon...But repentance must precede the right of pardon, and I have not repented.

Remembering...all which has been suffered, all that has been lost, disappointed hopes and crushed aspirations, yet I deliberately say, if it were all to do over again, I would do again just as I did in 1861."

Demanded by Honor

"We could have pursued no other course without dishonor. And sad as the results have been, if it had all to be done over again, we should be compelled to act in precisely the same manner."—General Robert E. Lee, C.S.A.

Unchanging

An excerpt from pages 750–752 of *The Lost Cause*, by E A. Pollard, 1866:

"The people of the South have surrendered in the war what the war has conquered; it has not conquered 'ideas'...The South must submit fairly and truthfully to what the war has properly decided. But the war properly decided only what was put in issue; the restoration of the Union and the excision of slavery; and to those two conditions the South submits. But the...things which the war did not decide, the Southern people will still cling to, still claim, and still assert in them their rights and views."

An Impossibility

From the *Southern Historical Society Papers XXII, 1894*:

"On the death of Jubal Early, John W. Daniel said, 'Indeed, my countrymen, it is impossible to conceive that a cause espoused and led by such men as Davis, Lee, Jackson, the two Johnstons, Early, and their compatriots was wrong, while that led by Lincoln, Seward, Stanton, Sherman, Thad Stevens, and Ben Butler, et id omne genus, was right.' "

Traditions

When we talk of Southern traditions and heritage, we do not mean just the way we stand proudly when the Confederate flag is displayed nor to our happily joining in to sing "Dixie" as often as possible. We are referring to such ideals as sacredness of duty, honesty, patriotism, independence, courtesy, self-reliance, and self-respect. Tradition holds society together; it was defined by Edmund Burke as a partnership between the living, the dead, and those not yet born. Our ancestors honored their obligations to the partnership when they passed on these ideals to us. We must defend our traditions so that those not yet born may have an opportunity to join in and enjoy the partnership.

Black Confederate Honored

At West Point, Mississippi, the UDC recently placed an iron Confederate Cross at the grave of Silas Chandler. Silas was twenty-one years old when he left the plantation where he was a slave to accompany sixteen-year-old Andrew Chandler when the youth joined the 44th Mississippi. The ceremony was attended by descendants of both Silas Chandler and Andrew Chandler. A photograph of Silas and Andrew printed in the local newspaper in 1909 shows them both in Confederate uniform, holding knives, with rifles across their knees. When Andrew was wounded at Chickamauga, Silas took him first to Atlanta then home rather than allow surgeons to amputate Andrew's leg. After the war Andrew gave land to Silas for his home and for a church that still stands. Silas received a Confederate pension from the state of Mississippi.

Change

Reverend B. M. Palmer, addressing the 1900 Confederate Reunion in Louisville:

"Whatever may have been the occasion of the war, the hinge on which it turned was this old question of state sovereignty as against national supremacy. As there could be no compromise between the two, the only resort was to the law of force. The surrender at Appomattox, when the tattered remnant of Lee's great army stood guard for the last time over Southern liberties and rights, drew the equatorial line dividing the past and the future of American history. When the will of the strongest, instead of 'the consent of the governed,' became the basis of our national structure, a radical transformation took place. The principle of confederation gave way to that of consolidation, and the American nation emerged out of the American Republic."

Unrepentant

"Nothing fills me with deeper sadness than to see a Southerner apologizing for the defense we made of our inheritance."—Jefferson Davis, President of the Confederate States of America

Knew His Customers

During the Congressional session preceding the passage of the 1867 Reconstruction Act, a Washington hotel-keeper posted the following notice on his dining room door: "Members of Congress will go to the table first, and then the gentlemen. Rowdies and blackguards must not mix with the Congressmen as it is hard to tell one from the other."

You Better Believe It!

"If I ever disown, repudiate, or apologize for the Cause for which Lee fought and Jackson died, let the lightnings of Heaven rend me, and the scorn of all good men and true women be my portion. Sun, Moon, Stars, all fall on me when I cease to love the Confederacy. 'Tis the cause, not the fate of the Cause, that is glorious!"—Major R. E. Wilson, CSA

Unchanging

Jubal Early was perhaps the most Unreconstructed Rebel of all, remaining loyal to the Confederacy for the rest of his life and never forgiving the North. In a letter to General D. H. Hill, Early referred to the biblical instruction to forgive one's enemies, "I am clearly of the opinion that the Yankees furnish an exception. At any rate, if my salvation depends upon my being able to love, I fear I shall be lost." In a similar vein he wrote to General Thomas Rosser, "My hatred of the infernal Yankees is increasing daily, if possible, and I do not speak to any of them that I meet. My motto is still *War to the Death*, and I yet hope to have another chance at them." Fitzhugh Lee described Early's attitude: "When Early drew his sword in that conflict he threw the scabbard away and was never afterward able to find it."

Forever

From a sermon by Rev. James S. Vance, reported in the July 1897 *Confederate Veteran*:

"The South is not ashamed of the lost cause, which can never be lost as long as men preach patriotism, glorify valor, and worship sacrifice."

To the Confederate Dead

In a small park in Charleston, South Carolina, stands a monument to Major Henry Timrod, C.S.A. (1829–1867), sometimes called "the Poet Laureate of the Confederacy." These words are engraved thereon:

> Sleep sweetly in your humble grave
> Sleep, martyrs of a fallen Cause
> Though yet no marble column crave
> The pilgrim here to pause.
>
> In seeds of laurel in the earth
> The blossom of your fame is blown
> And somewhere, waiting for its birth
> The shaft is in the stone.
>
> Stoop, angels, hither from the skies
> There is no holier spot of ground
> Than where defeated valor lies
> By mourning beauty crowned.

Inscription on Confederate Memorial in Arlington National Cemetery
Written by Dr. Randolph McKim

> Not for fame or reward
> Not for place or rank

Not lured by ambition
Or goaded by necessity
But in simple obedience to duty as they understood it
These men suffered all, sacrificed all, dared all and died.

Jefferson Davis Said It

"Our cause was so just, so sacred, that had I known all that would come to pass, had I known what was to be inflicted upon me, all that my country was to suffer, all that our posterity was to endure, I would do it all over again."

— The Author —

RALPH GREEN is a descendant of several Confederate veterans. Born in Dallas, Texas, he graduated from SMU after his service in the U.S. Army Air Force in WWII. Retired from Electronic Data Systems, he is highly active in adding to our under-standing of the history of the War Between the States. He is a founding member of the Descendants of Confederate Veterans, as well as a past commander in chief of the Sons of Confederate Veterans. He has received many awards and honors, in-cluding the Jefferson Davis Chalice, the SCV's highest honor. He is president of the board of advisers for the Texas Heritage Museum at Hill College in Hillsboro, Texas. In addition, he is the editor of the *Rebel Rouser*, an award-winning newsletter, where he has published many of the stories in this collection.

"Ralph Green has cracked the code with his new book. Not only does his book provide us with great history lessons, the material presented is both fascinating and intriguing. Block out some time to read this book, even if you are not a Civil War buff. You will learn something and have a lot of fun in the process."

—John C. Perry, Author of *Myths & Realities of American Slavery*

"Ralph Green's stories and anecdotes are rare gems about life, valor, humor, and conflict. Every Civil War library should have a copy of this great collection that will bring enjoyment to Civil War enthusiasts and historians."

—Walbrook D. Swank, Author/Historian and recipient of the National Henry Timrod Southern Culture Award

— Of Related Interest—

Strange Tales of the Civil War
Michael Sanders

Strange Tales of the Civil War presents readers with a collection of strange stories from America's greatest conflict. Includes omens, predictions, dreams, and many other mysterious events.

ISBN 978-1-57249-271-4 • Softcover $9.95

More Strange Tales of the Civil War
Michael Sanders

This second installment of stories of the unusual, bizarre, and peculiar from America's greatest conflict includes chapters on dreams, predictions, coincidences, medical oddities, animals, and more.

ISBN 978-1-57249-383-4 • Softcover $9.95

The Complete Book of Confederate Trivia
J. Stephen Lang

Are you a Confederate History Buff? Do you know everything there is to know about Confederate History? If you answered "YES!" to these questions, test your knowledge with *The Complete Book of Confederate Trivia*!

ISBN 978-1-57249-007-9 • Softcover $14.99

— COVER ILLUSTRATION —
Illustration by Matthew Archambault, © 2007

Cover Designed by Angela Guyer

WHITE MANE PUBLISHING CO., INC.

To Request a Catalog Please Write to:
WHITE MANE PUBLISHING COMPANY, INC.
P.O. Box 708 • Shippensburg, PA 17257
e-mail: marketing@whitemane.com